WHAT BASEBALL MEANS TO ME

WHAT BASEBALL MEANS TO ME

A CELEBRATION OF OUR NATIONAL PASTIME

Edited by Curt Smith
and the National Baseball Hall of Fame
and Museum

WARNER BOOKS

An AOL Time Warner Company

Warner Books, Inc.
1271 Avenue of the Americas
New York, NY 10020

Visit our Web site at www.twbookmark.com.

• • •

An AOL Time Warner Company

Printed in the United States of America

First Printing: April 2002
10 9 8 7 6 5 4 3 2 1

• • •

ISBN: 0-446-52749-1
LCCN: 2002100281

• • •

Book Design: Judith Turziano

• • •

All photography courtesy of the *National Baseball Hall of Fame and Museum* with the exception of the following contributors:
Corbis: I, II–III, 4, 18, 22, 31, 33, 36, 61, 66, 68–69, 77, 130, 134, 143, 169, 186, 191, 217, 221, 230;
The Associated Press: VI, 5, 9, 19, 25 (bottom), 80 (left), 89, 92-93, 96, 101, 124, 135, 170, 172, 190, 200, 203, 251;
Photofile: 15 (bottom right), 74, 82, 88, 102–103, 124 (bottom left), 152 (right), 184 (left), 188, 196, 200, 204, 234, 237, 266;
Walt Barry: 38, 116, 165, 264; *Milo Stewart Jr./National Baseball Hall of Fame:* Endpaper, III (inset of baseball), 111; *Don Sparks:* 2, 232;
Al Tielemans/Sports Illustrated: 41, 270; *Chicago Sun-Times:* 46, 148; *Shreveport Times:* 62, 63; *Charles Shoup:* 151, 216; *Orion Pictures:* 207, 208; *Jack Goldstein:* XI;
Carl Kidwilee: XII; *Stan Grossfeld/Boston Globe:* 10; *Atlanta History Center:* 12; *New York News:* 17; *Robert Gorman:* 23; *Dick Raphael/Sports Illustrated:* 25 (top);
Barney Stein: 27; *Jonathan Busser:* 29; *Yale University:* 43; *Ron Jenkins/Ft. Worth Star-Telegram:* 45; *Courtesy of Jerry Reuss:* 50–51 (bottom);
Chris Hamilton: 52; *CBS News:* 57; *V.J. Lovero/Sports Illustrated:* 75 (top); *Dr. Gary Laine:* 75 (bottom); *Courtesy of Marlin Fitzwater:* 78;
George Bush Presidential Library: 84; *John Cordes:* 95 (left and right); *Courtesy of Kay Bailey Hutchison:* 119; *Doug Griffin/Toronto Star:* 122;
Chicago Historical Society: 132 (top); *Robert Obojski:* 136; *Mike Rucki:* 140; *Louis Requena:* 158; *Tom Ryder:* 159; *Pat Kelly/National Baseball Hall of Fame:* 179;
Richard Lasner: 192 (top); *Brooklyn Public Library:* 197; *Mark Hertzberg:* 198; *Tom Zimmerman:* 202; *Ron Kuntz/Reuters/Timepix:* 206; *Rochester Democrat
and Chronicle:* 214; *Fred Roe/National Baseball Hall of Fame:* 225; *Adrees Latif/Reuters/Timepix:* 238–239; *Daniel Aquilar/Reuters/Timepix:* 240;
Herb Scharfman/Sports Illustrated: 245; *Tony Triolo/Sports Illustrated:* 246; *Dennis Brearley Collection:* 254–255.
Copyright Status Unknown: 21, 73, 108, 131, 141, 142, 144, 226, 248, 261.
Illustrations by *John Corbitt:* XVIII–1, 15, 86, 138, 243.

Dave Barry's essay is copyrighted and reprinted by permission of the author.
Jack Cavanaugh's essay is copyrighted and reprinted by permission of the author.
Doris Kearns Goodwin's essay "From Father, With Love" is copyrighted and reprinted by permission of *The Boston Globe*.
Marvin Hamlisch's essay is copyrighted and reprinted by permission of the author and Charles Scribner's sons from *The Way I Was*.
Ernie Harwell's essay "The Game for All America" is copyrighted and reprinted by permission of the author.
Essays by the following contributors have appeared, some in a slightly different version, in the book *Baseball Days*
(Contemporary Books, 2000, copyright by Garret Mathews): Dave Barry, Julian Bond, Bill Bradley, Patrick J. Buchanan,
Clive Cussler, Mike Ditka, Thomas Eagleton, Marlin Fitzwater, Bud Greenspan, Frankie Laine, Johnny Majors, Billy Mills,
Ty Murray, Rick Reilly, Dick Schaap, Mickey Spillane, Eli Wallach, Tom Watson, and Fuzzy Zoeller.

TO COOPERSTOWN

"Here all was unchanged; the river still rushed through its bower of trees…the mountains stood in their native dress, dark, rich, and mysterious; while the sheet glistened in its solitude, a beautiful gem of the forest."

—James Fenimore Cooper,
The Deerslayer

THE LINEUP

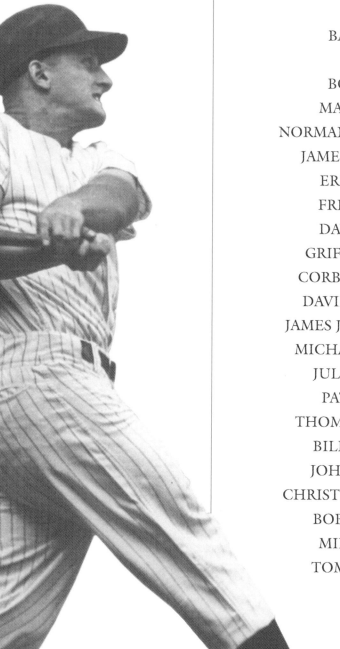

BATTER UP

The actor Desi Arnaz was once asked how television's *I Love Lucy* had changed his life. "That's a silly question," he replied. "Ask what it *hasn't* changed." It is silly to ask what baseball doesn't mean. What it does is more gainful—thus, the title of this book.

Plato said, "Before we talk, let us first define our terms." What tastes like chocolate to you may seem vanilla to me. Baseball is individual—hence, its lure, especial. *What Baseball Means to Me* explores what so many— here, over 170 essayists—love so much about America's oldest and greatest game.

This book airs the largest group of household names—actors, politicians, writers, and athletes; an entrepreneur here, an ambassador there—to fill a funhouse of baseball memory.

Each was asked to write about the sport. They replied as vividly as your first visit to a park—a blur of caps and hose and emblem across the chest of heaving, billowy woollies, yet indelible: the vendor, police, and skim of smoke across the yard; sunlight of early summer or darkness of early fall; timeless tableau of fielder crouched, batter cocked, the pitcher draped against the grandstand—above all, the surety that there was no place on earth that you would rather be.

Paradise: Safe at home.

Bud Selig writes of visiting Yankee Stadium, Ebbets Field, and the Polo Grounds, at fifteen, in 1949. Muses Rudolph Giuliani: "Sitting next to my father at Yankee Stadium during my first baseball game, I felt like the luckiest kid in the world." Tom Brokaw, Dan Rather, and Rick Reilly are less ooh-ah: respectively, touting Strutz Field, Buffalo Stadium, and Prairie Dog Field. George W. Bush hails Nolan Ryan. His dad recalls Lou Gehrig, averring, "Baseball has it all." Another ex-President etches game 7 of the 1992 National League Championship Series. Says Jimmy Carter: "You can still hear the noise."

What does baseball mean? To composer Marvin Hamlisch, a Yankee fantasy camp; actor David Birney, a poem to his son; writer David Maraniss, his father listening to Harvey Haddix's 12-inning perfect game. Jack Larson— TV's Jimmy Olson—salutes his baseball-loving father. Corbin Bernsen recounts a fight in Little League: Two players' mothers, "a catfight, straight out of the WWF." Faith, hope and charity: Dave Barry prayed that no one would hit to him.

Baseball means: Donna Shalala, throwing out the first ball at Camden Yards. Marlin Fitzwater, hurling a no-hitter, walking 21, and losing, 13–0. John Havlicek, bird-dogged by five big league clubs. Clive Cussler's gloveless catch. Cal Ripken plays his 2,131st straight game: Tim Russert rejoices. Roger Maris smacks homer 61: Sean Wilentz exults. Reg Murphy watches Henry Aaron's 715th. Bucky Dent's homer mimes Mike Dukakis's bid for Massachusetts Governor. "I can imagine a world without baseball," writes Leonard Koppett, "but can't imagine wanting to live in one."

What Baseball Means: The next pitch.

Baseball can mean odd plays, lost cards, an Oh-my-God, can-you-believe-it, how-about-that lilt. Football is an event—the greyhound you thrill to. Baseball is a fact of life—the cocker spaniel who steals your loyalty and love. One is showbiz—TV's Simpsons. The other mimes the Waltons—religion passed from one generation to the next. "It is...a game of fathers and sons," adds Frank Deford, and his link to "the broader community."

To Charley Steiner, baseball gives running home new connotation. To James Symington, it means hitching a pants elastic—and raising a coach's ire. Teresa Wright—film's Eleanor Gehrig—discovers "our rite of spring." Ann Richards jokes about changing batting orders. Julius LaRosa recalls Brooklyn's 1940s and 1950s Dodgers.

Ask Christine Brennan. Baseball means love: the Toledo Mud Hens. John Updike: courage to face big league smoke. Lisa Fernandez: intellectual. Martin Sheen: befriending a boy in Cooperstown. Doris Kearns Goodwin writes that baseball is the "most timeless of all sports." This book shows why.

◆ ◆ ◆

You will recognize the vast majority of contributors. The less big-wigged deserve kudos, too. The wife of a newly inducted official once told visitors, "You're all invited to our house. No more big shots!" Her husband amended the gibe. "Of course, *all* of our visitors are big shots!" *Ibid. What Baseball Means to Me.*

Madelyn Pilkington, 100, etches TV baseball and the elderly; Evan Roberts, eighteen, America's youngest sports talk host, the 2000 Subway Series; Frank Capparelli, longtime Wrigley Field groundskeeper, tending "America's prettiest lawn"; Mike Brito, the Dodgers' Radar Man, his

Yankee Stadium, 1955 World Series: The Bombers bat against Brooklyn.

hope to be buried at home plate in Chavez Ravine.

"You can't describe baseball," Bob Costas once said, "without noting folks who constitute baseball." Thus, clubhouse man Jim Schmakel compares Tiger Stadium to Comerica Park. Bob Allen, an old-school players agent, tells why he liked it better, well, back then. John Franzen has seen more than 1,200 straight Brewers games. Tom Burgoyne—the Phillie Phanatic—remains "the only baseball celebrity [Phillie fans] never boo."

Baseball is people. Reading this book, you may see yourself.

◆　◆　◆

In 1982, Joseph Alsop wrote of Franklin Roosevelt a century after his birth. "Maybe I have become a sorry praiser of the past; but this is a personal memoir," he wrote, "and if I truly feel that there were giants in the land in the Roosevelt years, I claim the right to say so." This book is personal. Let me briefly claim the right to say what baseball means to me.

It is said that with the possible exception of the equator, everything begins somewhere. For me baseball began in the 1950s and early 1960s in Caledonia, New York—pop. 2,188, one bar, six churches, no traffic lights, and 300 miles from the nearest big league park—cleaving lowland of Lake Ontario and rolling scenery to the south. Hitting fungoes, citing batting averages, or trading two A's playing cards for a dog-eared Eli Grba, friends and I thought of little else.

Most baseballphiles ape a player. George Fisher revered Stan Musial; Larry King, Jackie Robinson; Bud Greenspan, Mel Ott; Curt Gowdy, Ted Williams. Monty Hall salutes Ernie Banks. Kay Bailey Hutchison rides the Ryan Express. Patti LuPone recounts her son catching a ball thrown by Buck O'Neil. Dan Jansen regales how Paul Molitor returned a ball—and kept his word.

My favorite player was Yankee second baseman Bobby Richardson—to my father, "a fine family man and Christian gentleman." Germane to me was Bobby's prowess at the double play. Winter ended with catch and Little League. (See pollster John Zogby: "For so many of us guys, it all boils down to Little League.") Summer brought pickup games in a field adjacent to a cemetery. Rites linked grass stains, broken glass, and our Holy Grail—a long belt, an

automatic homer—clanging off a stone.

One day a batter took me downtown *beyond* the farthest grave. *Requiescat in pace.* As a player, it augured my career.

◆　◆　◆

Baseball also means sites, built on a human scale, of quirk and personality. Tom Dreesen writes of the ivy at Wrigley Field. Skip Caray recalls a rainy day at Sportsman's Park. George Winston

The Phillie Phanatic remains "the only baseball celebrity [Phillie fans] never boo."

educes Forbes Field's stretch of acreage grown heavy with hits.

Forget mascots or exploding scoreboards. Nooks, odd angles, and strange shapes changed the game within. The Polo Grounds tied popgun lines and a Sahara of a center field. Shibe Park's double deck pricked even the 1961 Phils' godawfulness. A long out to left-center—Death Valley—in Yankee Stadium might be a home run at Griffith Stadium. It made a difference.

At Crosley Field, long pokes over the fence dented cars parked at an adjacent laundry. In

Kansas City, a mule—Charlie O, named for owner Charles O. Finley—grazed beyond right field. Someone put pen to a Lifebuoy soap ad on Baker Bowl's outfield wall: "The Phillies use Lifebuoy and they still stink." Tiger Stadium's right field overhang turned pop-ups into homers. Ebbets Field flaunted a Sym-Phony Band and cowbell-ringing Hilda Chester and pinball emporium. Still enduring: their Flatbush of the mind.

◆ ◆ ◆

If *The Graduate* meant "plastics," baseball also means falling in love with a team. Emeril Lagasse writes of the Red Sox; Larry King, Dodgers; Edward Cardinal Egan, Cubs; Tom Brokaw, a South Dakota town built by the Army Corps of Engineers. To me, the White Sox meant speed; Pirates, bloops and bunts; Yankees, high deeds and Holy Days; the Triple-A Rochester Red Wings, what I tuned to when the Bronx Bombers were rained out.

Each year began slowly, irreversibly, and built through climaxes, toward that New Jerusalem when the Phils would leave the cellar, or the Red Sox win their first title since the Wilson presidency, or the Senators—"First in War, First in Peace, and Last in the American League"—would finally shake their lot as the wretched of the earth.

Name a year. Nineteen twenty-seven meant Murderer's Row; '34, Gas House Gang; '68, Year

Lou Gehrig, Miller Huggins, and Babe Ruth monuments flank Mickey Mantle.

of the Tiger. In 1960, Pittsburgh oozed with a blizzard of "Beat 'Em Bucs" and "The Bucs Are Going All the Way" and a World Series that puzzled Ripley. By contrast, the 1962 Metropolitan Baseball Club of New York was so pathetic—40–120—that it became an enduring fashion in the ephemera capital of the world.

The Mets' metaphor of initials—*Marvin Eugene Throneberry*—mimed Alfonse at the plate and Gaston in the field. Tom Eagleton mocks his own limited range. At least he caught the ball. "Hey!" Throneberry flogged a Met fielder who dropped a fly. "What are you trying to do? Steal my fans?"

Once Marv tripled, but was called out by umpire Dusty Boggess for missing second base. Coach Cookie Lavagetto intercepted the angry Met skipper. "Don't bother arguing," he told Casey Stengel. "He missed first base, too."

Such a man deserved a coda, and found it in 1963. "Marv was upset the other day because the writers gave me a birthday cake," said Stengel. "He asked how come they didn't give him one. I told him, 'They would have, but they were afraid you'd drop it.'"

◆ ◆ ◆

To many, baseball means the manager. "Show me a good loser," blared Leo Durocher, "and I'll show you an idiot." Charlie Dressen bubbled egomania. "Just keep 'em close," he told his players. "I'll think of something." Walter Alston once pondered what he'd learned in baseball. "You make out your lineup card, sit back, and some very strange things happen." Crossing Joe McCarthy, you risked jobs, careers, legs, arms, and perhaps life itself.

As a child, my favorite manager was Stengel—clown, semigrammarian, and linguist—i.e., Sten-gelese. In 1949, he was named Yankee skipper after never placing above fifth in nine big league years. "I became a major league manager in several cities and was discharged," the Ol' Perfessor later told a U.S. Senate committee. "We call it discharged because there was no question I had to leave."

Rambling hid a street-smart hardness (albeit, not Casey's ten pennants and seven World Series). Said Stengel of his 1960 firing: "I'll never make the mistake of being seventy again." In 1992, Richard Nixon said, "If I had it to do over again, I'd name Casey Secretary of State. The essence of diplomacy is to confuse the opposition. The opposition never knew what Casey was talking about. He *always* knew."

Paid by the word, Stengel would have owned the world.

◆ ◆ ◆

Like Musial, Ted Williams, and Willie Mays, Stengel made of baseball almost existential pleasure. Too, announcers who from distant places spun a galloping globe of big league gloss.

If a Voice is good enough, lasts long enough, and has an easy familiarity, he becomes an extended member of the family. Hugh Sidey recalls a '30s Dutch Reagan, Bob Trumpy a transistor carted into bed, George Vecsey baseball radio on the road. Harry Caray sold beer, sacked pomp, and became a balladeer. The Phillies' Byrum Saam made English a second language. "Hello, Byrum Saam," he began his career, "this is everybody speaking." Joe Garagiola became baseball's Bob Hope of the resin bag. Mel Allen made you swear that a florist must have decorated his voice.

"Other sports limit you to play-by-play," observed Red Barber. "Baseball's tempo lets your personality show through." Dizzy Dean "commertated" how a batter "swang" and runner "slud" and slugger stood "confidentially" at the plate. Bob Prince mixed Bellevue and Faulkner. Ernie Harwell said nightly grace around your table. The lyric Vin Scully said, "It was so hot today the moon got sunburned."

Each, I suspect, might call baseball an Andy Hardy parable. Bart Giamatti was right to call it a winnowing force for good. The poet Walt Whitman wrote, "Where is what I started for so long ago? And why is it yet unfound?" The contributors to *What Baseball Means to Me* started loving baseball very young. They have never wandered far away.

◆　◆　◆

Eugene McCarthy observes, "Baseballs never absolutely go out-of-bounds." George Will adds, "I write about politics, mostly to support my baseball habit." Even beyond America, it is a habit hard to break.

Not long ago my wife and I adopted two small children from Ukraine. One day we traipsed to a sidewalk gallery in Kiev. In 1995, inducted at Cooperstown, broadcaster Bob Wolff played "Take Me Out to the Ballgame" on his ukelele. Now, nearly five thousand miles away, I saw a *bandura* for sale—Ukrainian for that instrument. "Let's buy it," I said, and began strumming sport's "Marseillaise."

A Ukrainian ukelele. Two Red Sox fans-to-be smiling seven time zones from Fenway Park. Odd tatters. Photographs and memories. A sonnet sung upon the heart. That's what baseball means to me.

—CURT SMITH, DECEMBER 22, 2001

Main Street on parade: The Hall of Fame and Museum opens, 1939.

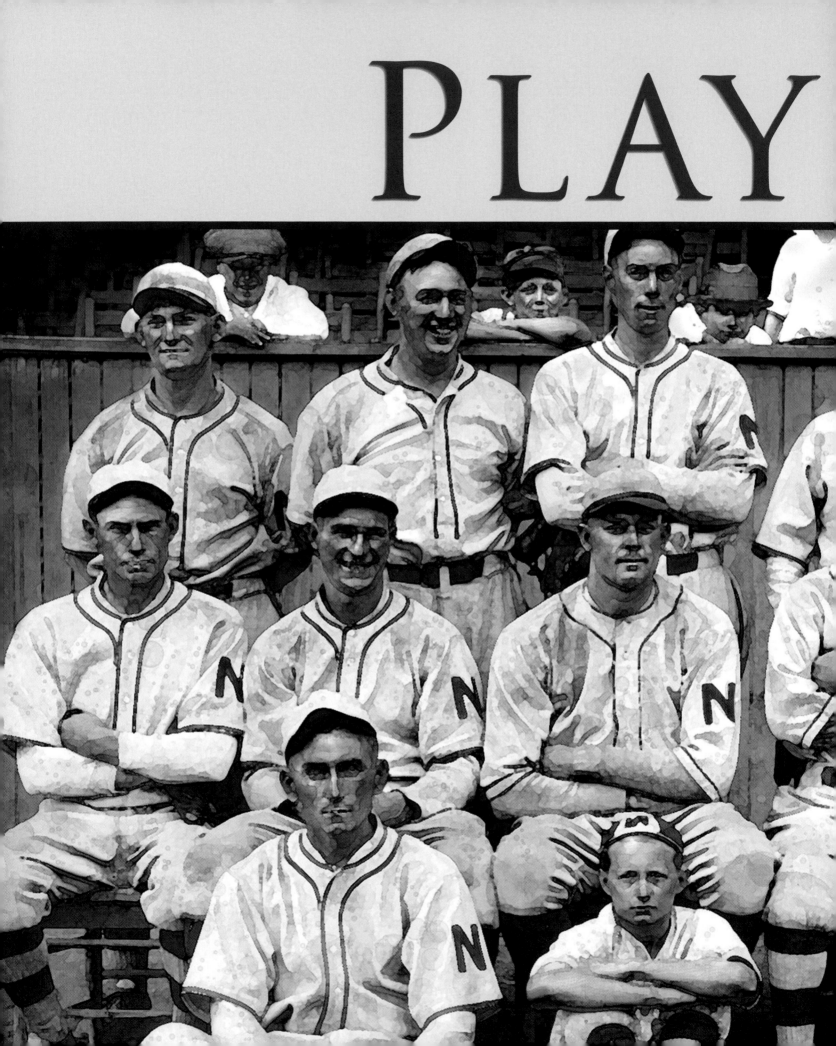

PLAY

BALL!

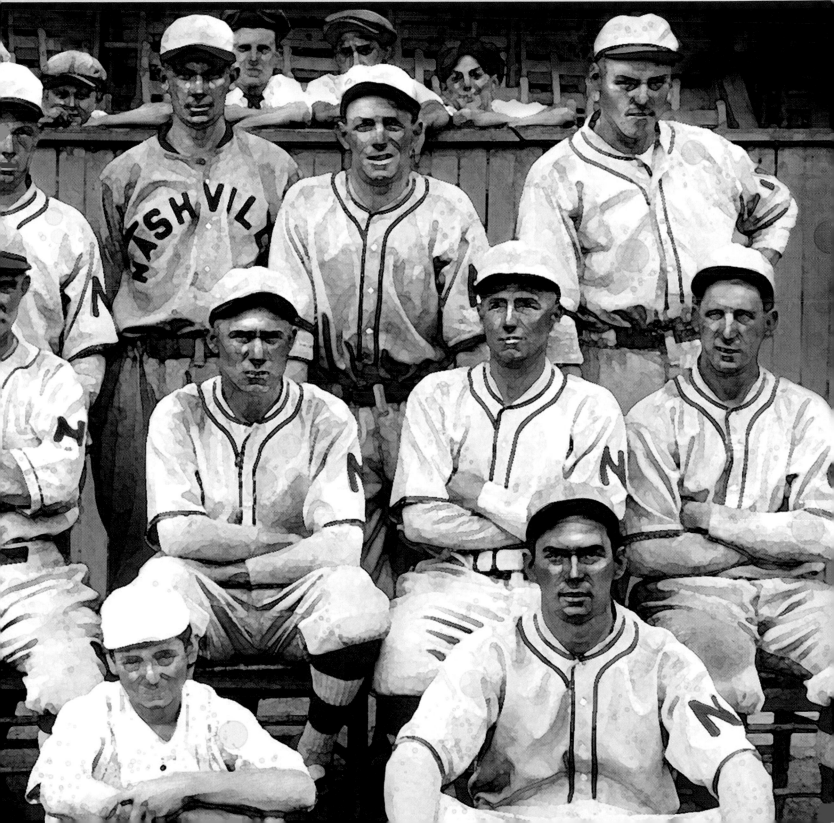

BOB ALLEN

◆ ◆ ◆

What does baseball mean to me? It means living the game I loved as a kid. In 1942, I was eleven years old and World War II was underway. The Milwaukee Brewers offered free admission to any child accompanied by an adult who donated an aluminum pot or pan to the war effort. Our American Association entry defeated the Columbus Red Birds that day. My lifelong affair with baseball had begun.

After that, I cleaned under the bleachers before every home game to gain free admission. Between games of a doubleheader I'd go to the concession stands and get Cokes and hot dogs for the players—forget food in the clubhouse! Then, in 1953, the Boston Braves arrived in Wisconsin—the first team in fifty years to move—and I became the only Milwaukeean to work in their publicity office. The next thirteen years were glorious as we won two pennants and a World Series. What excitement! The city of Milwaukee and its fans were the talk of the nation.

The Braves broke the all-time National League attendance record their first year and then drew over two million fans each of the next four years—another record. A sea of yellow charter buses on weekends. Trains stopping beyond the center field parking lot to discharge fans from throughout the Midwest. Divorce actions got nasty when both parties fought over their season tickets. Following deaths, some family members battled over these prized possessions.

When the Braves moved to Atlanta after the 1965 season, I resigned out of loyalty to my city and state. After all, I had my 1957 World Series ring. Since then I have been an agent to Hank Aaron, Johnny Vander Meer, Bill Mazeroski, Don Larsen, and Bobby Thomson, among others, and supplied players for baseball card shows. I've traveled coast to coast with Aaron and Eddie Mathews and players like Ernie Banks, Mickey Mantle, Willie Mays, and Ted Williams. You get to talk about how it was when they played—and you cheered. I have to tell you: I liked it better, back then.

Take talent. How appropriate it is that Hank Aaron is the first player listed in the records of the more than 15,000 major league players whose statistics are shown in the *Baseball Encyclopedia*. Or humor. Imagine: Our Braves

Eddie Mathews swings for the wall in the 1960s.

actually *enjoyed* their job! Warren Spahn won more games, 363, than any other left-hander. He was a cutup with a great pickoff move. A story goes that once he threw to first base—and the batter swung.

Spahnie was my favorite Brave even before they moved from Boston. Years later my wife and I went to Hawaii on a cruise with him for seventeen days—and I pinched myself: You can see why people have said they'd like to spend one day with me and rub shoulders with the greats. Which brings up Mathews. To me, he embodied what baseball meant, and had. Eddie always said his greatest thrill was being one half of its greatest one-two punch. He and Aaron hit more home runs as teammates than Babe Ruth and Lou Gehrig. Of their record 863, Aaron hit 442 and Mathews 421.

All told, Eddie hit 512. From his rookie year in 1952 through 1959, he had more homers than any-one—299. He was on time every day, in shape to play. He would play a position other than third base, if need be, and give everything he had. Teammates knew he'd back them in a fight on the field. Chuck Tanner told me: "He played every game like the world was coming to an end tomorrow."

Mathews was by far the toughest guy I ever met in or out of sports. Maybe it was because he threatened to "punch me out" on a cruise ship a few years back, and another time threatened to flatten me in Philadelphia. Once he asked me to join him for his first solo flight a week after he earned a pilot's license. I told him I would be happy to fly with him, but give me six months to get used to the idea. Eddie didn't speak to me for two years.

Not every player was as volatile. Mathews could change moods in an instant and become introverted and sullen. But if he liked you, he would do anything for you. He could spot a phony a mile away. What I liked is how players viewed *life* like Eddie did. He preferred a neighborhood bar to fancy hotel digs, the common man to big shots. Once he told me we would

He played every game like the world was coming to an end tomorrow.

always be friends, as long as I did not take advantage of his being Eddie Mathews.

In 1957, with the Yankees threatening to take a three-games-to-one lead, Eddie's two-run homer in the 10th inning evened the World Series. In Game 7, his ninth-inning, heart-stopping backhand stop of Moose Skowron's vicious liner over the bag gave the Braves their victory. Mathews was the only Brave to play all thirteen years in Milwaukee.

When Eddie died in 2001, I thought of the watch with his name on it he gave me in 1961, and how I wore it every day since, as a reminder of our friendship. You could believe anything he told you: Ask agents if that's true now! Players had less money when Eddie broke in, were less selfish, had to scrap. I'll never forget Eddie, Hank Aaron, Spahnie, and many other players arriving at the park via the Number 10 streetcar over the 35th Street viaduct and walking to the stadium with the fans.

There wasn't the distance between players and fans that we see today. I miss number 41. I miss his kind of baseball even more.

BOB ALLEN was the Milwaukee Braves' publicity director from 1953 to 1965. Today he is president of Bob Allen Sports, Inc., representing retired athletes.

MARTY APPEL

♦ ♦ ♦

What can we say about a game in which spring training begins every winter and the winter meetings are held every fall?

For one thing, you can set your watch to it, and if you are lucky, you can set your life to it.

I was born nine days before Babe Ruth died in 1948. When I turned fifty, people kidded me about getting old, but when you have devoted a life to being a baseball fan, getting older is a joy! It means you have personally catalogued so many memorable experiences with this National Pastime of ours. You possess the ability to speak firsthand of them. It's a gift.

I remember going to Yankee games in the mid-1950s and overhearing fans talk about the old-timers. I came to have a bit of envy for those who could talk about seeing Ruth or Gehrig or DiMaggio. I was always particularly fond of people who could remember Ruth playing the outfield or sliding into a base. It meant more than the recollections of those who invariably said "...and the Babe hit a home run that day!"

As a baby boomer, I was treated to the game in new and exciting ways. Baseball cards, for one, brought the player images to full color, right in the palm of your hand, and when collecting became all the rage, we got to know every player by his card. Mention Ted Kluszewski

to any fan over fifty today, and the image of his muscleman Topps card runs through the mind. Same with hundreds of others. Baseball cards have been the gateway to the game for generations now, but mine was the first.

Mine was also the first to have baseball on television.

Television not only let me see the long legs of Ted Williams and the running style of Jackie Robinson (side to side, arms flailing, hands out flat, recklessly accelerating), but the "low home" camera let you see the rising fastball of Sandy Koufax, and the center field camera, introduced in 1957, let you appreciate how Whitey Ford and Billy Pierce could work the corners.

And replays! They came in the early 1960s and forever changed the way we watched baseball. Imagine, that in 1951 viewers saw Bobby Thomson's homer only *one time* before they saw the replays in theater newsreels weeks later!

I love it when I can tell a younger fan about the Boys of Summer,

On October 8, 1956, Don Larsen pitched the World Series' sole no-hitter.

and Don Larsen's perfect game, and the Hollywood glamour of Mickey Mantle, with his twelve World Series in his first fourteen years. Or the move west by the Dodgers and Giants, the Maris-Mantle home run chase, the original Mets and the Miracle Mets. And Mays, Aaron, and Clemente in the same N.L. outfield for the All-Star Game.

I went to games at Ebbets Field and the Polo Grounds. And at old Yankee Stadium you would exit via the running track and walk through the bullpen, where Ryne Duren had been throwing just minutes before.

Not to mention the Washington Senators. Boy, they were awful.

The game, you see, belongs to the fans more than to the players or the owners. They're only passing through. You say Rickey Henderson played in twenty-three seasons? Big deal. I've had *forty-six seasons as a fan!* More than 175 new Hall of Fame inductees in that time. Forty-six World Series (all right, forty-five), and each one still conjures up memories of the Gillette theme song with Sharpie the parrot overlaid on the screen ("To LOOK sharp…") and how good the players look in their long-sleeved sweatshirts.

Baseball serves as a perfect gauge for measuring the milestones of my life.

I was twenty-eight when Hank Aaron retired. He was my last active player from my first year as a fan. I was twenty-nine when Maury Wills's *son* reached the majors! I was thirty-two when the first player born *after* Maris's home run record reached the majors. I remember when I first knew all the

By 1956 Larsen was using a no-windup delivery. In this game against Baltimore a year earlier, he winds up.

managers as players. I was thirty-three. Or when Ray Boone's *grandson* played in the bigs. I was forty-four.

I was forty-seven when Mickey died. That was what is called a reality check.

Some say the beauty of baseball is that it isn't played by the clock. But there is a timepiece governing it, and it is the timepiece of our lives. And if we are to measure our journey by the memories we store, the joy of the game on the field has given us plenty. Even Cubs and Red Sox fans would agree.

Thank you, Abner Doubleday, or Alexander Cartwright, or George and Harry Wright, wherever you are.

MARTY APPEL, former Yankee public relations director, has written sixteen books, including his autobiography, Now Pitching for the Yankees.

NORMAN R. AUGUSTINE

◆ ◆ ◆

Baseball means going with my father on the spur of the moment to Merchants' Park to see the mighty Denver Bears of the world-renowned Western League.

It means having gone with my son-in-law—and my son, who died recently—to see the Orioles at Camden Yards.

It means walking in the winning run as a kid in the local youth league championship game.

It means tearing up an ankle sliding into home, successfully stretching a triple into a homer, and realizing that the cheers of even a small crowd can completely eliminate pain.

It means having an office in my home generously adorned with autographed baseballs...the one of greatest pride having been given to me as a child by my uncle, accompanied by a letter saying that he had just seen "a kid pitch who was pretty fast and looked like he might amount to something." (The autograph on the ball reads "Bob Feller.")

It means in the years after graduating from college listening to Vin Scully and carefully scoring some 300 games so that I could produce my now widely unremembered copyrighted calculator for baseball managers.

*Oriole Park at Camden Yards, Baltimore's
idyll of turf, brick, and memory.*

It means as a young aerospace engineer cleverly constructing, as had many of my several hundred colleagues sitting at desks in a large bullpen-like office area, an early transistor radio to surreptitiously defy our bosses' pronouncement that we not listen to the World Series while at work...only to be exposed by the spontaneous roar that followed the explosion off Bill Mazeroski's bat...which in turn was followed by a whole series of explosions as our bosses one by one peered out of their offices like awakening gophers, each wondering—albeit momentarily—what had caused the uproar.

It means taking my fiancée from Sweden to watch a Dodger game in the hopes of hooking her on this strange American pastime called baseball...only to have Sandy Koufax pick that particular day to set a strikeout record—the stuff of somewhat limited excitement to the unwashed.

And, finally, it means as a business executive later in life the unparalleled thrill of standing on the pitcher's mound at Camden Yards and being introduced to the crowd alongside no less a celebrity than Cal Ripken.

And, yes, as I recall there was another fellow standing there on the mound that day—it seems to me it was the President of the United States.

*NORMAN R. AUGUSTINE is the retired Chairman
and CEO of Lockheed Martin Corporation, former
Undersecretary of the Army, and former President
of the Boy Scouts of America.*

JAMES A. BAKER III

◆ ◆ ◆

Bottom of the ninth, final game, one out, trailing 2–4. What memory could be sweeter than Bobby Thomson's homer in the 1951 National League best-of-three playoff series? I've read that it was the first baseball ever televised coast to coast. I watched the final game with some friends at college. No one who saw the game or heard it on the radio will ever forget it. That indescribable moment reminded a generation of Americans of an important lesson: keep swinging; it truly ain't over till it's over.

*JAMES A. BAKER III, former Secretary of State,
has served in senior government positions under three
Presidents. He is right: The 1951 playoff series marked
baseball's first national TV coverage.*

*Polo Grounds, October 3, 1951: Bobby Thomson
swings—and "The Giants win the pennant!"*

ERNIE BANKS

♦ ♦ ♦

To me, baseball means love, family, friends, and fun. Baseball has cultivated my love of life. People ask me what I've learned in my seventy years on earth. I tell them it's only love that matters. Part of the joy of playing for the Cubs was day baseball. I'd say, "The moon and the stars are destined for love." You'd finish playing and then have the evening for family—for your kids. Baseball by day, love at night. It gives new meaning to "Let's play two!"

What a lucky guy I am. I was the first player in the Cubs' more than 100 years to have his uniform number retired. I'm the only one to play for one team—the Cubs—under one owner—Philip K. Wrigley—in the city of one mayor—Richard J. Daley, "Da Boss"—under one light—God's—in one park—Wrigley Field. All that fostered a sense of family with the Cubs. I remember a commercial they used to run: "Come to Wrigley Field and get fresh air and sunshine—and see a major league game besides." The game was secondary. Family came first.

Only in baseball do you see a grandfather, father, and son trooping to the game together. It binds the generations. Every game is a new memory you'll be talking about generations from now. Remember the TV show *Eight Is Enough*? Not in my family! I had eleven brothers and sisters. I grew up before Jackie Robinson, so baseball didn't mean everything to me as a kid. My dad, on the other hand, loved it, and eventually so did I. I started with the Kansas City Monarchs. Buck O'Neil was the manager. Satchel Paige played there. Man, they loved the game— and I learned from them. I eat, drink, and sleep baseball. It's the greatest life I know.

Baseball also means friends. You got to be one to have one. Guys like Warren Buffett and Bill Gates I know through baseball. They own half the U.S. economy. I've got other friends who can't afford to go to a game, or can't get seats. What brings us together is that baseball keeps you young. I even knew that as a player. Like everyone else, they get sick, hurt. But the game is like college, or the Army. Its dynamics teach teamwork. Think of confidence, heart, determination, focus, dedication: You need 'em to succeed in baseball. It's the best training ground for life.

The next time you're at Wrigley Field, look around at what you don't see. Violence, brutality, aggression, hate. Then look at what you do see—you sense it, feel it. Love matters even more than a world championship for the Cubs.

ERNIE BANKS played his entire career (1953–71) with the Chicago Cubs. He hit 512 homers, was the National League MVP in 1958 and 1959, and was inducted into the Baseball Hall of Fame in 1977.

Mr. Cub: His wrists were made for hitting.

Dom DiMaggio, "The Little Professor," played for the San Francisco Seals before joining Boston.

FRED BARNES

◆ ◆ ◆

When I was five years old, my father gave me a baseball autographed by all the players on a team he coached as an Army lieutenant in Monterey, California, in the late 1930s. One of the players was a seventeen-year-old private named Dom DiMaggio, who, my dad proudly pointed out, had grown up to become the center fielder for the Boston Red Sox.

And so I became a Red Sox fan. It's a passion that has never died in the half-century since then. The

Bucky Dent homer that kept the Red Sox out of the World Series in 1978 didn't chill my enthusiasm. Nor did the sixth game of the 1986 World Series with the Mets, as painful as the error by Bill Buckner and the wild pitch by Bob Stanley were. True, I switch off the TV or leave the room when replays of that game come on. But I'm still as big a Red Sox fan as ever.

Somehow when I was courting my wife, Barbara, I didn't fully reveal this. We got married on Labor Day in 1967 and went to the Gulf coast of Florida for our honeymoon. Each night, I would slip out to the car and try to pick up the Red Sox game on radio on WTIC in Hartford. The Red Sox, after all, were in a hot pennant race. Carl Yastrzemski was headed for the Triple Crown and Jim Lonborg for a Cy Young Award. At first, my wife didn't understand what I was doing. Then I explained—and she still didn't understand. When the Red Sox won the pennant on the last day of the season and my eyes teared up, she finally understood.

I didn't see my first game at Fenway Park until 1977 when I moved to Cambridge for a year-long Nieman Fellowship at Harvard. In fact, one of the reasons I applied for the fellowship in the first place was the prospect of going to games at Fenway. I had grown up in Arlington, Virginia, across the Potomac River from Washington. So I'd only seen the Red Sox play at Griffith Stadium, then at RFK Stadium, then at Memorial Stadium in Baltimore after the Washington Senators moved away. I had seen Ted Williams hit a homer off Camilo Pascual. And I had seen Reggie Smith make one of the greatest catches ever, reaching over the low center field fence at RFK to rob Hank Allen of a homer and holding up his glove with the ball sticking out like an ice cream cone as he ran back to the dugout. But I hadn't seen Fenway, the shrine.

Bill Buckner's error in Game 6 of the 1986 World Series will forever be remembered.

The sad part is I was in Boston for the 1978 season. That's when the Red Sox were well ahead at the All-Star break, then lost the pennant in a playoff game to the Yankees. Anyway, I must have seen thirty or thirty-five games, often in the bleachers, often alone, since my wife and daughters weren't always interested in going. There's no place like Fenway.

A wonderful thing happened to me and my son during the 2000 season. I spoke one Saturday in May at a conference on Christians and the culture, or something along that line, at Harvard Law School. Meanwhile, my son Freddy and son-in-law John Kurcina went to see the Red Sox play at Fenway. At the conference, I met Walt Day, the Red Sox chaplain. Having heard me speak about my faith, he asked if I'd talk to the Red Sox chapel the next morning. I agreed instantly, as long as I could bring my son along.

I don't remember exactly what I said beyond telling how I'd become a Christian and how it had changed my life. What I do remember vividly is looking out at roughly fifteen Red Sox sitting and listening to me. My son was sitting there, too, right next to Nomar Garciaparra. Hours later, the Red Sox beat the A's.

FRED BARNES is executive editor of The Weekly Standard *and a Fox News Channel regular contributor.*

DAVE BARRY

◆ ◆ ◆

I was on a team called the Indians and had a Herb Score–model glove, named for a player who went on to get hit in the eye by a baseball.

I particularly remember this one game: I was in deep right field, of course, and there were two out in the bottom of the last inning with the tying run on base, and Gerry Sinnott, who already had to shave, was at bat. As I stood there waiting for the pitch, I dreamed a dream that millions of other kids have dreamt: that someday I would grow up and I wouldn't have to be in Little League anymore. In the interim, my feelings could best be summed up by the statement "Oh, please, please, please, God, don't let Gerry Sinnott hit the ball to me."

And of course God, who as you know has a terrific sense of humor, had Gerry Sinnott hit the ball to me. Here is what happened in the next few seconds: Outside of my body, hundreds of spectators, thousands of spectators, arrived at the ball field at that very instant via chartered buses from distant cities to see if I could catch the ball. Inside my body, my brain cells hastily met and came up with a Plan of Action, which they announced to the rest of the body parts. "Listen up, everybody!" they shouted. "We're going to MISS THE BALL! Let's get cracking!"

Instantly my entire body sprang into action, like a complex, sophisticated machine operated by earthworms. The command flashed down from Motor Control to my legs: "GET READY TO RUN!" And soon the excited reply flashed back: "WHICH LEG FIRST?" Before Motor Control could issue a ruling, an urgent message came in from Vision Central, reporting that the ball had already gone by. In fact, it was now a good thirty to forty yards behind my body, rolling into the infield of the adjacent field. Motor Control, reacting quickly to this surprising new input, handled the pressure coolly and decisively, snapping out the command "OKAY! We're going to FALL DOWN!" And my body lunged violently sideways, in the direction opposite the side the ball had passed a full two seconds earlier, flopping onto the ground like some pathetic spawning salmon whose central nervous system had been destroyed by toxic waste, as Gerry Sinnott cruised home.

Embracing baseball is as natural as a smile.

DAVE BARRY, a leading American humorist, is a best-selling author and Pulitzer Prize–winning Miami Herald *syndicated columnist.*

Atlanta's Ponce de Leon Park, circa 1950. A magnolia tree once anchored deep right-center field.

GRIFFIN B. BELL

◆ ◆ ◆

I am by no means an expert on baseball, but you don't have to be to understand its meaning to America. In my early years our law firm in Atlanta had a close association with the minor league [Southern Association] Crackers and, as a young lawyer, I frequently attended their games. They played in Ponce de Leon Park, and a magnolia tree in center field was actually in play. I hate to admit it now, but I was a great New York Yankee fan. There was something special about October in the Bronx. I attended the World Series twice when the Yankees were playing and have always thought they had—and still have—a lot of magic. Now that we have big league baseball in Atlanta, I have become a Braves fan still trying to get over 1996 and 1999. Whoever you root for, baseball is clearly our greatest national sports institution.

GRIFFIN B. BELL served as U.S. Attorney General from 1977 to 1979 under President Jimmy Carter. Today he is a senior partner of an Atlanta law firm.

CORBIN BERNSEN

◆ ◆ ◆

Of course it would be easy to say that baseball brings with it the sweet smell of eucalyptus drifting on a summer breeze across the Little League field, barbecues urging the game to be finished and blue clear pools of water offering to take the sting off scraped knees and bring "cap hair" back to normal. Ahh, maybe I should just stop here.

Unfortunately, I can't. You see, all that is a romantic notion, a memory stored under "youth and undiscovered wisdoms." You start to learn as you grow older that the game is in fact like a gentle snow that sits quietly, patiently, on top of an active volcano. Even today I try to teach my children, all of whom are devoted to the game, that it is never okay to just sit back in the outfield and let your mind drift. That's a killer. A ball may never come to you once during a game but you must always be ready! You never know when the mountain will blow, and if you are caught sleeping, the lava will run you down and burn you to death.

All this is to say that there is a severe, tightly wound tension beneath the ballet. Look at the way entire teams pound onto the field to brawl when given the chance. It comes out of nowhere.

This was most identified to me when, in my sweet youth, an incident happened during one of my brother's games: My brother was stealing second and he, as was always his fashion, dove toward second like a wild horse, spikes up, willing to take out anything in his path. In this case it was the shortstop, a kid with a turned-up nose and equally bad attitude. The mountain blew! Fists started flying, bases turned into weapons. The teams, however, for the most part stayed calm. The umpire saw to that. Instead, it was the shortstop's mother who raced onto the field to aid her son in attacking my brother. In turn, my mother leapt from the bleachers and onto the diamond to attack her!

A catfight, straight out of the WWF, right there on second base on our Little League field. Don't ask why, but the fathers never really got involved. Their only job was to...and I mean this literally...bail their wives out of jail. Ahh, the sweet smell of the city holding tank. Now that's baseball...when you rip the hide from the cork!

Okay, now I know that's an extreme example and, yes, of course, I remember days sitting in the Los Angeles Coliseum watching the Brooklyn Dodgers become my Los Angeles Dodgers, bonding with my dad, but I'm acutely aware that at any given moment, the oh-so-beautiful field of green can turn ugly, become a battlefield, where warriors roam in search of the good fight.

CORBIN BERNSEN played Arnie Becker from 1986 to 1994 on the TV series L.A. Law. *Art miming life: Bernsen brought his love of baseball to film in the classic* Major League.

October 6, 1959: A World Series record crowd (92,706) packs the oval for Game 5 at the Dodgers' 1958–61 home, Los Angeles Memorial Coliseum.

DAVID E. BIRNEY

◆ ◆ ◆

In 1993, my son Peter and I attended an Indians game at old Municipal Stadium. I got to thinking about fathers and sons, and teaching sons about heroism, and baseball as a portal to a world of myth and legend. So I wrote a poem, *Peter at Ten*. Below are my favorite segments:

Peter at ten,
Ears crushed and curled
Like tiny flowers spilling
Beneath his bright blue
Cleveland Indians hat,

Smiles at me from behind his headgear—
The bright grace of his sunlit face
Barred for the moment,
Prisoner of the orthodontist.
"Dad, is Pena a better catcher than Piazza?"

We are at an Indians game,
Extra innings—the fourteenth—
The stadium a bright arc
Against the midnight black,
And the Cleveland catcher is at bat.

Like Piazza and Pena, Peter catches
For his Braves, his team at home.
Masked, armored in pads and guards,
Kneeling, erect,
His glove centered

Precisely in front of his chest,
His small fist clutched behind his back,
He kneels, intense, formal,
Like a warrior in a Samurai movie,
Fierce, concentrated, precise;

Or the captain of a lunar module
Guiding his pitcher's fastball
To a pinpoint landing
In his
Mitt.

Pena swings.
A strike.
"Probably Piazza," Peter meditates
Behind his wire smile. "A really good hitter."
"Can I get some ice cream?"

He does, running up the steps
Toward the sweating vendor
Those steps, the same steps—
(Not the same, but the same)—
I climbed as a boy
On endless afternoons
Of summer baseball.

The field at my back
I climbed, into the infinity
Of Lakefront Stadium
Staring into the crowd,
"Coke, Orange, Pepsi!"

A bucket of sodas and ice,
Its wire handle
Cutting my forearm,
Cash folded in my pocket,
Dazed, exhausted,

Into a wall of faces,
I climbed, alone and oblivious
To the summer giants
In the vast grass
Far below.

Pena takes a called strike
And Peter returns with chocolate mouth
Behind his headgear.
He is his own minstrel show,
Blackface in negative image,

Leaping and strutting the steps,
A smile for every aisle
Cohan and Kelly and Callaway
Vaulting the last seat beside me.
"Yeah, a much cooler hitter...Piazza."

His life is primary colors,
Sunlight and sea green and buccaneer red,
He learns the world by embrace and
Joyful collision. He does,
And by doing, knows.

He is the stream shouting over rock,
Crystal with light,
Celebrating the journey,
The spring wind, alive in blossom and
   bright,
Light-shimmered air.

Both flag and wind,
Plow and loamed earth
Is he, simple as grass,
Knotted and far as stars and galaxies,
Learning the way and why of the world.

[Editor's Note: at 12:30 A.M., Cleveland slugger Albert Belle came to bat. The count went to 2-0. Peter began chanting, "Belle, Belle! Ring the bell," and bouncing on his father's knee.]

Belle, motionless, regards an outside pitch.
Impassive. "Ball, three."
"Come on. Come on!" Peter turns his
Hat backwards again and jumping,
Imprisons me in his joy.

I hug him back—
And hear him sing at church,
A duet with his sister,
Twin heroes of my life,
And I am imprisoned again.

And later, a "credo,"
Alone before his school choice,
Vivaldi, I think,
His voice, so simple on high, so pure,
It suspends the air,

Sunlight stilled
And my heart startled,
Stops, weeps. This blessing
Which like the music itself,
Dissolves even as it is made.

His boy's soprano,
The breath of hope and heart
Lights my soul,
And in that moment
In spite of loss

And the death of heroes,
And all that must die,
Dust at last,
His breath breathes in me,
And I believe.

He graces the world,
Losing it even as he learns it.

"Stee...rike"
"Oh, no. Not a strike!"
Peter turns his hat backwards again.
Belle steps back out of the box,
His bat arcs slowly, gracefully,

His great shoulders and arms,
Rehearsing, reliving,
The massive serenity,
The power of his
Epic swing.

"Oh, Dad,
I love this game,
This is the best game."
And he tumbles back
To his seat alongside me.

He means, this time,
This second,
Endless, unbearably bright,
Poised, suspended in the light,
Past and future giving way to now,

And we three become one now...
Belle coiled, radiant,
Peter, yearning,
Time stretched between his joy and
    the plate,
And I engulfed, adrift in love
For this wild and precious boy.

It is a moment like that second before
We light the rocket
Peter has built himself
From an endless array of fragments.
Two days of concentrated work.

Newton calculating the apple's fall,
Galileo discovering the moons of Saturn,
Cone and fins and chute become
Shape and silent grace,
Peter exuberant, intense,

With discovery and intuition
And frustration,
Tears falling in dismay,
Streaking his laughing face
As fit refuses fit,

In 1995 Albert Belle led
the American League in runs,
doubles, homers, slugging,
and runs batted in.

Tube and thumbs tumble
And try again, and again,
And once again,
As fin finally notches into silvered body,
The cone capping the sleek shape.

And trial and fumbled fit
Become space and time and beauty.
And Peter's eyes moving
Between flame and ignition point.
Mouth open, no breath, no sound
No...

This second
Burnt by a blush of flame
And the shockingly beautiful arc of the
craft,
Blooming,
Its scarlet chute

Falling like a rose from the sky
A single blossom, floating...
Peter and I statues in the grass.
"Did you see, dad? An Angel...
Did you see?"

The crack of the bat.
Silence,
Like a great bell in the haloed night,
Reverberates, re-echoes,
As the ball rises against the black,

To become another point of light
A shooting star among a cloud
Of stars. Peter steps,
Sleepwalking, onto the seat of his chair
Cap clutched in hand, watching,

As the star falls
Slowly through the light,
Beyond the light,
Beyond the shadowed
Left-field wall into myth.

The noise is dense,
Palpable.
Like darkness far undersea,
Or a roiling surf over rock,
Belle moving through the fierce and
    festive storm.

And Peter, "Yes."
Laughing. Amazed.
And, "Yes!" again.
His arms raised.
"We win, Dad." "Dad, Indians win."

He leaps,
Leaps into my arms,
Joy leaping to joy,
This instant
Becoming for this boy,

Legend, in this moment,
Incandescent,
Myth blooms to myth.
Belle and Pena and Piazza,
Gehrig and "The Babe."

Achilles and Hector,
St. George and St. Joan and Davy
    Crockett,
Daniel Boone and Alan Shepard,
Leaping lightly
Onto the moon.

DAVID E. BIRNEY is an actor and director who has starred in such TV films as Love and Betrayal, The Five of Me, *and* The Long Journey Home.

Babe Ruth chooses his lumber on opening day at Yankee Stadium, 1932.

JAMES J. BLANCHARD

◆ ◆ ◆

Forget a straight line being the shortest distance between two points. As a boy growing up in Michigan I dreamed of being a major leaguer. My baseball coach knew better. He told me, "You know, you're very good at student government." My shortest distance to the bigs was becoming Governor of Michigan.

The trip began very early. I was like most kids in mid-century America. I got hooked on the game, listened even to exhibition games on the radio, and collected baseball cards. Of course, my collection was the best around! The first team I followed was the 1950 Tigers, who lost the pennant by only three games to New York. God, they were the most important thing in my life. I can still tell you their entire lineup.

You're so impressionable as a child. Events that happened fifty years ago seem like yesterday. I still remember the first game I saw in Boston. My parents were divorced when I was young, so it was hard going to games: no father, no brother. Neighbors'd take me. This one day a family friend, John Ham, took his son, Steve, and me to Fenway Park. We get to the last inning and the game is tied. Red Sox up, bases loaded, Ted Williams up. He gets a walk to win the game, but is mad 'cause he didn't get a pitch to hit. He throws his bat in the air, the crowd gets on him, and he goes over near the fans and starts arguing. Controversy. Excitement. Was it baseball—or politics?

As a teenager, I once ran on the field at Tiger Stadium to shake Mickey Mantle's hand. They didn't eject you right away back then. It happened a couple innings later, I guess to protect your dignity. Talk about a passion for the game. Who could guess that I'd get elected to Congress, become Governor, and throw out the first ball at Michigan and Trumbull? Or have a collection of autographed baseballs—Feller, DiMaggio, Connie Mack. I have an actual ball signed by Al Kaline and Charlie Gehringer—legends thirty years apart. I'd go to spring training games at Lakeland, where the Tigers

September 24, 1974, Memorial Stadium:
Al Kaline gets hit 3,000.

trained, and when they played at Sarasota (White Sox) and Winter Haven (Red Sox).

Baseball is a people game. Maybe that's why so many public officials like it. Kaline, of course, is Mr. Tiger. I got to know Kirk Gibson, who campaigned for me. Sparky Anderson became a dear friend. I mentioned Williams. Once in Florida Sparky took me over and introduced me.

Ted took one look and said, "You're an R, aren't you?" He's a conservative Republican.

Sparky didn't miss a beat. "No," he said, "he's a D, but a great guy." Williams went, "Aww," then put me in a head-lock—he's one big guy, 6-3, over 200 pounds. I still have the picture of the three of us.

Sometimes I worry about the game. It's like the rest of culture. Too much money. Strikes. Guys moving to and fro. I just hope they remember their loyalty to baseball, just like I did as a kid, like many kids do today. Short or long, I can't think of a better line than the one to baseball.

JAMES J. BLANCHARD has served as U.S. Congressman, Governor of Michigan, and Ambassador to Canada. He is also the author of Behind the Embassy Door.

Kaline, the A.L.'s youngest batting champion, robbing Mickey Mantle in 1958 at Yankee Stadium.

Mickey Mantle in 1959 (left). "He had more talent," said Casey Stengel, "than most fellas ever dream of." Mike Garcia was asked how to pitch the three-time MVP in a close game. "Easy," he replied. "You don't."

MICHAEL BOLTON

◆ ◆ ◆

I was seven years old when my father bought me a glove and began my "pitching" lessons. In my front yard, he threw the ball to me, encouraging a "hard" throw back. Then hitting the ball to me, again and again, harder and harder, admonishing, "This is the way it'll be coming to you on the field"—a metaphor that would apply to my later years in life (as well as my performance in Little League baseball and other games down the road).

It's been a long time since my five years of Little League that began at age eight, but the memories in between then and now are poignant.

In the early 1960s, I was riveted to the radio or TV when the Yankee lineup was announced from Richardson, Kubek, Maris, through number 7, Mickey Mantle. Nineteen sixty: the amazing loss of the World Series and Casey Stengel—and Kubek taking one to the throat. 'Sixty-one: Mantle and Maris neck in neck hitting home runs—losing Mantle to an injury, but cheering as Maris finally broke the Babe's record. The excitement I felt as an eight- and nine-year-old then seemed beyond replication. I didn't yet realize that the Yanks—my champions—would be a permanent source of enjoyment and inspiration in my life.

Within the last few years, Paul O'Neill joined my team, the Bolton Bombers, in a softball game held as a fund-raiser in the Midwest. At the end of the game, I thanked him and told him about the Yanks' legacy I was witness to as a kid. He said, "God, we'll never live that team down." Now that he's retired, I can't wait to see him again and tell him about *these* Yankees, *his* Yankees! I want to tell him how they've done the Yankee pride proud.

One of the most interesting things about baseball is the game's ability to affect everyone in such an exclusive way. Baseball is a lot of things, depending on who you are. It conjures so many images. One of mine: Joe Torre's—tears streaming down his victorious and humble face. Another: Billy Crystal and I were talking about the Yankee phenomenon and how for a moment, when Mickey died, it felt like we had lost an integral, innocent part of our youth.

Baseball is respect for the opposition. Bobby Valentine and the amazing 2000 Mets forced the Yanks to play harder. So many friends who are die-hard Mets fans don't believe me when I tell 'em I love their club. They are such a great team and never had a moment of smug, false confidence. They can win anytime—just not over my club.

Baseball is great voices. I miss the familiar voice of Mel Allen, Voice of the Yankees, exulting "Going, going, gone!" The one and only Phil Rizzuto, the Scooter, who moved to the booth from the field right around the time I was born, takes me back to that gentler time even today. Holy Cow!

As the years pass, work and other adult responsibilities take over, and the only way I can play ball as I travel is fielding a semipro team who tours with me and my band, playing all games for various charitable causes. At night, we go on stage. We play as many as forty-plus

games per tour. My uniform number is 7. The Bolton Bombers play hard and though it's for charity, there's something about it that's for us—the field, fans, sunshine, sense of nostalgia, and promise of fun. Yet this pastoral seduction is not really what most of us love about the game. Baseball is hard, and that's what keeps us coming back. On the road, it's our version of the Clash of the Titans: Aches now don't heal as quickly. There is a lot of pain on stage if we have a show the night of the game—but the extra adrenaline helps.

I talked about number 7. Another number is 5. One day in 1993 in Fort Lauderdale, Florida, home to the Joe DiMaggio Children's Hospital. I met Joltin' Joe. I was privileged to play in Joe's annual Legends Game, which raises money for charity, and we became

Joe DiMaggio in the Yankee clubhouse. Baseball named him the greatest living player in 1969.

As the crowd stood and cheered for Joe DiMaggio he turned to me and said, "Gee, Mike, they really like you here."

The Yankee Clipper at his retirement in 1951. Asked why he hustled, DiMag said, "Maybe there's somebody here who never saw me play."

friends. We supported one another's causes. Suddenly, he began to show up at my concerts, always with his grandchildren and great-grandchildren (who, fortunately for me, were the ones who probably *really* wanted the tickets). At my shows that they attended, we literally could not begin the show until the standing ovations died down.

Once, during a charity softball game against Barry Bonds and the finest of baseball pros, my assistant told me that Joe had arrived. Of course I met him to escort him across the field. As soon as we were visible, the crowd stood and howled as we walked across the field, toward our *opponents*. Gentleman Joe wanted to pay his respects. As the crowd stood and cheered for Joe DiMaggio he turned to me and said, "Gee, Mike, they really like you here." Astonished, I looked at him. I'll always remember the subtle wink he gave me, as he ambled, "humbly," across the field.

During our time together, backstage, at a charity event or on the phone, he shared personal stories, tales about his life in pinstripes, and great advice. I am a member of the multitudes who loved Joe D. When we lost him, I was proud that mine was one of three CDs that he listened to while in the hospital. Imagine how I felt—the great Joe DiMaggio listening to *my* music. His passing was one of the saddest days of my life.

Joe believed that baseball was timeless. He knew that probable future legends Derek Jeter and Bernie Williams with their fresh, raw edge bring different personalities from those who took the fields before—but bring legions of new fans who feel the same about the game.

He knew that baseball is athletic giants battling with fierce game faces—and it's also America's heroes, jumping up and down like little kids, like eight-year-olds at a Little League game, hugging each other in triumph.

Baseball is a paradox, and I love it. Just like I did on my front lawn, my father challenging me. What's true about baseball is that baseball belongs to all of us and we all have our reasons. The core remains the same. For most, to be a part of baseball, in whatever capacity or fantasy, is to be a part of the American Dream.

MICHAEL BOLTON, singer-songwriter, has won two Grammys and six American Music Awards, been nominated four times for Best Pop Vocals, Male, and sold more than 52 million albums and singles worldwide.

JULIAN BOND

◆ ◆ ◆

I grew up on the campus of then-small Lincoln University in rural Pennsylvania, fifty miles from Philadelphia, much more remote than today. During the summers, when students went home, the campus was empty. I can't remember there ever being enough children to field two full teams. But we played anyway. We had five- or six-person teams and simply rotated at bat. I can't say I was any great shakes as a batter, but I was a good fielder. I was quick and could catch almost any batted ball, but I never threw what could be called a rifle shot. My memories aren't of home runs or spectacular catches, but of pleasant summer afternoons on a large field—the campus center mall—with friends you thought you'd always have, playing ball.

JULIAN BOND is Chairman of the Board of the NAACP, America's oldest civil rights group, and a Distinguished Scholar in Residence at American University and faculty member of the University of Virginia.

Connie Mack Stadium (nee Shibe Park): The 1909–54 and 1938–70 home, respectively, of the Athletics and Phillies.

PAT BOONE

◆ ◆ ◆

My favorite baseball moment doesn't involve Mickey Mantle, Hank Aaron, or even Mark McGwire. It involves me—and a black bat.

Growing up in Nashville, I loved our Nashville Vols, and played pretty good shortstop in grade school. We came to a climactic season-ending game with another school when I was in the eighth grade, and the first time I stepped up to the plate I was wielding a black bat borrowed from somebody and on which I had written the name "Joan" in dust.

Joan Askew was a beautiful little blond girl, and I was terribly infatuated with her. I swung the bat, connected, and arced a home run over the left field fence! I rounded the bases and glanced bashfully at Joan, who was standing and applauding along with everybody else.

Not smart enough to quit while the quitting was good, next time I came to the plate I repeated the process, carefully writing "Joan" on that black bat. And this time I connected again, sending the ball deeper over the fence in center field!

Next time up, the other team gave me an intentional pass—in the eighth grade!

I rode home on the city bus with Joan, and though that romance phased out, that exhilarating memory never has. And never will, for me.

PAT BOONE linked white bucks, a next-door image, and box-office wow. From 1955 to 1961 the teenage idol made the singles charts sixty times.

The 1955 Nashville Vols. The team anchored the Southern Association for 61 years.

Pilgrims at Lourdes: Fans spy green grass upon entering the ballpark. The 1970 Red Sox host the White Sox at Fenway Park.

THOMAS BOWDEN

◆ ◆ ◆

Before the first pitch is thrown, before the first batter strolls to the plate, even before the home team charges onto the field amid the cheers of its fans, comes my favorite moment in baseball.

It's the moment when I first glimpse the bright, lush green grass of the playing field. That little patch of green—so vivid in contrast to the gray concrete of the narrow tunnel that frames my view as I walk up the ramp toward the seats—is my private welcome to a different world, the sporting world, where all my values come into sharper focus and brighter reality.

That brilliant flash of green reminds me that I'm entering a world where every player must earn his way onto the field with superior ability—where the rules are clear and fairly enforced—where the outcome is just—and where I can immerse myself guiltlessly in an exciting, suspenseful contest for no other reason than my own personal pleasure.

To me, that first flash of green beckons me to a world where I can relax and celebrate human skill, dedication, and success in a spirit of simple joy.

THOMAS BOWDEN is senior writer for the Ayn Rand Institute, a global research group.

BILL BRADLEY

◆ ◆ ◆

I played a lot of baseball when I was growing up in Missouri. The game taught me lessons about teamwork, perseverance, and hard work. It also provided insights into life off the field. I remember staying in a run-down hotel in Joplin, Missouri, during a Little League playoff because the better places wouldn't accept the team's black players. I also remember traveling to New Madrid—that part of Missouri that protrudes into Arkansas—and being refused service at a restaurant there because our catcher and left fielder were black. Because we were a team, all of us left the restaurant. Baseball put me in multiracial situations at a very early age. It was there that I realized that we will not fulfill our ideals until we can see deeper than skin color to the individual.

BILL BRADLEY played baseball and basketball at Princeton, buoyed the New York Knicks, and served as a U.S. Senator from New Jersey from 1979 to 1997.

In 1947 Jackie Robinson broke the color line by leaving Brooklyn's Montreal farm club for Ebbets Field.

JOHN BRANCA

◆ ◆ ◆

I grew up in a baseball family in Mt. Vernon, New York. You may have heard of my uncle, Ralph. Bobby Thomson has. He pitched for the Brooklyn Dodgers for ten years and was a three-time All-Star. My father, John, was named New York High School Player of the Year and later became the New York State Athletic Commissioner. So it was no surprise that my earliest dreams were to become a major league baseball player. (Only later, when I joined a rock band and signed my first record deal at sixteen, did I dream of becoming a rock star!)

Yet growing up, I was somewhat of a traitor—a Yankee, not Dodger, fan. And my idol was Mickey Mantle. (Babe Ruth, dying in 1948, was more of a god on Mt. Olympus than a living idol like the Mick.) My earliest baseball memories were watching Yankee games on Channel 11 in New York. The broadcasters changed over the years—but who could forget Mel Allen?

My strongest childhood memories, though, are baseball cards. My father was our town's Recreation and Parks Commissioner, so I spent summer afternoons with him at the parks. Between playing ball, we collected and traded cards. The Yankee cards were in the highest demand—and Mantle's cards were golden. Mick's earliest cards, including the 1951 Bowman rookie and 1952 Topps, were not common. The 1956 Topps card from Mantle's Triple Crown year was terrific. But my favorite was the 1957 Topps Mantle card, which features photography and not artwork with the Mick in a full-swing pose. His cards had a magical quality—like Mantle.

Years later I attended UCLA Law School. My card collection, stored in my mother's rental property, was stolen. You can imagine how for more than two decades I turned away from any glimpse of a baseball card. I had no interest—it was too painful. Yet sometimes one can "heal" such loss. Recently, the sports collector Barry Halper put most of his collection for sale

Ralph Branca, who pitched for the Brooklyn Dodgers from 1944 to 1953 and one game in 1956.

through Sotheby's. What attracted me was that my uncle's Dodger uniform from 1951—number 13—was being auctioned. This was the kind of thing that should stay in the family, so I bought it. The auction featured virtually every significant baseball card set from the twentieth century! In one fell swoop, I replaced my card collection—and improved it!

I am not a psychologist, but it's said that addictions stem from childhood wounds. And I've noticed that, as a collector of antiques, there is a fine line between "collecting" and "addiction." During the last two years, I've found that my collection skirts that line. My Mantle collection is now one of the best in existence, including his 1951 Bowman and first 1952 Topps, both in Mint (PSA-9) condition. I also have the Babe Ruth and Jackie Robinson rookie cards.

I often ask myself, "Why am I collecting baseball cards since basketball is the sport I

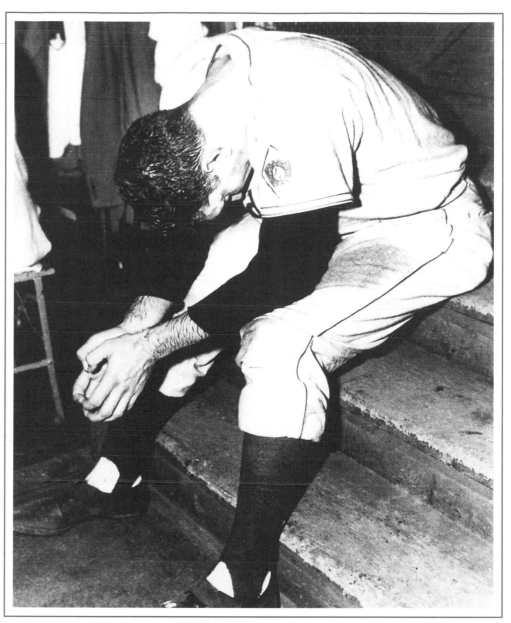

"Why me?" Branca laments after Bobby Thomson's Shot Heard 'Round the World.

formerly played?" The answer is that nothing comes close to baseball as the strongest form of twentieth-century Americana, with its traditions, folklore, and statistical analyses and compendia. Baseball's lure transcends the game and players. Babe Ruth is as much a part of American history and culture as Abraham Lincoln or Elvis Presley, as much a part of any kid's dreams. And like any great sport or form of entertainment, baseball—and its collectibles—offer a wonderful diversion from everyday reality. That's what it means to me.

JOHN BRANCA has been called the leading representative of rock and popular music artists, with more artists in the Rock and Roll Hall of Fame than any lawyer in rock music history.

CHRISTINE BRENNAN

◆ ◆ ◆

Baseball and I first became acquainted through a radio sitting on an end table in our living room. It was the summer of 1969. The sport turned 100 that year. I turned eleven.

Every night, I would sit by myself on the couch in our living room in the Toledo suburbs, turn on that radio, and listen to my Mud Hens. Often, I would keep score, a skill my father taught me the previous summer, and that I would I use for decades to come in my chosen career.

After listening to the game the previous night, I devoured the morning newspaper stories. I pored over the box score and analyzed the International League standings to see who had gained a game or who had fallen back. I couldn't get enough of this team, its young players, its promise. Soon, the radio wasn't good enough for me. I had to see the Mud Hens in person, so my father bought season tickets, and he took my younger siblings and me to dozens of games.

My dad is the man who gave me my first mitt at five and played catch with me in the backyard at a time when most fathers in America never would have allowed a daughter to do such a thing.

But the fellow who brought the Mud Hens to life in our living room every night was Frank Gilhooley, a local Toledo sportscaster. He was a play-by-play man, and one night he announced a contest to name an all-time Mud Hens roster, position by position.

A couple of weeks later, he took time away from calling the game to read one submission.

As he read the names, I listened very carefully: "Bob Christian. Don Pepper. Ike Brown. Tom Timmermann..."

Every name he read was a current Mud Hen, a player who was playing in the game I was listening to that night.

As the list was being read over the air, my father,

Ex-Toledo Mud Hen Bob Christian hit .224 for the 1968 Tigers and 1969–70 White Sox.

Ned Skeldon (née Lucas County) Stadium housed the 1965–2001 Toledo Mud Hens.

a broad-shouldered man of forty-three, walked into the room. He stopped and stood over me, listening intently with me as the announcer finished the list.

"Must be from a young man," Gilhooley said to his listeners.

I could hear a smile in his voice. He sounded very amused.

"But there's no name on it," he said, "so we'll never know who sent it in."

I don't remember what Gilhooley said next, although I do know he chuckled. I looked straight ahead. My father started to leave the room.

"Dad?"

My voice stopped him.

"That was me."

Years later, as I think about it, I didn't put my name on that piece of paper because, at eleven, I thought voting for an all-time team was the same as voting in an election—an anonymous act. I remember feeling embarrassed about this until my father looked down at me and smiled.

"You know that was yours," he said softly.

"That's all that matters."

Baseball was my first serious sports interest, and the Toledo Mud Hens were my first true sports love. I cheered Tom Timmermann and Ike Brown when they made it up to the Detroit Tigers. I shed a tear when Bob Christian died of cancer in 1974 after a few seasons with the Tigers and White Sox. Years later, I asked LPGA star Dottie Pepper if she was related to Don Pepper. Related? Absolutely, she said. She's his daughter.

These were my Mud Hens, the first athletes I followed, the first athletes I cheered. They were my earliest heroes, and no matter how many thousands of athletes I have met since I first heard their names, I will never forget them.

And, thanks to the Mud Hens, I'll never forget this, either: Everything I've written since, I've put my name on it.

CHRISTINE BRENNAN, author, ABC-TV analyst, and USA Today *columnist, is a leading voice on the Olympics and women's sports.*

BOB BRINKER

◆ ◆ ◆

Growing up in Philadelphia in the 1950s was a great time to be a baseball fan. The 1950 Whiz Kids, also known as the Fightin' Phils, were National League champs for only the second time, and took on the mighty New York Yankees in a World Series they lost in four straight...but three times by just one run.

Putt-putt Richie Ashburn, who covered the vast acreage of Shibe Park's center field with speed and grace, three times led the National League in base hits. Richie got down to first base running like a deer, and frequently bunted his way on to lead off an inning.

Willie "Puddin' Head" Jones, who owned the hot corner and batted fifth behind cleanup ace Del Ennis for years, earned only $5,000 in 1950 for his trouble. Colorful Willie returned to South Carolina in the off season to put food on the table selling used cars.

Granny Hamner held down shortstop... and was a very good all-around player. But Phillies ownership placed a private detective on his trail when he was away from the ballpark and things were never quite the same with Granville and the Phils.

The Phils had a solid mound contingent led by 20-game winner Robin Roberts, Curt Simmons (who lost a couple of toes cutting his lawn in the Philly suburbs), and

Richie Ashburn twice won the National League batting title. Said Ted Williams: "That kid has twin motors in his pants."

Jim Konstanty in the clutch, who bailed the Phils out of many jams back then. Roberts refused to brush back sluggers and paid with a high home run count. In 1950, Dick Sisler clobbered the "other"

Shot Heard 'Round the World in Brooklyn to win the pennant just one year before Bobby Thomson took another pennant away from the Dodgers. Two straight years they lost on final-inning home run blasts. Sisler's will never be forgotten in Philadelphia. Phillie fans can still tell you where they were when President John F. Kennedy was assassinated...and when Sisler's blast went skyward at Ebbets Field in the 10th inning of the pennant-deciding game.

What does baseball mean to me? Gene Kelly, one of the greatest baseball voices of all time, reminding Phils fans on the radio to get ready for the seventh-inning stretch with his famous call to "rub your nose, cross your fingers, tug on your cap, and knock on wood." Kelly was poetry in motion on the radio, with few peers before or since. Gene brought baseball play-by-play

to its highest level, and must be classified among the best ever with Bob Prince and Ernie Harwell.

Who could ever forget the Duke of Flatbush, Duke Snider, climbing high on the left-center field wall at Shibe Park to pull down a would-be game-winning drive by Willie Jones in extra innings to save another win for the Dodgers on Memorial Day?

Who could forget watching Roberto Clemente his first year in the majors go 5-for-5 at Shibe with speed, power, and grace that had Hall of Fame written all over it?

I will always remember one Saturday when Lew Burdette, the brilliant Braves right-hander who won three games in the 1957 World Series, threw me a bullpen baseball during pregame warm-ups. Needless to say I spent the rest of his career pulling

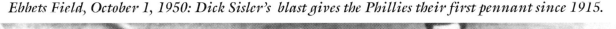

Ebbets Field, October 1, 1950: Dick Sisler's blast gives the Phillies their first pennant since 1915.

for him every time he took the mound—even though he was not pitching for the Phillies.

I still remember Smoky Burgess...one of the most prolific pinch batters of all time, coming off the pines night after night to strike fear into the hearts of opposing pitchers. Smoky would frequently wind up on first or second with a solid base hit.

❖❖❖

...I realized every generation has its boys of summer.

❖❖❖

Sitting in the stands years later with my son and taking in the new wave of Phillies stars of the 1970s...Mike Schmidt, Greg Luzinski, Larry Bowa et al., I realized every generation has its boys of summer. For the Dodgers the boys of summer led to a best-selling baseball book. But for the Phillies there was no best-seller...just an unlikely conglomeration of talented young athletes playing at a time when it was all about winning...and not very much at all about money. And they had names.

Eddie Waitkus...Mike Goliat...Granny Hamner...Willie Jones...Andy Seminick...Del Ennis...Richie Ashburn...Johnny Wyrostek... Robin Roberts...Curt Simmons...Bob Miller... Jim Konstanty...Smoky Burgess...and Gene Kelly bringing all the action into your home.

BOB BRINKER hosts the national radio weekend financial talk program, MoneyTalk.

MIKE BRITO

◆ ◆ ◆

Without baseball, I'm dead. I'll tell anybody I meet. Most guys know me as the fella who stands behind the plate at Dodger Stadium with the radar gun, clocking each pitch's speed. You've seen me a million times on television. I'm the one with the panama hat, the suit, and the big cigar. I'm also a Dodger scout who's brought twenty-two players to the big leagues in twenty-three years. Baseball has been my life. I'd be lost without it. I'm like Tommy Lasorda—I bleed Dodger blue. I hope I die on the grass of Dodger Stadium. You won't have to look far to see me. I'll be buried at home plate.

I grew up in Cuba before Castro. In 1955 I signed my first contract with the Senators. Joe Cambria, their scout, found guys like Camilo Pascual, Zoilo Versalles, Tony Oliva. The only mistake he ever made was signing me! He did in Cuba what I did in Mexico: prowl for players. Minnie Minoso was my favorite player. I'd get out a broomstick and hit rocks. Couldn't believe I'd ever make the bigs. People today talk of Santo Domingo as the fount for talent. Man, then it was Cuba. Before Castro there were sixty-five Cubans in the major leagues one time in the 1950s. When Castro dies, we'll have a hard time finding enough visas to handle all the players headed for the U.S. I can't wait. I'll love baseball even better then!

The Dodgers were our team. Snider, Reese, Robinson—in Cuba we loved him. "Maybe I can join them!" I remember dreaming, but I hurt my arm after six years in pro ball. Try being a catcher with a dead arm. So I retired, became a scout in the Mexican League, and kept hoping. You remember Al Campanis, the Dodgers' general manager: God bless him. In 1978, I signed Fernando Valenzuela.

The next year we had a pitcher, Bob Welch, struggling. Didn't know if he'd lost speed. Just sensed that

Washington Senators scout Joe Cambria (second from right) with Cuba's ambassador to the United States, Cuban player Bobby Estalella, and Nats president Clark Griffith.

maybe he had a sore arm. One day, Al said, "Mike, what you are doing tonight?" I said, "Nothing special. Why?" Campanis said, "I want you to go down to field level, stand in the boxes behind the plate, and clock Welch." I did, and he *had* lost speed—five miles off his velocity. I made a report to Al, and he said, "From now on, whenever we're at home, you go down there and time pitches." Today everybody uses the radar gun. We were first.

I love scouting. Tell ya what you want. At tryouts you look at a guy's body, his age. If he's a pitcher, the movement. He's gotta control the fastball, curve, change-up, throw strikes. Look at the hands—we want big hands, long fingers. His catcher ought to be at least 5-11, have good range, be flexible behind the plate, have a strong arm and back. Used to be even weak-hitting catchers could play if they handled pitchers.

Not now. We want power. The shortstop and second baseman—the hands, you want a rifle of an arm, range each way, hit to all fields. First and third—give me punch! Center, excellent speed. If he can homer, you're talkin' superstar. Left, you want power, don't care about the arm. But right field? Give me a cannon—and distance. That kind of team'd clobber Murderer's Row.

What baseball means to me is difference—each day's a story. People—you deal with all kinds. Talent—how'll this kid come out? You never know. But man, I do know. There hasn't been a second I haven't loved this game.

MIKE BRITO is as much a Dodger Stadium institution as Vin Scully, the Dodger Dog, and late-arriving traffic. Since 1978 baseball's "Radar Man" has been a managing instructor and scout.

TOM BROKAW

◆ ◆ ◆

As a baseball fan I've been present at some magic moments. As a seventeen-year-old, visiting New York from South Dakota, I managed to find my way to Ebbets Field, home of my beloved Dodgers, to see what remained of their dynasty against the New York Giants. My idol, Jackie Robinson, had retired the year before but the Duke was still in uniform and Campy was behind the plate. The great Mays was right there in front of me in that storied and cozy little ballpark.

Later I'd go into the press box at Dodger Stadium in Los Angeles on nights when Koufax was throwing to wonder, "How does ANYONE hit that guy?" Or I'd arrange my schedule to catch my home-state friend Dick Green, the second baseman for those championship Athletics teams of the 1970s. I was in a Yankee locker room with Mantle and Maris.

I was sitting with my family behind the Yankee dugout the night Reggie Jackson hit three home runs in a row off first pitches in the deciding 1977 game of the World Series against the Dodgers. My kids discarded their Dodger heritage on the spot and became Yankee fans. Later I was in Dodger Stadium the night Kirk Gibson limped to the plate against Dennis Eckersley and hit the most electrifying home run I will ever see.

I got to know Joe DiMaggio, and Ted Williams sent me an autographed picture for Christmas a few years back. As a reporter I traveled with Hank Aaron for a month the summer before he hit home run 715. We're still in touch.

For all of that, I cherish the memories of two summers in the mid-1950s in a small-town yard by the Missouri River in South Dakota. It was a town hastily constructed by the Army Corps of Engineers to house the workers who streamed in from all directions to build a massive dam across the Missouri.

I was part of a collection of eleven- and twelve-year-old boys who were athletic and competitive. The group broke neatly along the age lines so we formed two teams: the Pheasants (my team) and the twelve-year-old Warriors. We organized bake sales and mowed lawns to raise money for red sweatshirts and caps for the Pheasants and blue outfits for the Warriors. Baseball was the defining competition. We played every day during the summer on the town field, a dirt infield diamond with an uneven outfield. We had no umpires or adult supervision but we managed to

Ebbets Field was demolished in 1960, but this Brooklyn Little Leaguer kept the faith alive.

get along surprisingly well, arriving at balls and strikes and outs by consensus. When there was an irreconcilable dispute we often turned to the only nonplayer in our crowd, Johnny Strutz, a quiet and studious only child. He was always fair and we accepted his rulings.

I can still remember the players: Chuck Gremmels, the chief Warrior, with his blistering fastball; Marc Rhoades, his best friend, behind the plate; my pal, Jimmy Brown, a tough little catcher and daring base runner; I played second base, like my hero, Jackie Robinson, and swung his signature bottle-handed bat.

From time to time we'd arrange games with nearby towns, persuading our mothers to drive us. The opposition would be surprised when we'd show up without a grown-up manager, but our two captains would have settled on an all-star lineup and we'd take the field. Somehow it worked.

In those hot South Dakota summers the games were almost always in the mornings so we could reserve the afternoons for swimming in the nearby river or at a pool seven miles away. We'd wind up the day at the drugstore, teasing the high school girls who served us fountain Cokes and double-dip ice cream cones for a dime.

The town was dismantled when construction on the dam was finished and families scattered around the world. I have gone back a few times to drive the deserted road past the overgrown field that was our main ballpark. I almost always drive by another patch of prairie grass that was a place where we often practiced, the Pheasants and the Warriors in their red and blue sweatshirts and caps.

It was there that we assembled in the second summer, each team lined up solemnly along the first and third base lines, our caps off. The preceding winter our friend Johnny Strutz, the quiet and fair arbiter, had died of leukemia. His house was just across the street and Chuck Gremmels gathered us to declare, "This will be known as Strutz Field—forever."

I learned a lot about baseball, friendship, and life during those two summers with the Pheasants and the Warriors.

TOM BROKAW, the Peabody and Emmy Award-winning anchor and managing editor of NBC Nightly News with Tom Brokaw, *is the author of the best-selling book* The Greatest Generation.

HEYWOOD HALE BROUN

◆ ◆ ◆

Green and nervous, I became a baseball writer in 1941 because of two staff illnesses on the New York newspaper *PM*. I had spent a winter writing column fillers and opening mail on the night shift at the paper, and was startled to be told that I would be covering the Yankee season opener against the Washington Senators.

On the train to D.C., knowing no one and hoping not to be taken for an invasive autograph seeker, I was dwelling on my insufficiencies when an elderly man of military bearing stopped beside me.

"Are you young Broun?" he asked, and at my nod continued. "I'm Sid Mercer of the *Journal*. I broke in your father in 1915. How can I help you?"

So began my membership in that friendliest and most helpful clan, the Baseball Writers Association of America, the BBWAA. Sid Mercer taught me how to keep a scorebook, Tom Meany of my paper combed away my extra adjectives, Roscoe McGowen of the *Times* caught me up on the past, the magisterial Dan Daniel of the *World Telegram* introduced me to rare book dealers all around the league, and Al Laney of the *Tribune* knew a good French restaurant in the grittiest of industrial towns.

When I went off to the Army in August of that year, I left behind a group whose generosity had brought me, if not to their level, to a reasonable competency in my job.

I came back to baseball in 1946 and one day, standing alone in the large lobby of the Benjamin Franklin Hotel in Philadelphia, found myself approached by Joe DiMaggio with an invitation to coffee. I realized at once that he had no axe to grind with a little-known writer from a small-circulation paper. He was simply and warmly welcoming me back into the fraternity of the game. Later, after his retirement, he was often called remote and cold, but I remember an immortal with a mortal's sensitivity and kindness.

Kindness comes to mind when *PM* folded while I was on a road trip with the New York Giants. Club secretary Eddie Brannick offered to carry me as a guest of the team until I could get another job.

The *New York Star* immediately succeeded *PM*, but when that folded in turn, I decided, perhaps encouraged by success in baseball writers shows, to try my hand as an actor.

A last kindness was an offer from Bob Cooke of a job on the *Tribune*. The lure of the footlights was too strong but even though my Broadway plays are forgotten and my old press box friends are gone, I hear their lively voices, in the tavern room of my personal Hall of Fame.

HEYWOOD HALE BROUN was a writer, stage, film, and television actor, and son of Heywood Campbell Broun, the 1970 recipient of the Baseball Hall of Fame's J.G. Taylor Spink Award. He died in 2001.

Toastmaster Sid Mercer, postmaster general James A. Farley, and Yankee president Edward G. Barrow (left to right) at the 1940 New York Baseball Writers dinner.

Griffith Stadium, the Senators' 1911–61 home.

PATRICK J. BUCHANAN

◆ ◆ ◆

I grew up in Washington in the age of the baseball Senators. "First in war, first in peace, and last in the American League." Perhaps that explains my lack of playing inspiration. As a lad I took the mound, at eighty pounds, against the league's leading hitter, Bill Russell. With the bases loaded, I struck him out on three pitches. For a minute or so, I stood on the mound, gazing at the outfield and savoring the moment. It did not last long. The next batter, Charlie May, had figured me out. My control was excellent, and everything I threw was up in the strike zone. May had observed that his friend Russell had gone around swinging before the ball reached the plate. Digging in, Charlie May waited and drove the first pitch deep into the trees above our center fielder, Mike Loh, who waited beneath the branches as the bases emptied. The Lord giveth; the Lord taketh away.

PATRICK J. BUCHANAN is a columnist, commentator, and author. The former aide to Presidents Nixon and Reagan was the 2000 Reform Party candidate for President.

JACK BUCK

◆ ◆ ◆

I remember the 1966 All-Star Game. It was played at our new park, Busch Stadium, in St. Louis. The temperature was 103, and it registered 130 on the Astro-Turf. They asked Casey Stengel, "What do you think of the new ballpark?" He said, "It sure holds the heat well."

You can't treat the game like Armageddon. It's every day. You'll wear your audience out. You also treat it with respect. The baseball audience knows more

Mark McGwire waits to hit.

about *its* sport than, say, football's because it includes the ladies. A lot of the ladies have been brought up in the game and it's a simple game if you start with it as a kid. So as a broadcaster you're kind of giving already bright people the inside dope—telling what you know because you're on the scene and they're not.

With football it's mechanical, calling each play,

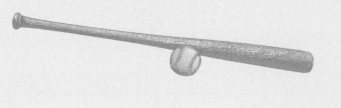

telling where the ball is, the down, and distance. In baseball you tell a story as the game goes along. I enjoy *winning* baseball more than anything and I've had the pleasure of seeing the Cardinals win in '64-67-68 and '82-85-87-96-2000. When you have a bad club and you're out of it in August, baseball can become drudgery because you get spoiled. There's nothing like winning baseball when it engulfs the city and lasts through the winter. A successful baseball team has no parallel in sport. It's just a wonderful thing to observe.

I haven't even mentioned Mr. McGwire. He's been sort of wonderful, too.

JACK BUCK, wounded in World War II, spent V-E Day in a Paris hospital. In 1954, he became a St. Louis Cardinals broadcaster.

"Baseball gets in your blood," muses Jack Buck. "It stays with you far longer than any other sport."

JOE BUCK

◆ ◆ ◆

I refuse to fill a page about what baseball means to me with the typical syrup that is found in just about every account of childhood and the national pastime. Once you get on the inside of this sport on a professional level all the feel-good "smell of the fresh popcorn" or "look of the freshly painted foul lines and beautiful green grass" stories do not mean much, but then again I'm jaded.

I grew up with this game as a constant background and soundtrack for my life. I was born in spring training in 1969 in St. Petersburg, Florida. That is my birthplace because that is where the St. Louis Cardinals trained. If they had trained in Norman, Oklahoma, then that is where I would have come out cryin'. My father has been the play-by-play voice of the Cardinals since the 1954 season, and from the day I was able to consciously keep my voice volume low, without constantly having to be reminded, I was with him in the booth. I followed him down to the field. I followed him into the clubhouse. I followed him into the parking lot after games, and held his beer while he signed autographs for fans he delighted from spring to fall, year after year. I know what baseball means to me. Baseball is that which binds me to the man I most admire.

It is the sport that took him away from our family for road trips, and delivered him back to us a little weary and very much appreciated. Our "together" time was dictated by the schedule printed by Major League Baseball, not by school sessions or Little League calendars. The game came first and everything else followed. It was always that way, and it continues to this day as he enters his sixth decade behind the mike. The game provided us with a more than comfortable way of life: It was worth it.

Now I am trying to be him. Following in my father's footsteps was never something I was told I should do. It wasn't necessary. I like that lifestyle. I love baseball. The game can be a wonderful ride through the warm months, or it can be an excruciating journey filled with frustration and false hope. What I have come to realize over the years is that those who play it professionally don't care about it as much as die-hard fans do. The players have the ability to let go of a loss before they leave the ballpark. They don't have their next day's mood depend on the previous night's game. Real fans do, at least I do. It is the last thing I think about before I fall asleep, and the first thing I think about when I wake up in the morning. It has to be this way, or you couldn't survive as a broadcaster.

Other than being with my wife and two girls, I would rather be at the ballpark than anywhere else. It is my stock market, my assembly line, my court case,

my operating table. In the morning the sports page comes first and if the kids are still asleep I'll learn about the world around the ballpark. It is a great game filled with good-hearted people and surrounded by fans who care about it. No sport celebrates its history like baseball. The growth of the game mirrors the growth of this nation. It links generation to generation, father to son—oh, God, pass the syrup.

JOE BUCK has announced the Cardinals since 1991. He is also Fox Television's voice of the Game of the Week, All-Star Game, *playoffs, and* World Series.

TOM BURGOYNE
◆ ◆ ◆

Bob Uecker says that Philadelphia is so tough that fans go to the airport to boo bad landings. People say to me, "Man, they must be brutal." I disagree. I'm the only baseball celebrity they never boo. I'm the Phillie Phanatic.

The Phanatic is perhaps the most famous mascot. I love the guy. To many, he *is* the Phils. Mascots matter more in baseball than other sports. It's the pace. First of all, you've got lots of time between innings to entertain, do skits. There's also time *during* innings to roam the stands, get people stomping, cheering. I know a lot about that—because I was a fan before I put the costume on.

I remember the first game at Veterans Stadium [April 10, 1971]. I was one of six kids, grew up in the Philly area, and we'd go as a family. I love the feeling when you come through the entryway—seeing the

The Phillie Phanatic. One writer called the pear-shaped, green-haired, elephant-nosed mascot "a big blur of fur."

> *Some mascots are told where to sit, what to do, have a walkie-talkie to their boss. Not the Phanatic. He runs the show.*

players, the smells and sounds, the green of the grass. Okay, so at the Vet it's a patchwork turf. But we'll open a new stadium soon, and it'll have real grass—the emerald kind. The Phanatic can't wait.

In 1989 I became the backup, then the main Phanatic in 1994. My favorite time is the pregame: For those twenty minutes the Phanatic comes alive. He tries to knock enemy players off their game, get them upset, give the Phils a home field advantage. You try to humanize the players—they're more accessible than at any time. Yeah, you root for the home team, but the aim is to have fun.

The Phanatic gets the same reaction at the park and when I make appearances around Philadelphia. It's priceless—the smiles and kisses. I get asked why he's so popular. My answer: It takes three things to make a mascot beloved.

One, the costume. The Phanatic's frumpy, got the big belly, the tongue that extends, he's made so the whole body moves. His head sits on top of mine, not around it, so when I move my face, his goes with me. I spot a beautiful girl, do a double-take, and the costume follows suit. Not every mascot's built that way.

Two, the team has to back you up. The Phillies do

in terms of money and philosophy. Some mascots are told where to sit, what to do, have a walkie-talkie to their boss. Not the Phanatic. He runs the show. Anyone who tried to interfere—Phillie fans would run 'em out of town.

Third, you need the right performer and personality—and it's not easy. It gets *hot* in Philadelphia. Our turf can reach 160 degrees. And here I am, with a thirty-five-pound, shag-carpet costume, baking inside. I take some breaks, have a fan blowing on me, drink lots of fluid. You gotta be a little loopy. Which brings me to the players, who love the whole affair.

Joe Carter's not exactly the most popular guy in town—for good reason. He hit that last-game homer [for Toronto, in 1993] off Mitch Williams to beat the Phillies in the World Series. Four years later we start interleague play and he comes to town—first time since breaking our hearts. The Phanatic was ready. So was Joe. That first game I mimicked him in batting practice. He came back smiling. I brought out a dummy dressed like Joe. He sees it, races out of the dugout, grabs the dummy, takes it back, gets high-fived by his teammates.

The next night I didn't do too much. Carter didn't like it. "Gee, Phanatic," he said a day later, "you didn't put on much of a show." So in pregame he leaves the dugout to flip the Phanatic's four-wheeler on its side, and we start wrestling in the outfield. I declared victory. Just like I did the year after Mitch was traded to Houston. He'd always walk from the dugout to the bullpen in the fifth inning. The night of his return I came out with a water gun and start spraying him. Mitch puts his arms up, surrendering.

Mitch's nickname is "Wild Thing." I can't think of anything wilder, or more rewarding, than being a character I love.

TOM BURGOYNE is married with two children. They have not told their father if they intend to follow in his garb.

In 1948 Yale University baseball captain George Bush (second from left) received Babe Ruth's official papers.

GEORGE BUSH

◆ ◆ ◆

It is said that you never forget your first love. For me, that is Barbara. But a runner-up is baseball. My first memories came as a boy, growing up in Connecticut. I followed the game, and memorized its box scores. My favorite team was the Boston Red Sox. My favorite player was the Pride of the Yankees.

His name was Lou Gehrig, the Hall of Fame first baseman. He was a good and quiet man about whom teammate Bill Dickey observed, "Every day, any day, he just goes out and does his job." More than half a century ago, the Iron Horse was stricken by a form of paralysis that now bears his name. In a speech at Yankee Stadium, he said, "I consider myself the luckiest man on the face of the earth." Lou Gehrig was, and remains, my hero.

In 1989, presenting his memorial postage stamp to the Hall of Fame, I thought of how Gehrig enriched baseball—like baseball enriches America. Someone asked me why I love it. I said, "Baseball has it all." In the major leagues or Little League, what counts is your heart and dreams.

Babe Ruth, whom I met in 1948 when he presented his papers to Yale University, had both. "Baseball comes up from the youth," he said. "You've got to start from way down, when you're six or seven years old. And if you try hard enough, you're bound to come out on top." Baseball enchants kids of *every* age. Our family marks chapters of our lives by baseball moments we recall.

After graduation, Barbara and I packed up our red Studebaker in 1948 and left the Northeast for Texas. I coached Little League for a while, and all four of our boys played. One of them, George W., became Managing General Partner of the Texas Rangers. As for Barbara, well, even then thousands of Texas kids played Little

League—and there were times when I thought she was car-pooling them all! She also knows how to score a game along with the best of them.

Our entire family followed the career of a dear friend—and the greatest hitter who ever lived. I admire Ted Williams for many reasons. The first is character. Ted couldn't stand what he termed "politicians"—phonies. Teammates adored him. Rivals asked for batting tips, and Ted never turned them down. Finally, Red Sox owner Tom Yawkey said, "Ted, I know you're generous, but why are you helping the enemy?"

Ted faced *other* enemies in Korea and World War II. He met gunfire in thirty-six combat missions, but never complained about five and a half years robbed from the prime of his career. Curt Gowdy calls Ted "the most competent man" he's ever met. I've seen that fishing and hunting. He also raised millions of dollars for charity—a point of light before my administration coined the term.

Ted's Red Sox never won the World Series. In 1967, however, the Bush family hailed their Impossible Dream. By now, even our youngest child, Doro, loved baseball. We watched the 1969 Miracle Mets, Brooks Robinson devastate the 1970 Reds, and 1971's Roberto Clemente. Then came what has been called the greatest game ever played—Game 6 of the 1975 World Series. Carlton Fisk smacked his 12th-inning homer at 12:34 A.M. Eastern Time, giving Boston a 7–6 triumph over Cincinnati. I was stationed in Beijing as Envoy to China at the time, and recall how our embassy's Red Sox fans—nearly 11,000 miles from Fenway Park—were cheering Fisk's blast almost as soon as it occurred.

Later, as President, I saw how baseball hit a grand-slam home run. I remember greeting Little Leaguers on the South Lawn of the White House, hailing the world champion Oakland A's in the Rose Garden, and telling Polish boys and girls in Warsaw, "Few things show America's love like bringing our national pastime to you." Always, it was America's ambassador of goodwill—linking teamwork, generosity, and dedication. Each day it shows why two of the most beautiful words in *any* language are "Play ball."

GEORGE BUSH was the forty-first President of the United States. At Yale, as team captain he played first base and batted eighth. He called it "second cleanup."

GEORGE W. BUSH

◆ ◆ ◆

I have many great memories of baseball parks all over America, and the best have been with a member of my family.

I remember the first time I saw my hero, Willie Mays, when my Uncle Buck took me to the Polo Grounds. I well remember seeing my first game in

A. Bartlett Giamatti, 1986–89 National League president and 1989 commissioner. "It breaks your heart," he wrote of baseball. "It is designed to break your heart."

the Astrodome and watching little Joe Morgan homer off of Warren Spahn. My mother took me to that game. I remember going to my first major league All-Star Game with my mother and dad.

The greatest memory of all was watching Nolan Ryan achieve a historic record—his 5,000 strikeouts. At the time [1989], I was the Managing Partner of the Texas Rangers. My wife, Laura, and our twin daughters attended the game with a great American, Bart Giamatti, National League President.

Arlington Stadium was completely full and energized. Every pitch that our hero "Big Texas" threw meant something. As he approached the magic number of the 5,000th strike-out, the energy level rose appreciably. Flashbulbs sparkled all around the stadium every time he threw to the plate. Little Barbara said it looked like our ballpark was suddenly filled with fireflies.

Finally, Nolan Ryan struck out Rickey Henderson for his 5,000th strikeout. The place went wild: Nolan graciously received the accolades, but insisted that the game go on. After all, baseball is a team sport.

GEORGE W. BUSH is the forty-third President of the United States. From 1989 to 1994 he was the Texas Rangers' Managing General Partner, helping design and oversee The Ballpark in Arlington.

Nolan Ryan pitched the seventh no-hitter of his career in 1991.

FRANK CAPPARELLI

◆ ◆ ◆

People ask me what it's like taking care of America's prettiest lawn. There's nothing I'd rather do. Wrigley Field is the most beautiful park in America. The groundskeeper feels that you're preserving something that's a member of the family. The outline of the park, the way bleachers kick into the field, the vines on the wall, the crowds and breeze and fun—that's what baseball means to me.

I remember my first day: March 13, 1959. I started out working the field, laying sod down, and cleaning the park. Today maybe four guys are responsible for only keeping up the field. Not then. We tended to the whole park. I didn't mind. I'd go to games and say, "Gosh, wouldn't it be great to work here." One day I saw a man who worked there and I introduced myself. "If's there any opening," I said, "I'd like to apply." A year later he called—and I was at Wrigley for almost the next forty years.

First, about those vines. In the spring you'd go out to the wall and fertilize. It wasn't warm, and the vines were scraggly. With heat they'd bloom. Each morning you'd get to Wrigley, take off the canvas, and put screens up for batting practice. Later you'd remove them, clean bases, draw the batter's box and baselines, and water the grass. Our games were all day then, so we didn't have a lot of time—especially when I added the job of clubhouse man for the umpires' room. What great guys they are—Doug Harvey, Andy Olsen, Chris Pelekoudas, from Chicago. Jerry Crawford. You got to know them, exchange Christmas cards. Try putting a price tag on that kind of friendship.

When Leo Durocher came [1966], he made the old Dodger center fielder, Pete Reiser, a coach. We'd talk baseball. Same with Billy Williams. Ernie [Banks] was always a jokester. You remember the visitors— Sandy Koufax was so nice. Or the funny things. Each day I'd sit in the home dugout in the ninth inning. That way I could get to the field fast and collect the bases. One day Randy Hundley hit a homer in the ninth to win it for the Cubs. Another groundskeeper was so excited he raced out to third and started removing it before Randy gets there! "Put it back!" he starts yelling. Spahnie [Warren Spahn] and Lew Burdette were always practical-joking. Every day the grounds crew digs the infield in the fifth inning. This one day they put a lit cigarette in a groundskeeper's pant cuffs. He was smoking by the time he got to second base!

But, hey, these are the Cubs. You remember the sadness. In 1969 we had an eight-game lead over the Mets and lost the pennant by eight games. Come '84, we take the first two games of the playoff against San Diego. We go west and need one win to make the World Series—first since 1945. We lose twice, so the series is tied, but we're still feeling good. The Cubs lead, 3–0, in the final game and we can smell the Series. By then I'd become supervisor of groundskeepers and am back in Chicago preparing the field. Two days later the Series starts. I'm thinking, The whole world'll see us. Then we lose, 6–3. What a letdown.

That still doesn't keep people from coming to Wrigley—it's an outing, a place to spend the entire day, let's see the charisma of the park, maybe hit a restaurant. There's no place like it. That's why it's always packed— that, and maybe because of a lawn as pretty as they come.

Wrigley Field, 1969: Roberto Clemente fights for Jim Hickman's drive. This time the ivy won.

FRANK CAPPARELLI, now retired, was a Wrigley Field groundskeeper from 1959 to 1982 and later spent another fifteen years as supervisor of the grounds crew.

Stan Musial homers against the Mets. The Cardinals' number 6 took a .331 batting average, 3,630 hits, and seven batting titles into the Baseball Hall of Fame in 1969.

SKIP CARAY

◆ ◆ ◆

It was spring 1954 and the Cardinals had a double-header with the Giants at Busch Stadium. There had been a rain delay, and it was about eight o'clock when Stan Musial batted late in the second game. The Cardinals had won the first game but were behind in game two. A large crowd was there, and virtually no one had left despite the lateness of the hour. Stan was at the plate. He hit a high pop fly that

was caught by the first baseman. As he trotted off the field Musial received a standing ovation. Those who stood and applauded never sat down again. They grabbed their umbrellas and headed for home. Why had they stayed? Why had they cheered a pop to first? Because in that doubleheader Stan had hit five home runs. Everyone was rooting for number six. I often wonder how many arguments there were around the dinner table that night started by wives who had their Sunday dinners ruined by the late hour. In St. Louis, Stan was king. You go back to St. Louis today. Nothing's changed. The Man still is.

SKIP CARAY became a Braves announcer in 1976. In 1991, he made history: Three generations of Carays—he, son Chip, and dad Harry—broadcast a game from Wrigley Field.

Musial was named "The Man" by Brooklyn fans. "The key to hitting," Stan mused, "is relax, concentrate—and don't hit a fly to center field."

BOB CARPENTER

◆　◆　◆

I love ushering. I was a man—really, boy—in red long before I began broadcasting the Big Red—the St. Louis Cardinals—at Busch Stadium. Ushers are like announcers—the game's face to the fan. You talk up close, get to know people. It's a big part of what baseball means to me.

My sister Judy started working for the Cardinals in 1967, and became administrative assistant to several general managers. The one who hired her, Bing Devine, helped move the outfield fences in the 1970s. It made the distances shorter, but created a gap between the wall and the bleachers. One day he asked me, "What do you think?" I said, "I don't like how it separates the fan from the field." The next year the temporary fences were removed. Ushers never want to keep fans away.

Even then, you had to be at least sixteen to be an usher. I couldn't wait: It's still the best way to learn baseball. It also drew my future. One of my locations was level 4 in deep center, where a ramp between the scoreboards circles the stadium. In one place you can lean against the rail and see home plate. Ushers were told to patrol it and keep the aisles clear—of other people and ourselves. Here's the kicker: When nobody was looking *I'd* lean on the rail, fix on the batter, and see from about 500 feet the difference between a fastball and change-up. I began doing play-by-play—*for* myself, *to* myself. Nobody'd confuse me with Jack Buck. Still, I got to thinking: I can do this.

Ushers get asked where's your seat, the nearest rest room, the concession stands. That's why I loved another location: those center field bleachers. You'd have people coming from Arkansas, Tennessee, Oklahoma, hundreds of miles away. They'd have loved how ushers get to go on the field. Three innings each game I sat at the end of the dugout on a little folding

stand. You learned that if a foul ball came, get up and remove that stool! Three more innings you spent behind a wall door in right and left field. The final three you sat on a bullpen chair farther beyond the dugout. Some advice: Watch out before you're decked.

One day I was sitting past the Cardinal dugout when Ron Fairly hit a foul ball right at me. I dove straight ahead and fell on my face. The ball hit where my head would have been. Those fans are tough: They booed me for bailing out. But for memory I love the time Jerry Reuss was pitching for the Redbirds. The

Jerry Reuss won 220 games between 1969 and 1990.

The Cardinals' roost. "The Greeks had their Parthenon," wrote Sports Illustrated. *"St. Louisans have Busch Stadium."*

Expos' Bill Stoneman hit our Richie Allen. Allen walked to the mound, both benches emptied, and from my location I glimpsed into our dugout and saw Reuss—the only player who didn't go on the field. I said to a photographer, "Look at that!" The guy snapped the picture, whereupon next morning page 1 of the *Globe Democrat* shows two photos—the brawl, and Reuss sitting it out!

Fast-forward twenty years later. I'm working with Reuss on an ESPN telecast. I tell him the story, and he's flabbergasted. "*You're* the guy who caused that picture. Some usher. I've been waiting to deck you." Next time we worked together he brought in his scrapbook and there they were—the brawl and Mr. Reuss. That's the thing about ushering. Full circle. Full life.

BOB CARPENTER began calling Cardinals baseball in 1984. He has also broadcast the Rangers, Mets, and Twins, and for ESPN since 1988.

"I came to the Braves on business," Hank Aaron said, "and I intended to see that business was good as long as I could." He retired in 1976 with 755 homers.

JIMMY CARTER

◆ ◆ ◆

As a farm boy, I grew up immersed in baseball. I played on a team, my dad and uncle managed a league and spent their vacations in different major league cities every year, and my mother was an avid Dodger fan.

As a state senator, I watched the Braves' stadium being erected. I was delighted to be present for Hank Aaron's historic home run when I was serving as Georgia's Governor. While waiting to start my presidential election campaign, I played softball games in Plains with my brother, Billy, and teams of Secret Service agents and news reporters. At one time, the entire Atlanta Braves team came to visit us.

The most exciting baseball moment I've ever witnessed was during the final playoff game between the Atlanta Braves and the Pittsburgh Pirates in 1992. Pirates up, 2–1. Then Francisco Cabrera pinch-singles, and the

Game 7, 1992 N.L. Championship Series. Atlanta's Sid Bream beats the tag to score the pennant-winning run in the ninth inning.

Braves win, 3–2. Sid Bream slid across the plate. I'll never forget that heart-stopping play in the ninth inning that won the Braves the National League championship. You can still hear the noise.

JIMMY CARTER was President of the United States from 1977 through 1981. The author of the Camp David Accords is now active in Habitat for Humanity.

JACK CAVANAUGH

◆ ◆ ◆

The next time you see a big league bat boy remember Monday, August 18, 1941. The St. Louis Cardinals were a half-game back of the Brooklyn Dodgers in the battle for the National League pennant. The Cardinals, riddled with injuries throughout the season, had split a doubleheader in Pittsburgh the day before and were to open a three-game series in Boston against the Braves on Tuesday. With pennant pressure building, the players would have welcomed a day's rest in Boston after the long trip from Pittsburgh.

However, the Cardinals' train stopped first in Stamford, Connecticut: There would be no day of rest. Because a Stamford promoter had come up with a guarantee that met the demands of the Cardinals' penurious owner, Sam Breadon, St. Louis was booked to play an exhibition game with a team of local semipros that Monday night. After all, the players could still get some sleep on the train to Boston later that night. Besides, the first game with the Braves was not scheduled to start until 3:00 P.M. the next day.

All this may be difficult to comprehend in an era when players use every possible ruse to avoid appearing in the All-Star Game and when the Major League Baseball Players Association dictates much of what a ball club can do during the season. One of the things the Cardinals definitely could not get away with now would be scheduling an exhibition on an off day in a town such as Stamford. But back in the 1920s, 1930s, and 1940s such games were commonplace. Breadon reasoned that if a promoter could guarantee $1,500 for an exhibition, that was almost enough to pay a rookie's salary for the whole season. What difference did it make if such games were anathema to the players and the manager?

Thus, the Cards found themselves playing under makeshift lights on off days (even before major league night ball was introduced in Cincinnati in 1935), then spending the night in Pullman cars en route to a league game the following afternoon. "We were like a carnival, playing in towns we had never heard of," said Terry Moore, the Cardinal captain and center fielder in those days. "We hardly ever had a day off. But few of the players complained, because most of us had never been with any club other than the Cardinals. To us, it was a way of life." To his death in 1995 Moore believed such exhibitions cost the Cardinals the 1941 pennant.

The Cardinals' 1941 visit to Stamford was not their first. As the fabled Gas House Gang, they had played an exhibition there three years earlier,

John Leonard "Pepper" Martin, the Wild Horse of the Osage, keyed the Gas House Gang.

I heard the ball slam into the catcher's mitt, then the roar of the crowd. To me it was as if the Mighty Casey had struck out again. Spiers—and Stamford—had been avenged.

trouncing a local all-star team, 20–4. That game had been halted prematurely when the supply of three dozen experimental yellow baseballs ran out. The Cards had lost about half of the balls by clouting batting practice home runs. The rest disappeared during the course of play despite the efforts of retrievers who had been posted at strategic locations to run down foul balls. "We would try to lose as many balls as possible, both during batting practice and in the early innings, so that we'd eventually exhaust the supply and they'd have to call the game," Moore said. "That way we could get some rest at the hotel before heading to the train station."

When I read that the Cardinals were returning to Stamford, I wrote to the club, asking if I could be its bat boy. To my astonishment, I received a reply from the Cardinal vice president informing me that the job was mine. For weeks I was in ecstasy. On the big day, hundreds of Stamfordites, including the mayor, the Holy Name Church Fife and Drum Corps, and me, welcomed the team at the Stamford station. Butch Yatkeman, the Cardinals' clubhouse man, greeted me

warmly and told me I could ride to the Roger Smith Hotel with the team. Later I went for a walk with shortstop Marty Marion, showing him the town, and that evening I had dinner with the players at the hotel. Then I rode to Mitchell Field with manager Billy Southworth, coach Mike Gonzalez, and the Cards' famed brother battery, Mort and Walker Cooper. My friends, who were gathered outside the hotel, looked on enviously as I jumped into the limousine.

St. Louis's opponents that night were the Stamford Pioneers, a good semipro outfit made up of local talent and a number of ringers from New York City. The Pioneers were probably the equivalent of a Double-A minor league club, and they regularly played against strong barnstorming teams such as the bearded House of David and the old Black Yankees. From the 1938 Cardinal team that had devastated the Stamford all-stars, only Moore, first baseman Johnny Mize, and outfielders Don Padgett and Enos Slaughter remained on the roster. And because of an injury, Slaughter was not with the Cardinals on this occasion. The new faces included Marion, the Cooper brothers, left fielder Johnny Hopp, third baseman Jimmy Brown, and second baseman Frank Crespi.

At the outset, another Cardinal rout appeared likely. Brown opened with a double, but was thrown out trying for third. Hopp then tripled and scored on a single by Mize. The Pioneers tied the game in the second and scored again in the third to lead, 2–1. During the 1938 game, the jittery Stamford team had committed seven errors and was pitiful at bat. The Pioneers were more poised. When Mize struck out in the third with Moore on first, and when Hopp, one of the league's best hitters, fanned with the bases loaded in the fourth, the crowd of 5,000 went wild.

In the bottom of the fourth, a local hero named Joe Yaeger belted a home run over the left field fence to make it 3–1. The spectators, many of whom had witnessed the 1938 massacre, were delirious. Was it possible? Could the Pioneers beat the mighty Cardinals? It appeared highly possible when most of the St. Louis regulars left the game in the fifth inning. I felt crushed. My friends would never let me forget it if the Pioneers won. I became even more apprehensive in the seventh inning when the Pioneers scored two more runs to take a 5–1 lead.

Going into the ninth I was near tears. The Cards were my adopted team. (I had switched my allegiance from the Yankees the day I received that letter from St. Louis.) I had gotten to meet and talk with most of the players. How could they let me down? Some of my friends began to ridicule me. "You wrote to the wrong team, Jack," yelled one.

Compared to the 1938 Cardinals, this club was more businesslike, more solemn. There was no raucous pepper game, no Pepper Martin waving a flash- light to dramatize the inadequacy of the lights, and no levity on the bench. Per- haps the players

were thinking about the Dodgers and their half-game lead. They seemed to be going through the motions, eager to leave town and resume the pennant race.

Then in the ninth inning the Gas House spirit flared. Hopp doubled, Estel Crabtree walked, Coaker Triplett singled, Padgett doubled, and Crespi walked. Suddenly, the Cards were within one run of the Pioneers, the bases were loaded, and Walker Cooper was at bat with two out. I was so overjoyed that I tripped as I went to hand Cooper his bat and fell flat on my face, evoking derisive laughter from my friends sitting nearby. Fuming, I besought Cooper to get a hit off Al Spiers, the losing pitcher in the 1938 game. He swung lustily at three sweeping curves. On the last one, I closed my eyes. I heard the ball slam into the catcher's mitt, then the roar of the crowd. To me it was as if the Mighty Casey had struck out again. Spiers—and Stamford— had been avenged.

Walker Cooper, a catcher for the Cardinals in the 1940s, took his first big league pitch for a strike. "If this is a sample of your work," he told the umpire, "you won't be here too long."

The Cardinals hurried to their waiting cars for the trip back to the hotel, where they would change before their all-night train trip to Boston. While they had been losing to the Stamford Pioneers, the Dodgers had been beating Pittsburgh to go a full game in front. (Brooklyn went on to win the pennant by two and a half games.) Crestfallen, I clutched a used baseball that most of the players had autographed for me and picked up a broken Estel Crabtree–model bat that he had given to me. Then I began the long walk home where I cried myself to sleep, deeply anguished but a Cardinal fan the rest of my boyhood and beyond.

JACK CAVANAUGH writes sports for the New York Times *and teaches writing at Fairfield and Quinnipiac universities in Connecticut.*

JERRY COLEMAN

◆ ◆ ◆

I don't know what it was, but Joe DiMaggio had an eye-catching grace, almost an imperial presence on the field unlike any other player in any sport. When I made the Yankees, he was at the end of his career. He still handled himself like a king in America's court. Once, he was asked, "You're beating the St. Louis Browns, 22–1. Why are you out there running around like it's a one-run game?" He said, "Because there may be someone who never saw me play before." What a way to look at life. Sometimes it's hard to bear down when you're way ahead. Why care? It's pride. All the greats had it. They never give anything away.

DiMaggio was unusual in a way. Many players don't know all the rules beyond their own position. I was an infielder who had played second, third, and shortstop and knew what it was all about in the field. But I was not an expert at all the positions. DiMaggio had a keen sense for the entire game. Suddenly I became a broadcaster. That's a role where you must understand all that goes on on the playing field, especially the rules. It's the only sport where the officials (umpires) don't designate "traveling" or "15 yards for unnecessary roughness." You must know the rules.

My first attempt at play-by-play as a broadcaster was spring training 1963 at Fort Lauderdale. I'm hoping for a quick inning, three up, three down. Instead, in that first half-inning twelve men came to

Mel Allen made "How about that!" a household phrase. The 1939–42 and 1946–64 Voice of the Yankees called twenty World Series.

the plate. Passed balls, wild pitches, errors, you name it. At that time I couldn't keep score very well and I was totally confused by all that happened. Mercifully, the half-inning finally ended. I was supposed to do the next half-inning—but Mel Allen, sensing my discomfort, said, "Jerry, I think you've had enough for your first game." I thankfully said, "You're right," and departed the booth.

Baseball games can be tricky. In my first year broadcasting baseball for CBS-TV along with a couple of great personalities, Dizzy Dean and Pee Wee Reese, I was doing a pregame interview with Cookie Lavagetto when suddenly the National Anthem began. Frankly, I didn't know what to do. Do I keep going with the interview? Do I just stop? The director should have cut me and shot the American flag but this was live TV so I thought, "Well, I guess I keep going." So I went right through the Anthem with the interview. Afterward CBS got more than a few letters concerning the broadcaster who talked through the National Anthem. Believe me, today when the Anthem starts— I don't care whether I'm taping, talking, or eating a banana—I stop in mid-stride.

Another day in Kansas City Phil Rizzuto and I were doing Yankee radio and TV. It was so hot that we took off our pants to cool off and were broadcasting in our undershorts. About the fifth inning someone put his hand on my shoulder. When I turned around I was staring at a Kansas City policeman who told me to put on my pants. You apparently could see us from the seats below and a woman had complained. Hm-m-m. You know, I didn't take my pants off ever again—anywhere.

Above all, what baseball means to me is getting it right, and explaining the plays properly, bringing listeners to the park through the medium of radio so that they can visualize what we see. So that the game is there in their minds to take with them. That's what broadcasting is all about.

Baseball, the game, is the magic, the ebb and

Dizzy Dean (left) was baseball's Falstaff behind the mike. He, Bud Blattner, and Pee Wee Reese (right) made CBS-TV's **Game of the Week** *an institution in the 1950s and 1960s.*

flow on a summer evening—nothing can match it. Sometimes, of course, that magic takes a twist. Once Rizzuto and I had the wrong pitchers for four innings. Birdie Tebbetts, then managing Cleveland, said okay when I asked him if Sam McDowell and Jack Kralick were pitching the doubleheader. So I told everybody it's McDowell and Kralick: Unfortunately, Kralick pitched the first game! In the fifth inning someone in New York said to me through the earphones, "You've got the wrong pitcher." I asked Cleveland broadcaster Bob Neal, "Who's pitching?" When he said, "Kralick," we both started laughing. Oh well, you can't be perfect!

JERRY COLEMAN served as a Marine in World War II and the Korean War and played for the Yankees from 1949 until 1957. He broadcast Yankee games from 1963 to 1969 and has aired the San Diego Padres since 1972.

BOB COSTAS

◆ ◆ ◆

What baseball means to me...A sense of continuity...A cavalcade of characters... Enough anecdotes to fill a hundred rain delays...Debates that always rage, and are almost never settled...Familiar surroundings, always holding the possibility of something you'd never expect...

BOB COSTAS has done the World Series, Game of the Week, Summer and Winter Olympics, and has virtually retired two awards—the Emmy and National Sportscaster of the Year.

Ralph Kiner won seven N.L. home run titles.

CLIVE CUSSLER

◆ ◆ ◆

When I was ten, I wanted to play on my grammar school baseball team so bad I'd go to bed every night and dream about it. Those were the days long before Little League, and there were no tryouts. Team members were selected mostly on a clique basis by class buddies who had played together since the first grade, and they naturally assumed there was no one else in the class who could catch or bat as well as they.

The times when the team was short of players due to chicken pox or measles, I'd beg to substitute, but the team captain—his name was Buzzy Bennett— always picked someone else.

Undaunted, I went home and attacked the problem as if it were a war. I began by coaxing my dad into being my trainer. We lived on a hill, and Dad would stand at the top and hit balls while I waited at the bottom to catch them. This gave the illusion that the balls were coming

Bob Costas (front row, far right) in Little League.

from a far distance at a staggering height.

I couldn't afford a mitt. This was the Depression, and every cent counted. I learned to catch with my bare hands. I soon built up calluses, but not before I bent fingers, sprained a wrist, and tore off fingernails. But before long, very few lofted balls got past me.

Then I had a stroke of luck. A college student who lived just up the block from me played baseball at a nearby city college. He caught fly balls with me and showed me how to hit. His name was Ralph Kiner, a guy who later had an outstanding major league career and became a broadcaster.

The day finally came when our class team was scheduled to play the team from the class above us. When you're ten, a kid who is eleven looks as big as a mountain and twice as athletic. The whole school turned out, and everybody expected our guys to lose in a rout. I begged to play, but was totally ignored. There was a little blond girl I wanted to impress, but since I wasn't on the team she didn't give me the time of day.

Then, in the middle of the third with the score nothing to nothing, our team's first baseman was knocked flat by a runner and cracked a rib. Buzzy brought in his right fielder to play first. He then looked around the crowd. Finding no one who looked like he could throw a ball, he stared a long minute at me.

"Okay, Cussler," he finally said. "Go play right field. You should be all right. Nobody ever hits 'em out there."

I ran to the position, still without a glove.

The fourth inning looked like the start of a massacre. We got two outs, but the big guys loaded the bases. The next batter looked like a cross between Babe Ruth and Roger Maris. The impact with the bat sounded like a cannon shot and the ball lifted high in the air. Like a movie in slow motion, every eye on every face was on the ball. I began running back. I stole a glance at the kid in center field. He was just standing there. Now that I recall, he was eating a candy bar.

I ran. Oh, God, how I ran. Out of the corner of one eye I saw the chain link fence coming closer. I ran two more steps and then jumped. I felt the fence become one with my right hip and shoulder. The ball smacked into my open hand. I had made a one-handed catch of a ball that should have been a home run. And without the help of a mitt.

There was stunned silence on the school ground. Plays like that just didn't happen in grammar school. The months of perseverance with the able assistance of Dad and Ralph Kiner had paid off. The force was now mine. I walked from right field to the bench, slowly tossing the ball up and down, trying to look cool. Only when I passed near home plate did I nonchalantly flip the ball to the opposing pitcher.

Nor did it stop there. I went on that day to hit a single and a triple. Sure, we lost, 6–3, but I was still the hero of the hour.

And the little blond girl who ignored me before the game? Her name was Joy, and she became the first girl I ever kissed.

CLIVE CUSSLER wrote his first Dirk Pitt novel in 1973. The series has now sold nearly 100 million copies.

Kiner hits one of his 369 dingers. Pirate general manager Branch Rickey turned down his request for a raise, explaining: "I know you hit all those homers, but we could have finished last without you."

ROBERT A. DALY

◆ ◆ ◆

When I think back to my childhood in Brooklyn and remember the first time that I went to Ebbets Field and actually saw a major league baseball game in the late 1940s, I remember falling instantly in love with everything about the experience. It was my first time of ever being in a major league ballpark with 30,000 fans, looking around at all the activity taking place in the stands, the total involvement the fans had with what was happening on the field—and thinking how great this is.

From that day on, I have had the same passion for baseball and for the Dodgers. There was a brief hiatus when Walter O'Malley moved the team to Los Angeles, where I felt somebody took away part of my family, but after moving to Los Angeles myself it renewed all of those wonderful memories, especially of the 1950s. Those Dodger teams were very exciting. Jackie Robinson was

Jackie Robinson was a lion at the plate and a tiger on the bases. "Here was a man," said Branch Rickey, "whose wounds you could not feel or share."

clearly my favorite player and it was a thrill to watch him play. I also loved Pee Wee Reese and felt so good when he stood up for Jackie.

One of the toughest experiences was Bobby Thomson's home run against Ralph Branca. I remember being in high school and our teacher let us listen to the game on radio. I remember like it was yesterday, after Thomson hit the home run she said to us, "Now that the Dodgers have won you can turn off the radio." Obviously my teacher was not paying attention and it was a miracle that I was not thrown out of the school based upon my reaction to her comments. To read today that the Giants were allegedly stealing signals does not improve this memory.

There have been many wonderful moments in this journey and there were many tough winters thinking about what could have been. I never thought that the intensity of my passion could ever increase, but ever since I became Managing Partner of the Dodgers, fulfilling a lifetime dream, the wins do feel better and the losses are much harder to take. Regardless of whatever happened in my business career both at CBS and Warner Bros., my family and my friends could always tell by my face whether the Dodgers had won or lost.

Notwithstanding the total emotional roller coaster, I love every minute.

ROBERT A. DALY is Chairman and CEO of the Los Angeles Dodgers, arriving from Warner Bros. and Warner Music Corp., where he was Chairman and Co-CEO.

FRANK DEFORD

◆ ◆ ◆

It is an article of faith, nearly a cliché, about how baseball is a game of fathers and sons. I'm sure this is true, too. I can remember talking to my father about baseball, and him taking me to my first real game, to watch the old minor league Baltimore Orioles of the International League play the Syracuse Chiefs.

But I think this sweetness camouflages a larger point. As much as baseball might bring a father and son closer together, it does a better job of introducing a young boy—or girl—to the wider world. I already knew my father. I already loved my father. I didn't need baseball to deepen that affection. Rather, what baseball did best for me—what it does for children yet—is to help take us out of our own neighborhood and welcome us into the broader community. In a sense, because we tend to be so much more isolated nowadays—closeted as we are, with our own TV shows and our favorite Web sites— baseball might have come to play an even more important role now.

Going to a baseball game was learning to be a part of my whole city, suddenly sharing something I cared about with other people—new people, different people, strange people, but people I realized I had something in common with. What a wonderful discovery. That I was a fan? No, more than anything, in an immediate, even visceral way, going to a baseball game made me realize that I was...well, I was a citizen.

So, in the matter of baseball, what I remember best about my father is not that he took me to a baseball game, but that he let me go back by myself.

FRANK DEFORD is an author, HBO-TV commentator, and Sports Illustrated *senior editor.*

The eyes have it. Janet Reeves of Richmond, Virginia, prepares to separate the ball and stationary target.

Ken Guettler, the minors' Babe Ruth, was a phenom who somehow never wowed the bigs.

TOM DeFRANK

◆ ◆ ◆

There was no major league baseball in Texas when I was growing up in the 1950s, but I was a big fan nevertheless. I remember every summer listening religiously to the Mutual Radio Network's *Game of the Day*. I used the earphone on my transistor radio to keep from driving my mother crazy. I was also a regular viewer of the television *Game of the Week* on Saturday and Sunday, with the irrepressible Dizzy Dean talking about frozen ropes, Texas Leaguers, and how someone slud into third base.

My favorite team was the St. Louis Cardinals. In part, it was because my dad was from St. Louis, and while I never saw a Cardinals game—we usually got to St. Louis for Christmas, well after the season ended— I considered them my home team. I followed Stan Musial's slugging exploits in the box scores every day, and in the late 1950s I finally got to watch him play.

During spring training the Cardinals always played an exhibition game in Houston at Buffalo Stadium. The Houston Buffs were the Cardinals' farm club in the old Texas League. My father took me to the game one year and I'll never forget one of the Cards tossing a ball into the stands to me during batting practice. I still have that baseball, autographed by several players. But the highlight of the game was watching Stan the Man launch a mighty shot over the right field fence. It cleared the stadium and landed in the middle of Milby Boulevard. I had never seen a baseball hit that far. In my mind's eye, it conjured up all those tape-measure shots Mickey Mantle was smashing up north.

My other memory of that stadium was the outfield fence—all green, no ads, and elevated in left-center so that it took a huge shot to get out. Whenever I see the Green Monster at Fenway Park I always think of the wall at Buffalo Stadium. I'm sure it was smaller than Fenway—but not to a ten-year-old.

The Texas League was a Double-A outfit with teams that reflected the character of the state and region— the Buffalos, named not after the animal but Buffalo Bayou, where Houston was founded; the Dallas Eagles and Fort Worth Cats (a Dodgers farm team), who ran a spirited rivalry; the Austin Senators and San Antonio Missions; the Tulsa Oilers and Oklahoma City Chiefs. Even after my parents moved to North Texas, where I liked to watch the Eagles and Cats square off, the Buffs were still my favorite.

I remember being thrilled to learn in 1956 that Ken Guettler, a slugger for the Shreveport Sports of the Texas League, broke Babe Ruth's record by belting 62 home runs. As I remember, it was a real success story because he had a problem with one of his arms. He never made the majors, and I've always wondered what happened to him.

Of course, Buffalo Stadium is long gone. The site of the field, which was located where the Gulf Freeway to Galveston intersects Milby Boulevard just east of downtown, is now part of a furniture store complex. When I'm in Houston, I usually find a way to drive by the site and remember those halcyon days of yore. In a corner of the store, the furniture company erected a little shrine, including the actual home plate from the stadium and other mementos. It's a little sad but very nostalgic, and a comfort as well, a reminder that, as a folk song about Roy Rogers says, "Memories, like heroes, they never grow old."

TOM DeFRANK is Washington Bureau Chief of the New York Daily News. *From 1970 to 1995 he chronicled six U.S. Presidents as* Newsweek's *White House correspondent.*

Guettler from above—a downtown cut.

MIKE DITKA

♦ ♦ ♦

My biggest thrill was my first time at-bat in Little League. I hit a high inside pitch over the left field fence for a home run. I got a baseball signed by Pie Traynor, the great third baseman for the Pirates. I cherished that baseball for many years.

MIKE DITKA made the Pro Bowl team from 1962 to 1966 as a Chicago Bears tight end. He later coached the Bears to a 112-68 record and the Super Bowl XX title.

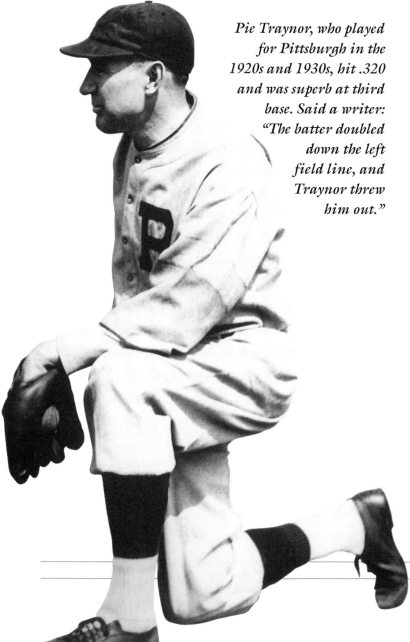

Pie Traynor, who played for Pittsburgh in the 1920s and 1930s, hit .320 and was superb at third base. Said a writer: "The batter doubled down the left field line, and Traynor threw him out."

ROBERT DOLE

♦ ♦ ♦

When you think about it, baseball is a small-town sport—the grass, the sky, the emphasis on the individual—sort of what I learned growing up in Russell, Kansas. You're out there by yourself—it's a little like track—at bat or in the field. The team can support you, but not like basketball or football, where everything is muddled. Baseball's a competitive sport, a personal sport, where you have to prove yourself. Maybe that's why I love it.

I grew up a big Yankee fan. Sure, we had the Kansas City Blues and Monarchs, and I'd listen to

A portable lighting system for night games let the Kansas City Monarchs play twice or more a day, making them black baseball's most popular 1930s touring team.

games on the radio, but the Yankees were the thing. Actually, the Blues were their top farm club, so I'd follow Ruth and DiMaggio. I knew all the batting averages, who had the most doubles, triples, I couldn't get enough. And I'd play it Sunday afternoon, at picnics, like everybody else. Baseball was our big sport—what Middle America was all about.

Many games now last too long. We need to change that. And we need a better way to have balance, whether it's revenue sharing or what, I don't know. Sure, a Yankee fan loves winning the World Series every year—but what about small-market teams like the Royals? I wouldn't mind seeing a Series back at Kauffman Stadium.

Today I live in Washington and chair the Federal-

City Council, which explores ways to make the District a better place. One of our priorities is to get baseball back. Maybe I could start memorizing those batting averages again. Blue sky, green grass, pitcher facing batter. Washington, or Russell? That's the great thing about baseball. It doesn't matter.

ROBERT DOLE served from 1969 to 1996 as U.S. Senator (Kansas). In 1996, he was the Republican nominee for President.

TOM DREESEN

◆ ◆ ◆

As far back as I can remember, I loved baseball and played it every chance I could find—not only as a child, but as an adult. As a boy growing up in Harvey, Illinois, I played on sandlots and school grounds. I went into the navy at age seventeen and played even if it was only tossing catch aboard ship. After leaving the service I went back to Harvey and immediately joined a softball league and played three nights a week and on weekends.

When I went into show business and had to move to the West Coast, it broke my heart to leave my fellow teammates. I knew I was going to miss the camaraderie and the competition. So when I arrived in Los Angeles, I immediately joined a team in a fast-pitch softball league and stayed on it until I was fifty-six years old. To this day I'm in touch with many of my former teammates and whenever we get together, it's a glorious time of reacquainting and reminiscing.

My introduction to baseball came from listening to the Chicago Cubs games on radio when I was a little boy, five years old. To this day I love listening to announcers describing play-by-play on my car radio while stuck in

Charlie Root warms up at the Cubs' 1936 training camp on California's Catalina Island.

traffic anywhere in the U.S.A. (and it seems like if you're anywhere in the U.S.A., you're stuck in traffic).

But the greatest thrill of all for a child is the first time you walk into a major league park. Picture this. You're in Chicago driving through a busy neighborhood. You come to a stoplight, look to your right, and lo and behold, there's a ballpark right in the middle of this neighborhood. And not just any ballpark. It's Wrigley Field! This is the ballpark that legend has it where Babe Ruth pointed to the wall after Charlie Root had a 0-2 count on him and then proceeded to hit it out of the park. This is

❖═◎═❖

As far back as I can remember, I loved baseball and played it every chance I could find—not only as a child, but as an adult.

❖═◎═❖

where Hall of Famer Ernie Banks hit his 500th homer and so many great baseball moments too numerous to recall.

In the hustle and bustle of human life, this is also the place where you can take your son and put him in a seat that you sat in as a child and his grandfather sat in and, in fact, his grandfather's grandfather sat in. He'll watch a game that all those before him watched. For a moment—for a precious wonderful moment—time stands still.

The smell of hot dogs, the cheers of the crowd, the bonding with people around you that you'll probably never see again. Take it all in, son. It's a grand time in a grand place, watching a great game.

TOM DREESEN, termed by ex-Cub Mark Grace "our greatest good-luck charm," has made more than 500 appearances on national TV, including more than sixty on The Tonight Show.

───────

MICHAEL DUKAKIS
◆ ◆ ◆

Baseball was a part of my life from the time I was three or four years old. I saw my first Red Sox game when I was four and a half. (Lefty Grove was the pitcher.) I was swinging a bat at the same age. Since I was one of the few students at my elementary school who could catch a swinging strike behind the plate, I became the catcher for the seventh-grade team when I was in the fourth grade. In those days, there was no Little League. We just went out and played and played and played.

Like all Bostonians, I live or, more frequently, die with the Red Sox. I was at Fenway when Carlton Fisk hit the famous home run against Cincinnati. I had just returned from a gubernatorial debate with my Republican opponent in 1986 when the ball went through Bill Buckner's legs. I live within twenty minutes walking distance from Fenway Park and, while I understand the economics of modern baseball, I love that park and hate to think of it being torn down.

Needless to say, Bucky Dent's home run in 1978 may mark the low point in my relationship with the Red Sox. I had been forty points ahead in the polls for reelection that year and lost the primary. The Red Sox were 14 games ahead after the All-Star

Winner takes all in the A.L. East, Fenway Park, October 2, 1978: Bucky Dent's seventh-inning homer gives the Yankees a 3–2 lead; New York ultimately won 5–4.

break and Dent killed us. For me and my family, 1978 was a terrible year.

MICHAEL DUKAKIS is a former Governor of Massachusetts and was the 1988 Democratic candidate for President. He now teaches at Northeastern University in Boston.

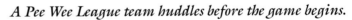

THOMAS EAGLETON

◆ ◆ ◆

I could catch a thrown ball and about 50 percent of the ground balls, if they were hit directly at me. My range was two feet either way. As a hitter, I could hit a slow pitch down the middle. Anything else was a pitiful swing and miss.

THOMAS EAGLETON, a U.S. Senator (Missouri) from 1968 to 1987, has loved baseball since his father took him to Cardinals spring training camp as a child.

A Pee Wee League team huddles before the game begins.

BOB EDWARDS

◆ ◆ ◆

I was raised in the bushes. That's how baseball regards Louisville, Kentucky, though the city was a charter member of the National League and enjoyed big league status until the dawn of the twentieth century, when the great Honus Wagner and his teammates moved upriver to Pittsburgh. Baseball likes to let a town know exactly where it stands, and Louisville's clubs have been *farm* teams in *minor* leagues.

Baseball tries the patience of a minor league fan. The game embraces tradition, but baseball in the bushes has about as much loyalty as a free agent on a bad team. Louisville has been home to the Grays, Eclipse, Colonels, Redbirds, RiverBats, and now (thankfully) the just plain Bats. It's played at Eclipse Park, Parkway Field, Fairgrounds Stadium (renamed Cardinal Stadium), and now Louisville Slugger Field. It's been a farm club of the Red Sox, Senators, Orioles, Braves, Red Sox (again), Cardinals, Brewers, and Reds. In 1957 it had no working agreement with any major league team and only six players showed up for spring training. From 1962 through 1982, there were sixteen seasons during which Louisville had no team at all.

A kid learning baseball in a minor league town is hit with the harsh reality that his heroes will soon leave town if they're any good. I saw Juan Pizarro pitch a no-hitter in his only game with Louisville. The Braves called him up the next day. Joe Torre and the Niekro brothers stayed a bit longer.

Big league baseball was just over a hundred miles upriver at Crosley Field. Watching my first Reds game from high in the upper deck, I had a great view of Frank Robinson playing Crosley's quirky left field terrace, a berm that served as a sort of uphill warning track. Robinson jacked three homers that day and would have had the record-tying fourth if he had hit

it to either side of the scoreboard that towered above the wall in left-center.

This tasting of baseball in the bigs whet my appetite. I resolved that someday I'd live in a town that had major league baseball. Impatiently I waited to grow up, but I was stuck in the bushes through grade school, high school, college, and two years in the army. A grownup at last, I chose a graduate school in a major league town and arrived in Washington, D.C., in August of 1971. Thirty days later, the Washington Senators played their last game in RFK Stadium and moved to Texas. The absence of baseball in the nation's capital is more outrageous than the designated hitter. I would have better luck explaining the infield fly rule to a stranger from Borneo than I have trying to fathom why major league baseball does not offer its product to a recession-proof community that has the highest per capita income in the country. Red Barber told me that baseball owners were nineteenth-century men. Guess they still are.

We are told that Peter Angelos, owner of the Baltimore Orioles, is the man keeping baseball out of Washington. He thinks we will stop being interested in his team if we once again have one of our own. Angelos may be attracting some suckers to Camden Yards, but not me. I have never set foot there and have no

intention of ever seeing the place until baseball comes to its senses and returns the national pastime to the national capital.

In the early 1980s, local baseball groups enlisted the banks to offer savings accounts for fans interested in buying season tickets for our nonexistent team. The idea was to demonstrate to baseball that there is a huge fan base that would support a team in the Washington area. The point was made, but baseball ignored us. Mergers have changed the names of the banks and most depositors long since have closed their accounts, but I have kept the faith. My baseball account, covering the purchase (at 1980s prices) of two seats for ten games, earns about five dollars in interest each year. Like many a baseball fan, I wait for next year.

BOB EDWARDS is the host of National Public Radio's popular show Morning Edition.

Upon entering Cooperstown, Billy Williams said: "It's like an Oscar to an actor, a Pulitzer Prize to a writer, a Nobel Prize to a scientist."

EDWARD CARDINAL EGAN

◆ ◆ ◆

There are several things, in particular, for which I will be forever indebted to my parents. The first, of course, is my faith. The second might well be my lifelong affection for the Chicago Cubs.

Growing up in the Chicago suburb of Oak Park, Illinois, baseball was simply an accepted part of our lives. My father had been a semipro baseball player before going into business, and my brother, Jim, and my closest boyhood friend, Bobby King, each had tryouts with minor league teams. Bobby was good enough that he played minor league ball for a few years. Although I was never in their league as a player, that did not diminish my love of the game.

Going to Wrigley Field was a special treat, as we got to see our favorites—players like Stan Hack and Phil Cavarretta—in person. Through the years, I continued to get to Wrigley when I could, cheering such great players as Ernie Banks, Billy Williams, and Ron Santo. Like so many others, I was disappointed by the team's collapse in 1969. I was certain that was finally our year and I'd get to see the Cubs back in the World Series, something that hasn't happened since I was thirteen years old and we lost in heartbreaking fashion to the Tigers. It is a hope and a dream of mine that I will again see the Cubs in the Series.

I've spent many years away from Chicago, living almost twenty-three years in Rome, and now in New York. In all this time I've never lost my love for the game of baseball and, I must confess, for the Cubs as well.

His Eminence EDWARD CARDINAL EGAN was ordained into the priesthood in 1957. The former judge of the Tribunal of the Sacred Roman Rota is now Archbishop of New York.

From 1912 to 1999 Cobb, Gehringer, and Kaline graced the corner of Michigan and Trumbull.
The centerfield flagpole was in play, while an overhang turned routine flies into homers.

DICK ENBERG

◆ ◆ ◆

I grew up in Michigan, went to Central Michigan University, and visited Tiger Stadium many times as a kid. That's what made the second of Nolan Ryan's no-hitters so special. It happened in 1973 (July 15), and I was behind the mike with Don Drysdale for the Angels as Nolan scorched the Tigers.

Ryan pitched his most powerful game—16 strike-outs in the first seven innings—and the symbol of Tigers' frustration was a former American League batting champion (.361 in 1961). In his fourth at-bat, Norm Cash got in the box wielding a leg from a clubhouse chair as a substitute for his Louisville Slugger. Not until he saw strike one did the umpire notice that he was improperly equipped. Cash told

me later that when ordered to go to the dugout and fetch a bat, he said, "Why? It ain't gonna make any difference. I'm not gonna hit Ryan anyway."

This was a time when the Angels provided few moments of greatness. To paraphrase an old Braves pitching credo—it was Frank Tanana and Ryan and three days of cryin'. Today was different. I was in the park of my youth—and in a visitors broadcast booth so close to the field that you could feel and, yes, hear, a legend at his omnipotent best. Oh, my!

DICK ENBERG has announced the World Series, Wimbledon, Rose and Super Bowls, NCAA hoops final, and baseball Game of the Week.

MIKE ERUZIONE

◆ ◆ ◆

When I think back on my baseball days it always brings a smile. Baseball was my favorite sport growing up. Whether it was playing catch with my father or fielding grounders with my uncle and cousin, those memories will always be with me. I can remember waiting for my new glove every few years, making sure that my father had the oil to loosen the pocket, wrapping a ball in the glove and taping it shut before I put it under the mattress to make sure it would form perfectly. I played baseball right up until the Olympic Games and I continued to play for three more years afterward before softball took over.

For me, hitting a home run in Little League was just as great a thrill as winning the Olympic Gold Medal. It's something that you always dream about. As a matter of fact, when my ten-year-old son hit his first Little League home run he said to me after the game, "Dad, it was just what I had dreamed." To me, that's baseball. Playing and going to games at Fenway Park and watching Yaz, Carlton, and Rico are the memories that never leave.

MIKE ERUZIONE was captain of the 1980 United States Olympic hockey team, which won the Gold Medal at the Winter Games at Lake Placid.

LISA FERNANDEZ

◆ ◆ ◆

A long-ago song says, "Doing what comes naturally." Baseball came naturally to me. I was raised by a dad who played semipro baseball in Cuba and a mom who loved stickball in New York. They met in California. I came along, and was introduced to baseball as a child. It's been with me ever since.

Why do I like baseball? I like how the sport relates. It's team, yet individual. Hitting, for instance, is one of the toughest things in sports—striking a moving object with a moving object, both round. You face the pitcher. A shortstop faces a ground ball in the hole. There's nowhere to hide. And each at-bat is a new adventure. Maybe you're oh-for-four, striking out three times, and you bat in the ninth. Get a hit and nobody remembers the rest.

I like baseball because it's mental. What else is so hard that a person succeeding three times in ten is a hero? I like baseball because of its work ethic. You have to have the courage to get up and keep going. Guys like Paul Molitor, Tony Gwynn, or Edgar Martinez excel year after year. I like it because it caters to all individuals, and has a spot for everyone. You can be big and strong and bat cleanup, quick and small

The Man They Call Yaz. Carl Yastrzemski retired in 1983 after 3,419 hits and a record 3,308 A.L. games.

and lead off like the wind, or somewhere in between and bat seventh. Baseball means equality.

Finally, I love the challenges. Can I beat that pitcher? What'll he throw me? Why does the shortstop play toward third on a pitch, then move toward second? I love the intricacies, the nuance, how you anticipate, how you gut it out. I don't really admire the one-year wonder, a flash-in-the-pan, but guys who remain true to the game. Paul O'Neill, not really a huge name, but a *player*, or Derek Jeter, who focuses like a laser, or A-Rod, with his love of baseball history. What a breath of fresh air.

In the overall scheme of things, it really helps you prepare for life—get a goal, pursue it, brave success and failure, never despair, take the long view. I'm not very old and already baseball has taught me this. Thank goodness that my parents met.

LISA FERNANDEZ pitched the United States Olympic softball team to a Gold Medal in the 1996 and 2000 Summer Games. The four-time college All-America is now a UCLA softball coach.

Tony Gwynn topped .300 for nineteen straight years on his way to tying Honus Wagner's eight N.L. batting titles.

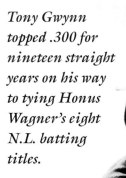

JEAN PICKER FIRSTENBERG

◆ ◆ ◆

Baseball has been part of my life since I was a child. My brother, who was five years older than I, loved sports. Since I wanted to do everything he did, I became a tomboy. While I was a good athlete, I was even more successful as a sports fan. Unfortunately, I was at least twenty years ahead of my time.

I did do color commentary for one baseball game. During my senior year at Boston University, I ran a great radio station—WBUR, 20,000 watts on your FM dial. One day, when the color announcer called in sick, I assigned myself as his substitute. I also did a half-inning of play-by-play. I called a ground ball up the middle a single before it even got through the infield. That's when I appreciated how difficult it is to do play-by-play.

My only other sportscasting occurred in my early teens in front of an eight-inch television set with a green magnifier on top of the screen. I kept the sound off and did play-by-play into a reel-to-reel tape machine. Years later, I found one of my tapes buried in a box at the top of a closet. I had it transferred to a cassette and with trepidation, I hit the play button. What a shock—I was a lot better than I remembered.

Eleven—that's how old I was when Branch Rickey signed Jackie Robinson to a Brooklyn Dodger contract, a seminal moment for baseball and America. Jackie was a superior athlete. Even better, he was a superior human being—turning the other cheek; hitting, stealing, running, and throwing out batters; showing in his unique way why baseball and America had to desegregate. Jackie made such an impression on me that as a young girl I wrote an essay about him for school. I remember my mother reading it over the telephone to every one of her friends. I was so proud. Jackie had opened the baseball world for Campanella, Newcombe, and others to follow. It's no wonder the

"I'm on a seafood diet," said Tom Lasorda. "I eat all the food I can see." The 1976–96 Dodger manager won seven division titles, four pennants, and two World Series trophies.

Dodgers—finally—won a World Series in 1955. Jackie showed me that you could be the best and still have far greater achievements ahead.

So when Walter O'Malley moved the Dodgers west, my world collapsed. It was a bitter blow that failed to diminish over time. Never did I believe that the Bums would enter my life again. But, in 1980, when I became Director and CEO of the American Film Institute, the girl who wanted to be a sportscaster was meeting face-to-face with Peter O'Malley, Tommy Lasorda, and Rachel Robinson. The girl whose life rose and fell on Red Barber's words was talking to Vin Scully—a young man who started as a Brooklyn announcer in 1950 and not only rose to the heights of the Old Redhead, but spoke poetically about sports.

I never would have dreamed that on opening day 2000, I'd be at Pac Bell Park to watch the Dodgers beat the Giants (definitely one of the few highlights of that season). And that I'd be front and center, sitting with the new Managing Partner, Chairman and CEO of the Dodgers, my dear friend, Bob Daly.

Outside Pac Bell Park is a bronze statue of Willie Mays. Now, there needs to be a bronze statue of Jackie Robinson. Preferably, it should be placed on the Mall in Washington, D.C. In many ways, Jackie was this country's first civil rights leader—using nonviolence and extraordinary skill as a ballplayer to show our country the value of tolerance.

Along with stealing bases in 1947, Jackie Robinson stole my heart. I'll always be grateful to a great man for the exceptional example he set and the lessons he taught that meant so much to baseball—and America as a whole.

JEAN PICKER FIRSTENBERG, Director and Chief Executive Officer of the American Film Institute, is a recipient of the prestigious Women in Film Crystal Award.

In 2000 the Giants opened Pacific Bell Park, the first privately funded baseball-only park since Dodger Stadium. Pac Bell has 40,800 seats and a 309-foot right field line.

GEORGE FISHER

◆ ◆ ◆

I grew up in a part of Illinois where a lot of people love the St. Louis Cardinals. I'll never forget how Yogi Berra's home town of St. Louis once honored him with a day. As usual, baseball's favorite philosopher proved equal to the moment. He said: "I want to thank everybody who made this day *necessary*."

I'd like to thank those who made *baseball* necessary. I played the game when I was young—even wanted to be a big league ballplayer. Then I hurt my knee. So long, Cooperstown. I left the exciting sports world behind for the more sedate world of business. Just kidding.

As a kid, I knew why Bill Veeck said, "Baseball is the only game where you don't have to be seven feet tall or seven feet wide." That's why it's the most democratic of sports. Of course, it's also the most republican. What Veeck meant was that anyone can enjoy baseball. Just like anyone can enjoy taking pictures—a ten-year-old or a pure professional.

In 1993, I became Chairman, President, and CEO of a company synonymous with pictures—Eastman Kodak Company. Baseball touches memory. So does photography—linking childhood and adulthood. After all, what are photographs other than giant baseball cards, if you will.

My favorite, of course, was Hall of Famer Stan Musial. I still remember how Ford Frick said: "Here stands baseball's perfect warrior. Here stands baseball's perfect knight." In twenty-two years with the Cardinals, Stan had 3,630 hits and won seven batting titles. I admired even more the attitude with which he played. "Every time I put the

uniform on I get a thrill," he said.

Bad knee or not, I still feel the same about this greatest game of all—the butterflies in my

Bill Veeck introduced midget Eddie Gaedel, players' names on uniforms, and an exploding scoreboard. "Make every game a carnival, every day a Mardi Gras, and every fan a king."

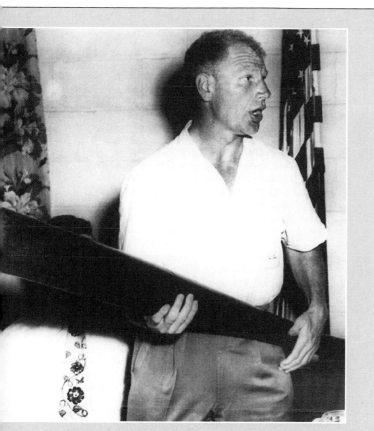

The then-Tribe owner swings a bat presented at a Cleveland dinner. It looked as big to the 1948 Indians, who won their first Series since 1920.

stomach at the sound of the game-starting "Star-Spangled Banner"; the amazement of a great shortstop play deep in the hole; the cringing sensation of a called third strike; the exhilaration of a grand slam; or just the feeling that winning is a team effort.

Every time I watch, the thrills are lived again.

GEORGE FISHER is the former Chairman of the Board of the Eastman Kodak Company.

MARLIN FITZWATER

◆ ◆ ◆

The Pee-Wee League in Abilene, Kansas, during the 1950s was the center of community activity, the social hub of every boy's world, and the surest way for a farm boy to get into town at least once or twice a week. I wanted that world, even at age eight.

One day, my father told me that tryouts for Pee-Wee were being held at Rural Center School, a new consolidated school about five miles from our farm. It was very important to be part of this new school and to play baseball. While I had thrown a softball around with my dad, I really didn't know much about this hardball business. But Dad dug out an old five-finger glove for me to use, and we headed for the pasture behind the school.

It was a wonderful sight. A ball diamond had been lined out, and kids in white T-shirts were running everywhere. The coaches, who were neighboring farmers, were giving batting practice. I lined up near the batting fence, hanging back until I was noticed.

"This your boy, Max?" the coach asked.

My dad nodded.

"Where's he play?"

"He can play anywhere," Dad said.

"Let's try him at second," the coach said.

I ran to second base and stood on it.

"Move to one side and bring it home," he continued, while tossing the ball and whacking it toward me.

It seemed to me that he was forgetting steps one and two—how to throw and how to catch. I was seized by fear, not of being unable to stop the ball, but of not knowing what "bring it home" meant.

I grabbed the ball with all four fingers wrapped around the seams and clutched it in the manner of a shot put. Then I mimicked the only players I had ever seen—the ones on Wheaties boxes—and took a full windup, kicked my left foot in the air, and flung that

Marlin Fitzwater (left), with brother Gary and canine companions, in his Abilene, Kansas, youth.

baby toward the catcher, which I assumed to be located some-place called "home."

The ball sailed and sailed, and it didn't stop until it hit the side of the school, behind the cars and a couple of cows.

The coach watched in amazement, in awe of my ignorance. He walked to second base.

"Have you ever thrown a hardball before?"

"No, sir."

He asked how I gripped the ball, and I showed him my four-fingered special.

"Okay, try it with two fingers, or if your hand is too small, three fingers, like this." He showed me how. "Don't put your little finger on it. Now throw to the catcher."

I did as he instructed. It felt funny. I wasn't sure I had enough finger strength to heave it home, although I was at least learning the jargon. I went into my deep windup, kicked my leg in the air, and let it fly straight to the catcher.

The coach looked at me, trying to figure out the kick I was using. I guess it never dawned on him that this was the only way I knew how to throw.

"I think maybe you are a pitcher," he said.

He led me over to a small piece of wood anchored in the pasture that was the pitching rubber.

"Throw a few from here."

Bursting with pride, I wound up again. I had thrown the ball exactly three times in my life and had been promoted to pitcher. Splat! Right in the catcher's mitt.

"Looks like we have a pitcher," the coach said.

But it was not to last. I had no real strength and even less control. I pitched our entire first game, which was a no-hitter. But I walked 21 batters and we lost, 13–0.

Years later, I asked the coach why he left me in the entire game.

"You had such a great windup."

MARLIN FITZWATER served as Press Secretary for Presidents Reagan and Bush before writing Call the Briefing, *a memoir of his White House years. He is now a novelist.*

JOEL FOX

◆ ◆ ◆

Like all my relatives going back to my grandparents' generation, I grew up in Boston in the 1950s and 1960s a die-hard Red Sox fan. When my father, Harry Fox, who had recently moved to California, passed away at the end of 1998, the funeral was held in the Boston area. My solemn eulogy spoke of his heroism as a man and a father, both recognized—a Bronze Star recipient serving under General Patton at the Battle of the Bulge—and unrecognized. My brother, Mitch, however, took a different tack. He started his remarks by saying, "I know for certain my father lived a long time because he was alive the last time the Red Sox won the Series."

The Boston audience appreciated the remark—just as it would have understood my story about the ball rolling through Bill Buckner's legs. I was watching Game 6 of the 1986 World Series at home in California. I had champagne on ice. But I knew I would have to be moderate in celebrating the Red Sox's first world title in nearly seventy years because I was scheduled to debate a California ballot proposition on KABC Radio in California from midnight to 2:00 A.M.

Because of the time difference from the East Coast, the game ended around 10:00 P.M. in Los Angeles. When the game came to its tragic end, I just picked up my notes and walked out of the house with a vacant gaze saying nothing to my family, including my puzzled in-laws visiting from Indiana. I got in the car and drove away from my home in the San Fernando Valley. I didn't know where I was going. I didn't turn on the radio. I was in a daze. I didn't even swear. I just drove, ending up along the coast in Ventura County. Finally, I followed the coast road to Los Angeles, arriving at the radio station just in time for the show—two hours of driving.

My wife forced herself to stay up until midnight and listen to the radio show to see if I had made it or if I had driven into the Pacific Ocean.

JOEL FOX, the former President of the Howard Jarvis Taxpayers Association, is senior research associate for the Rose Institute of State and Local Government at Claremont McKenna College.

One pitch could have ended the 1986 World Series. Instead, Boston lost Game 6—and the Fall Classic the following night.

JOHN FRANZEN

◆ ◆ ◆

*S*ports Illustrated gave me a Christmas present in December 2000. It named me "Milwaukee's Finest"—their number one fan. Since the Brewers came to town in 1970, I've seen more than 2,700 games, including a fifteen-year streak of over 1,200 at home. Some people say I'm baseball's number one fan. What could be greater?

Being a fan never leaves you, even when players and teams skip town. I remember when the Braves went to Atlanta in late 1965. There's a page one picture in the *Milwaukee Journal,* showing

Two-time MVP Robin Yount combined loyalty (Brewers 1974–93), durability (2,856 games), and longevity (3,142 hits) and was inducted into the Hall of Fame in 1999.

Warren Spahn was known for his pickoff move. It is said the left-hander once picked a man off first—and the batter swung.

me with an auto-graphed baseball just staring at the field. It was taken at their last-ever game at County Stadium. I kept thinking about being in high school when the Braves moved to Milwaukee in 1953. I bought season tickets from 1956 through 1965. How could you not feel blue?

What baseball means are memories. I remember 1957, when the Braves clinched their first pennant September 23. Then Lew Burdette won three Series games to beat the Yanks. Or May 1959. I was there when Harvey Haddix pitched 12 perfect innings only to lose in the 13th, 1–0. Joe Adcock hit the ball out of the park with two men on, but passed Hank Aaron on the bases and was called out. Only one run scored, but we won, 1–0. How about Spahn and Burdette throwing no-hitters in the early 1960s, or Warren's 300th win, or Willie Mays hitting four home runs April 30, 1961? I was there, saw 'em all. In baseball you remember.

It was great to see baseball return in 1970. I had joined the Army after the Braves left, and got out after the Brewers' first three games. I haven't missed many since. In 1980, I saw my 1,000th Brewers game. Two years later they won their only pennant. In 1992, I saw Robin Yount get his 3,000th hit. By then my streak ended after I collapsed while shopping. I spent April 1987 in the hospital. Maybe it was good luck: The Brewers started the year by winning thirteen straight. But after retiring as a postal clerk in 1991, I've seen almost every game. Same seat at County Stadium: eight rows behind home plate for twenty-eight years.

On the park's last Fan Appreciation Night, I was chosen by the club to turn the countdown number to the final game. Now I'm in a new home at Miller Park—front-row box in the loge level. There's no one in front of me. Can you imagine anything better than an unobstructed view of the Brewers? Well, maybe a pennant and that first World Series. I'll just keep watching till it happens.

JOHN FRANZEN's T-shirt says, "NO. 1 BREWERS FAN." "His apartment," wrote Sports Illustrated, *"would be unexceptional if not for the hundreds of books of scoresheets that spill out of his closet."*

RON FRASER

◆ ◆ ◆

In more than thirty-five years as a head coach in international and college baseball I've won three European championships, two College World Series national titles, and a world championship for the United States. But one of my most memorable experiences occurred in 1987 when I coached the United States Pan American baseball team.

During tryouts, the coach at Michigan called telling me about an outstanding nineteen-year-old pitcher he had on his team, Jim Abbott. I had heard about him—he was born with only one hand, his left. There was only a stump where his right hand would have been. I brought Jim in for a tryout, impressed not only with his pitching ability, but by his determination and spirit. He made the final cut.

The Pan American tour culminated in a trip to Cuba for a five-game series. The Cuban baseball team was the best in the world. The team was made up of men, twenty to thirty-five years old, who'd been playing together for years. At least 80 percent could be playing major league baseball. The rest would be in AAA. We were fielding a team of eighteen- and nineteen-year-old college players who'd played together for a few weeks. Quite a mismatch.

After losing the first two games, I decided to

Born without a right hand, Jim Abbott won a career-high 18 games in 1991.

The native Michigander pitched for four teams. Said then-Yankee manager Buck Showalter: "Jimmy does more with one hand than most do with two."

start Jim for the third game. Havana was buzzing with the news. "They can't beat us with their best pitchers, now they're going to field a pitcher with one hand?" I was concerned for Jim and what he had heard about the local reaction. I needn't have worried. I went to see him before the game and have never seen a player so focused on his mission. He told me not to worry.

The stadium in Havana was packed over capacity that day—way over 60,000. Our team was up first and went down quickly. The Cubans were up. Victor Mesa, the leadoff hitter, was an outstanding hitter and their fastest player. He stepped up to the plate and hit a high chopper to the mound. As Mesa sped to first base, Jim would have to wait for the ball to drop, catch it in his glove, which would have been transferred to his left hand to catch the ball, transfer the glove back to his right elbow where he cradled it, then throw the ball to first. It was an impossible task and everyone knew it—except Jim. Instead of switching the glove to his left hand for the catch, he cradled it in his right elbow, caught the ball in his glove balanced there, and threw to first with his left hand just in time for the out.

The crowd erupted in a roar not to protest the call—but to cheer an incredible play and great player. This was just the beginning. The Cuban fans, Communists who felt that all of their problems had been caused by the United States, continued to root for our young player. In the eighth inning, with the U.S. team firmly in the lead, I took Jim out of the game to give another pitcher some work. When he left the field, the fans would not stop cheering. The game was stopped as he took the field at least ten times to try to satisfy their gratitude for his ability. Finally the game continued despite the demands of the crowd.

After our victory, Cuban security asked that

I remain in the stadium with Jim while the rest of the team went back to the hotel. The crowd was assembled outside waiting for a glimpse of him. After a couple of hours, they led us outside for the long walk to the van. Thousands of fans were still waiting, forming a human tunnel. As we walked, they clapped their hands and chanted, "Abbott, Abbott, Abbott..."

Since Major League Baseball began its free agent draft in 1965, only seventeen selections have advanced directly to the major leagues without playing in the minors. Jim Abbott was one of them. In 1993, while pitching for the Yankees, he pitched a no-hitter—only the ninth pitcher to do so in the club's almost 100-year history.

I remember those moments. So do other fans. But it's the memory of Jim, and thousands chanting, "Abbott, Abbott" and all the other fine young men on our 1987 team that will remain with me for the rest of my life.

RON FRASER was the head coach from 1963 to 1992 of the University of Miami baseball team. He also was the head coach of the 1992 United States Olympic baseball team.

DOUG GAMBLE

◆ ◆ ◆

I spent the first three decades of my life in Canada, where the sound of pioneer hockey broadcaster Foster Hewitt's "He shoots, he scores" stirred the blood of most sports fans more than any baseball announcer's description of a home run. But if hockey is the father of all sports in Canada, baseball, for me, has always been a favorite uncle.

My earliest memories of the game were when my dad would take me to the ballpark in my native Montreal, where our family lived for only a few years before moving to Hamilton, Ontario, and then Toronto. I never did see the Montreal Canadiens play while in that city because hockey tickets were so hard to find. But the minor league Montreal Royals were more accessible and were my first exposure to baseball. Watching the Dodger farm team from which Jackie Robinson eventually entered the majors began both my love of baseball and my devotion to the Dodgers. Little did I imagine at the time that twenty-two years after they left Brooklyn for Los Angeles, I would move there myself.

Some of my fondest childhood memories include playing street hockey in the cold-weather months and sandlot baseball in the summer. But as someone who barely tolerated winter, the sport associated with the aroma of grass, the warmth of sunshine, light clothing, and glorious sunsets was special. I usually occupied third base, a not-so-hot player at the hot corner, but it didn't matter how I played. Next winter was far away, I was with the guys, and everything was fine with the world.

Perhaps my first big thrill as a sports fan, and one of the greatest ever, was the 1955 World Series when "next year" finally arrived for the Brooklyn Dodgers. It was back in the days when weekday World Series games were still played in the afternoon, making it either difficult or impossible for interested schoolkids to know the result of a game until classes were out for the day. Sometimes a kid or two would smuggle a small radio into school, and scores, or rumors of scores, would quietly circulate through the halls and classrooms.

The 1955 Series between the Dodgers and Yankees went the distance and, as bad luck would have it, Game 7 on October 4 was a school day. If anyone had managed to sneak a radio past school authorities that day it did me no good, for no scores reached my ears all afternoon. Until we were finally, mercifully, released at 4:00 P.M. my mind was preoccupied with baseball and the hope—no, the prayer—that the Dodgers would win.

But I knew I wouldn't have to make it all the way home, a long walk, before knowing the outcome. Halfway to my house was a drugstore where the proprietor had posted in the window the final score of each game throughout the Series, including the inning-by-inning breakdown. When the drugstore finally appeared in the distance I spotted the

President George Bush kept his college first baseman's mitt in the Oval Office desk.

YALE

George Bush

Yale   First Base

big, white sheet of paper taped inside the window, but I was still too far away to read the numbers. As I walked closer, almost not daring to look, the score came into view: Dodgers 2, Yankees 0. Pure joy! The rest of my walk home was on air. Jackie, Duke Snider, Pee Wee Reese, Roy Campanella, Gil Hodges et al., including winning pitcher Johnny Podres, could not have been much happier than I was at that moment.

I've seen a lot of baseball since then, some from the edge of my seat, much of it laid-back and comfortable. All in all, baseball has been a pleasurable constant in my life, an old friend always inviting me, in the words of the great Dodger announcer Vin Scully, to "pull up a chair." And although the impurities that have crept into the game over the years have diminished it, in my view, the way a declining culture has diminished America, it remains a great sport in a great country. Neither is quite what they once were, but because one is baseball and the other is America, there's always hope.

My career and baseball crossed paths during a time when I was honored to contribute humor to some of former President George Bush's speeches. In 1989, I prepared an opening joke for the President to use in welcoming the World Series champion Oakland Athletics to a Rose Garden ceremony. Poetic license is a key ingredient in humor, and I took full advantage of it having President Bush say, "One of my grandkids told me he wanted to be a baseball player, not a politician, because politicians never get their picture on bubble gum cards." It sounded funnier when he said it.

Although I made that up, the Topps trading card company took it seriously and produced 100 baseball cards with a picture of Mr. Bush in his uniform of the Yale team that went to the College World Series in 1948. He was presented with the card set, and *Newsweek* magazine

later reported the story and printed a photo of the card.

If only other politicians would restrict their distortion of the truth to jokes about baseball.

DOUG GAMBLE has written for many television stars, including Bob Hope and Johnny Carson. He has also been a humor writer for Presidents Reagan and Bush.

RUDOLPH W. GIULIANI
◆ ◆ ◆

Sitting next to my father at Yankee Stadium during my first baseball game, I felt like the luckiest kid in the world. At the time, I wasn't old enough to understand all the complexities that make New York City the capital of the world, but I was well aware that our city was the home of the Yankees and the capital of baseball.

My earliest memories of baseball are from an era when the Yankees won five World Series in a row—four of them Subway Series. But that day at Yankee Stadium is when my appreciation for the game—and what it means to so many fans—began to develop.

The Red Sox were in town. Joe DiMaggio was playing center field for the Yankees, and his brother Dom was playing center field for Boston. It seemed odd that two brothers would be on different teams, but that spirit of friendly competition was only the first of the game's many intricacies that I would learn. Through the years I've come to understand that baseball, with its roots in New York City, is not only an important part of my life, but a very important part of the city's life as well.

When the rules were first drafted in 1846, baseball was called "The New York Game." Players first gathered to practice in a part of Manhattan known as Murray Hill, and the first organized game took place between two New York City teams, who played across

the Hudson on the Elysian Fields of New Jersey.

The National Association of Professional Base Ball Players, considered to be the first major league, was founded in Collier's Cafe at 13th and Broadway in 1871. Since its earliest days, our city has been the birthplace of some of baseball's most enduring icons, including the hot dog, which was introduced in the early 1900s, and "Take Me Out to the Ball Game," which was first played in New York City in 1908. Our city has also been home to some of the most fabled teams in baseball history, including the Giants, the Brooklyn Dodgers, and the most successful team in the history of professional sports, the Yankees. And some of the greatest heroes of baseball have called New York City their home. In fact, more than 100 members of the Baseball Hall of Fame played for one of our city's teams during their career, and thirty-six members chose to be inducted wearing their New York uniform.

You would think, growing up in a city with such a rich tradition of baseball, that it would be easy to be a Yankee fan, but nothing could be further from the truth. My family lived in Brooklyn, in the shadow of Ebbets Field. I grew up in the heart of Dodger country. But my father was an avid Yankee fan, which was a point of contention with mother's family of Dodger fans.

Perhaps my father wanted to annoy the in-laws, or simply double the number of Yankee fans at family gatherings, because at a very young age he dressed me up in pinstripes and put a Yankee cap on my head. I endured a number of neighborhood confrontations, but my loyalty never wavered. And I've been a Yankee fan ever since.

When I was growing up, baseball meant everything to our city; it certainly meant everything to the kids in my neighborhood. The players were our heroes. Every sandlot ball game was filled with children who idolized Willie Mays, Jackie Robinson, Pee Wee Reese, Phil Rizzuto, Mickey Mantle, Yogi Berra—who was my favorite Yankee—and all the other players who

occupied a larger-than-life place in our imaginations.

As I grew older, my understanding of the game and its significance also grew. Living in New York City and being a Yankee fan offers more than just pleasant childhood memories; it is a continual blessing, a historical reference, and a cultural barometer. I remember times in my life—and the life of the city— in terms of Yankee seasons. Even my memories of learning math include the Yankees. As a child I learned

When I was growing up, baseball meant everything to our city...

to compute averages so I could figure out the batting averages of my favorite players. I could then offer timely analysis and prove why the Yankees were a better team than the Dodgers. This endeared me not only to my father, but also to my math teacher.

And while this may only be coincidence, it has always seemed to me that the success of the Yankees provided a rough gauge of our city's spirit during my life. For example, the 1950s and early 1960s were times of great hope and opportunity for the City of New York. The Yankees, led by manager Casey Stengel through 1960, and players such as Berra, Mantle, and Whitey Ford, embodied that spirit. When the city fell into decline in the early 1970s, culminating in the fiscal crisis of 1975, the once mighty Yankees were in decline as well. But the spirit of our city surged when Thurman Munson and Reggie Jackson led the Yankees to world championships in 1977 and 1978. Today the Yankees again mirror the city with possibly their greatest team of all.

Joe Torre's Yankees won four of five 1996–2000 World Series. In 2001 they helped inspire New York City after the terrorist attacks of September 11. The strengths of this most recent Yankee dynasty reflect the qualities that have always led to our city's success: a rich diversity, a commitment to hard work, and the achievement of personal excellence in the pursuit of team victory. At a time when our city stands as the capital of the world, the Yankees have again

helped New York reclaim one of its most cherished titles: the capital of baseball.

It is no accident that New York City—the city by which all other cities are measured—is home to the

"If I were a retired gentleman," said Casey Stengel, *"I would follow the Yankees around just to see Rizzuto work those miracles each day."*

baseball team by which all other teams are measured. Because of baseball's roots and our city's continued love of the game, baseball remains an expression of all that is great about New York City. It is a vibrant example of what Bart Giamatti meant when he wrote, "Baseball is one of the few enduring institutions in America that has been continuous and adaptable and in touch with its origins. As a result, baseball is not simply an essential part of this country; it is a living memory of what American culture at its best wishes to be."

RUDOLPH W. GIULIANI, the Mayor of New York City from 1994 to 2001, says that growing up a Yankee fan near Ebbets Field was treacherous: "Dodger relatives once tried—literally—to lynch me. It was great training for politics."

BILL GOFF

◆ ◆ ◆

In 1950, when I was a four-year-old Philadelphian, the Whiz Kids won the pennant. It must have made a deep impression because in '52 I was indignant when my father chose to take my mother instead of me to the All-Star Game at Shibe Park (a choice I still do not understand). He said something about its being a social event.

I went to countless games at Shibe Park/Connie Mack Stadium including, on my eighteenth birthday (June 4, 1964), a Sandy Koufax no-hitter. Koufax faced the minimum that day. Richie Allen, who walked, was the only Phillie to reach and was wiped off the bases caught stealing. Frank Howard hit a three-run homer over the left field roof to beat the Phils, 3–0. Another great game I later attended was at Yankee Stadium: Reggie Jackson's three-home-run World Series extravaganza in 1977. This had extra impact since Reggie and I were in the same high school graduating class (Cheltenham High School, Wyncote, Pennsylvania, class of '64).

Attending baseball games was special. As we approached the ballpark, the foot pace would quicken. So would the pulse. The turnstile. The stairs. The tunnel. The panoramic explosion of sensory assault. The game. Aside from the fact that the Phillies never seemed to win, I do not remember any unpleasantness that took place in the park. Only happiness.

Baseball has become more important in my life than I had ever dreamed. The memories of perceptions and emotions have translated into my profession, publisher of baseball lithographs. It began with ballpark panoramas, then still lifes, great moments, and players. Baseball contains so many basic elements of art genres: landscape, cityscape, portraiture, architecture, dynamic tension, and the elements of still life. And aren't the classic ballparks all shaped like an embrace—the stands

World Series Game 6, October 18, 1977: Reggie Jackson watches his third homer of the night. He retired in 1987 with 563 round-trippers and 1,702 RBIs.

hugging the field? Who doesn't need a hug every now and then?

My most meaningful baseball experience was one shared with my then nine-year-old son, Kenny. We were in the ballpark for the most unlikely of no-hitters. One-handed Jim Abbott threw wonder at the Cleveland Indians that day, September 4, 1993. Coincidentally, the same Frank Howard was coaching first base for the

Yankees. For fun I said to Kenny in the third inning, "You know, Abbott hasn't allowed a hit yet. We can't talk about it, though. We might jinx him. But every time he gets another Indian out we can wink." Seventeen winking outs later, with one to go, Carlos Baerga was at bat. Baerga was one of the toughest outs in the league that year. But he grounded out to short. No more winking, just an explosion of disbelief at what had occurred. What inspiration!

When we got home, my wife, who had watched the game on television, sat down with Kenny and said to him something so powerful it will stay with him forever. "I don't ever want to hear you say 'I can't.'"

BILL GOFF began in the art business in 1971. He is the leading publisher of baseball art lithographs, posters, and calendars.

NANCY GOLD

◆ ◆ ◆

Living in upstate New York, and not being travelers generally beyond an hour's ride thirty-five miles away, my family was very happy to go to a game in Yankee Stadium 180 miles away. In the car, my father listened to see which team my mother, brother, and I wanted to win (the Yankees, naturally) and then at the game he announced that he was for the other team! I don't think my mother, brother, or I were surprised: We knew my father wouldn't care what the other team was—as long as there was some excitement for our family. I remember the hot dogs, popcorn, soda, and sitting in the sun—eating and watching my brother and father rooting for opposite teams, both happy—and I even remember my mother's peaceful face. Which team won? Who cares now? We had a whole experience, a day with the excitement of our Yankees and another team competing—hitting the ball and running—a day with New Yorkers, and with ourselves.

NANCY GOLD, President of Tough Traveler Ltd., designs and manufactures luggage, backpacks, and other bag products—"just right," she says, "for any ball, bat, and glove."

The Cubs haven't won a World Series since 1908. By contrast, the Bronx Bombers have 26 championships, all since 1923.

DORIS KEARNS GOODWIN

◆ ◆ ◆

The game of baseball has always been linked in my own mind with the mystic texture of childhood, with the sounds and smells of summer nights and with the memories of my father.

My love for baseball was born on the first day my father took me to Ebbets Field in Brooklyn. Riding in the trolley car, he seemed as excited as I was, and he never stopped talking; now describing for me the street in Brooklyn where he had grown up, now recalling the first game he had been taken to by his father, now recapturing for me his favorite memories from the Dodgers of his youth—the Dodgers of Casey Stengel, Zack Wheat, and Jimmy Johnston.

In the evenings, when my dad came home from work, we would sit together on our porch and relive the events of that afternoon's game which I had so carefully preserved in the large, red scorebook I'd been given

for my seventh birthday. I can still remember how proud I was to have mastered all those strange and wonderful symbols that permitted me to recapture, in miniature form, the every movement of Jackie Robinson and Pee Wee Reese, Duke Snider, and Gil Hodges. But the real power of that scorebook lay in the responsibility it entailed. For all through my childhood, my father kept from me the knowledge that the papers printed daily box scores, allowing me to believe that without my personal renderings of all those games he missed while he was at work, he would be unable to follow our team in the only proper way a team should be followed, day by day, inning by inning. In other words, without me, his love for baseball would be forever incomplete.

To be sure, there were risks involved in making a commitment as boundless as mine. For me, as for all too many Brooklyn fans, the presiding memory of "the boys of summer" was the memory of the final playoff game in 1951 against the Giants. Going into the ninth, the Dodgers held a 4–1 lead.

First baseman Gil Hodges—the Quiet Man— anchored Brooklyn's postwar dynasty, with over 100 RBIs for seven straight years.

Then came two singles and a double, placing the winning run at the plate with Bobby Thomson at bat. As Dressen replaced Newcombe with Branca, my older sister, with maddening foresight, predicted the forever famous Thomson homer—a prediction that left me so angry with her, imagining that with her words she had somehow brought it about, that I would not speak to her for days.

So the seasons of my childhood passed until that miserable summer when the Dodgers were taken away to Los Angeles by the unforgivable O'Malley, leaving all our rash hopes and dreams of glory behind. And then came a summer of still deeper sadness when my father died. Suddenly my feelings for baseball seemed an aspect of my departing youth, along with my childhood freckles and my favorite childhood haunts, to be left behind when I went away to college and never came back.

Then one September day, having settled into teaching at Harvard, I agreed, half reluctantly, to go to Fenway Park. There it was again: the cozy ball field scaled to human dimensions so that every word of encouragement and every scornful yell could be heard on the field; the fervent crowd that could, with equal passion, curse a player for today's failures after cheering his heroics the day before; the team that always seemed to break your heart in the last week of the season. It took only a matter of minutes before I found myself directing all my old intensities toward my new team— the Boston Red Sox.

I am often teased by my women friends about my obsession, but just as often, in the most unexpected places—in academic conferences, in literary discussions, at the most elegant dinner parties—I find other women

Fenway Park, 1975 World Series. Boston's Carlton Fisk has just homered to beat Cincinnati, 7–6, in the sensational, spectacular, unanswerable Game 6.

just as crazily committed to baseball as I am, and the discovery creates an instant bond between us. All at once, we are deep in conversation, mingling together the past and the present, as if the history of the Red Sox had been our history, too.

There we stand, one moment recollecting the unparalleled performance of Yaz in '67, the next sharing ideas on how the present lineup should be changed; one moment recapturing the splendid career of "the Splendid Splinter," the next complaining about the manager's decision to pull the pitcher the night before. And, then, invariably, comes the most vivid memory of all, the frozen image of Carlton Fisk as he rounded first in the sixth game of the '75 World Series, an image as intense in its evocation of triumph as the image of Ralph Branca weeping in the clubhouse in its portrayal of heartache.

There is another, more personal memory associated with Carlton Fisk, for he was, after all the years I had followed baseball, the first player I actually met in person. Apparently, he had read the biography I had written on Lyndon Johnson and wanted to meet me. Yet when the meeting took place, I found myself reduced to the shyness of childhood. There I was, a professor at Harvard, accustomed to speaking with Presidents of the United States, and yet, standing beside this young man in a baseball uniform, I was speechless.

Finally, Fisk said that it must have been an awesome experience to work with a man of such immense power as President Johnson—and with that, I was at last able to stammer out, with a laugh, "Not as awesome as the thought that I am really standing here talking with you."

Perhaps I have circled back to my childhood, but if this is so, I am certain that my journey through time is connected in some fundamental way to the fact that I am now a parent myself, anxious to share with my three sons the same ritual I once shared with my father.

For in this linkage between the generations rests the magic of baseball, a game that has defied the ravages of modern life, a game that is still played today by the same basic rules and at the same pace as it was played 100 years ago. There is something deeply satisfying in the knowledge of this continuity.

And there is something else as well which I have experienced sitting in Fenway Park with my small boys on a warm summer's day. If I close my eyes against the sun, all at once I am back at Ebbets Field, a young girl once more in the presence of my father, watching the players of my youth on the grassy field below. There is magic in this moment, for when I open my eyes and see my sons in the place where my father once sat, I feel an invisible bond between our three generations, an anchor of loyalty linking my sons to the grandfather whose face they never saw but whose person they have already come to know through this most timeless of all sports, the game of baseball.

DORIS KEARNS GOODWIN is a Pulitzer Prize–winning historian who has written about Presidents Roosevelt, Kennedy, and Johnson. Her books include Wait Till Next Year, *on the 1950s Dodgers.*

ROBERT GOULET

◆ ◆ ◆

What baseball means to me is memory, above all. It starts when I was a nine-year-old dragged from the batter's box—by my hair, by my father—who castigated me for ignoring my piano tutor, who was waiting for me in our tiny apartment and to whom my father paid $1 a lesson. That was a lot of money for us. Or when I saw Ted Williams hit a home run out of Fenway Park. Or when Billy Martin gave my European wife and me his seats behind third base. He came out of the dugout, doffed his cap, and bowed to me. I rose, entered the aisle, saluted, and bowed to him to much applause from our audience. In the second inning Billy engaged in a chin-protruding, arms-behind-the-back harangue with the towering third base umpire. The late Ron Luciano then pointed Billy to the showers amid howls and guffaws from the fans. My wife, who had never seen a baseball game, asked me, "What happened?" I explained that our friend had been evicted from the playing field. She said, "Does that happen all the time?" Everyone who's heard this story inevitably says: "With Billy, yes!"

ROBERT GOULET is a film, stage, and television star.

"He's the kind of guy you'd like to kill if he's playing for the other team," Frank Lane said of Billy Martin, "but you'd like ten of him on your side."

CURT GOWDY

◆ ◆ ◆

Talk about right place, right time. I did Red Sox games from 1951 to 1965. Fenway Park is New England's nightclub. The Red Sox owner, Tom Yawkey, a multimillionaire, modest, dressed in khaki pants and a faded shirt, looked like he didn't have a dime, was the most marvelous man I ever knew. Then there's the Kid. Where would you find a copy in a million years?

Ted's eyes tested perfect in the Air Force. I've hunted with him when he said, "There are two ducks coming up at three o'clock." I have good eyes, and I'd say, "Where?" Two minutes *later* they'd show up. Ted's the best hunter I ever saw. The best fisherman, too. He got to like me because I'd talk fishing instead of baseball. When I think of Williams, I remember his final game [September 28, 1960]. I get to Fenway and equipment manager Johnny Orlando said, "Listen, this is the Kid's last game. He's gonna retire after today." It was Boston's last home game, but we had a season-ending series in New York. Johnny said, "Yawkey said okay. Ted's got a chest cold so he wants to call it quits." I went to Ted— nobody knew he wasn't going to New York—and said, "Is this your last day?" Ted said, "Yeah, don't mention it till the game starts." Before the game, we had a little ceremony behind home plate. Mayor Hines gave him a Revere Bowl and made a speech. Then, I got up.

I'd been late getting to the ballpark—did some commercials downtown and the recorder didn't work. So I got hell when I got there thirty minutes before the game. Bill Crowley,

Ted Williams— with six batting titles, the 1946 and 1949 MVP award, and the 1942 and 1947 Triple Crown—was arguably baseball's best hitter. He was inducted into the Hall of Fame in 1966.

the Sox publicity director, said, "You don't have a note." I said, "I don't need any about Williams." I stepped to the mike and said, "Today we honor a man who in my opinion and many of yours was the greatest hitter who ever lived. I didn't get to see Ty Cobb, Paul Waner, or Rogers Hornsby, who hit .400 four or five times, but I don't see how they could be better than Ted Williams. I could have pages of batting records up here—but what really made Ted was pride. He had an intense pride that every time up he wanted to produce a hit. Not only for himself, but for the fans at Fenway whom he secretly loved— who stood behind him amid ups and downs. Pride is what made him go and why he's here. The greatest hitter of all time, Ted Williams."

Williams grabbed me and said, "I want a copy. That's one of the nicest tributes to me ever." I said, "I don't have a copy." He says, "Oh, hell"—vintage Ted!—and walks to home plate. His first words were, "Well, I want to thank the knights of the key-board"—his sarcastic salute to writers in the press box. Then he thanked Tom Yawkey and [Sox ex–general manager] Joe Cronin and his teammates. But most of all he wanted to thank the New England fans who cherished him—and they did. You had to understand Ted—a perfectionist who got mad at himself more than anybody. If you know a perfectionist you know how they are. All the ashtrays have to be clean—everything in a row. I think New England forgave him more than he did himself.

Finally, the game starts. Ted goes out his first three times up. His third time he nearly had one— a long fly to right against the bullpen. In the eighth inning he's up against Jack Fisher. Today, they say Fisher grooved it. He didn't. It wasn't a good pitch. Williams never swung at a bad pitch.

His thesis was get a good pitch to hit, and you'll be a better hitter. Don't swing unless it's a strike. This time he did—and when I heard the crack of the bat and the ball started toward right field, I knew it was gone [at forty-two, Ted's 521st homer]. I was choked up. My heart was pounding, and as he rounded first and headed to second I made the statement about Ted's last at-bat. The media didn't say much about it then—but years later they replayed it—made a big to-do—at the 1986 World Series between the Mets and Red Sox. "How did you know it was his last at-bat? He was supposed to play the Yankees in New York." Because Ted told me, I said.

One last Williams story. In 1988, they had a tribute to Ted. David Hartman of *Good Morning America* came up to emcee. Thirteen public friends of Ted came together in a theater with 6,000 people to raise money for the Jimmy Fund [New England's cancer charity]. Each of us was inter-viewed by Hartman for about five minutes. I looked over and said, "That's John Glenn—the astronaut and Senator from Ohio. What's he doing here?" I introduced myself—"Senator, I'm Curt Gowdy. I used to broadcast Red Sox games. What's your connection with Ted?"

Glenn says, "I was his flight commander in Korea and that's how I got to be an astronaut— through my Air Force background. Williams used to fly a wing for me." I said, "What kind of a pilot was he?" Glenn says, "The best I ever saw."

CURT GOWDY has broadcast fifteen All-Star Games, twelve World Series, seven Olympics, and two decades of the Emmy Award–winning The American Sportsman.

Restaurateur Toots Shor was once talking with Sir Alexander Fleming when Mel Ott walked in. "Excuse me," Shor told the discoverer of penicillin. "Somebody important just came in."

BUD GREENSPAN

◆ ◆ ◆

When I was ten, we lived about ten minutes from the Polo Grounds in New York City, so, of course, I was a Giants fan. Many of the Giants rented rooms for the season in the apartment building next to mine, so I often saw my heroes leaving for and coming home from the ballpark.

I remember playing stickball in the street one day when I saw my all-time favorite player, Mel Ott, getting out of a cab. Just then it was my turn to bat, and I hit the hardest ball I ever hit—a magnificent drive that was a certain home run. I started for first base, looked up, and saw Ott going after my drive. He ran a couple of steps and leaped high to make a miraculous catch. My home run was lost forever. As he passed me on his

way into the apartment building, he said, "That was a home run in any park." From then on, I was looked at differently by the rest of my teammates.

BUD GREENSPAN is a writer, producer, and director. Among his seven Emmy Awards is the twenty-two part 1976–77 Olympiad. *He recently wrote* 100 Greatest Moments in Olympic History.

GILBERT M. GROSVENOR

◆ ◆ ◆

The setting: 1950 spring weekend home baseball game at Deerfield Academy in Massachusetts. Our big rival: Choate School. We're clinging to a one-run lead in the top of a late inning. We have two outs, but a runner dances off first base.

I'm pitching and fortunately my curveball is working. Without it, I'm nothing.

The batter hits a soft grounder to short. Inning over? Nope! The ball oozes between the shortstop's legs. Runners hold at first and second. The next batter hits a one-hopper to the second baseman, who scoops it up and throws perfectly to first base. Third out? Nope! The first baseman drops the ball! Bases loaded, still two outs! I'm ticked but hopefully don't show it.

The next batter hits a line drive to the pitcher's mound. I spear it but can't hold it. Picking up the ball, I race to first base touching the base, just before the runner, to end the inning. I trot to the bench, pleased with myself. Immediately the coach pulls me aside and angrily asks, "Why didn't you throw the ball to first base for that third out?"

"Another error and a runner scores," I shrugged.

"That was a poor play. I thought you had more character," he responded, walking way. We won the game by that one run, but the victory for me was hollow. I had clearly disappointed my coach, my mentor, and a man whom I idolized—and still do to this day. So who was that coach? Frank L. Boyden, headmaster at Deerfield for more than fifty years and perhaps the most respected and revered American prep school headmaster in the twentieth century.

The following Monday Dr. Boyden waved me to his desk strategically set in the main corridor of the school building. At some moment every day, each of the 450 students would pass his desk between classes.

"You disappointed me Saturday," he began.

A harsher reprimand I could not imagine.

"Winning is wonderful, but how you conduct yourself at Deerfield is more important," he continued. "Saturday you showed terrible judgment in not trusting the first baseman, your *teammate*. I chose you to be a

proctor in the John William House [a freshman dorm] because I liked your character, your Deerfield spirit of sportsmanship, and your sense of responsibility. You let me down." End of conversation. Total devastation. For ten days I was relegated to shagging fly balls in right field.

For our final game—as a senior I knew this would be the last competitive baseball game I'd ever play—we traveled to Cushing Academy for its graduation day. As usual, the headmaster-coach rode in his chauffeured Cadillac ahead of our bus. Periodically he would stop and have a player ride with him for a short chat, then repeat the process. I was summoned to the Cadillac. He quickly got to the point. "To be your best, you must make the best of what you have.

"Successful leadership requires you to set positive examples for others to follow. You must foster team-work if you expect others to contribute at their highest

Fifties baseball meant major league as well as prep school. The faithful leave Yankee Stadium after the Bombers sweep the 1950 World Series.

level. You must *be* a teammate if you are to earn the respect of those you wish to lead.

"How you conduct yourself, how you lead, and how you play on the baseball field, you will carry with you forever on life's field."

He stopped the Cadillac and summoned another player to join him. As I departed, he handed me a shiny new baseball. "You're pitching today."

His car roared off. For an instant I stood alone on that rural road surrounded by silent green sentinels guarding the Pocumtuck Valley. Those were the last meaningful words I would ever hear from that extraordinary man. The year of proctoring had ended, my almost daily chats with Dr. Boyden ceased, but that final message—a summation of the greatest educational year of my life—rang out clearly: Lessons learned on the ball field play out on life's field.

While I cannot recall that Cushing Academy baseball game fifty-two years ago (a euphemism for losing), Frank Boyden's final words have resonated within me for almost half a century playing on life's field at the National Geographic Society.

GILBERT M. GROSVENOR is Chairman of the Board of the National Geographic Society.

STEVE GUTTENBERG

◆ ◆ ◆

Baseball is the greatest time!

STEVE GUTTENBERG has starred on Broadway, TV, and in such films as Diner, Police Academy (1–4), Cocoon, *and* Three Men and a Baby.

The Red Sox looking good in spring training, 1936, in Sarasota, Florida.

MONTY HALL

◆ ◆ ◆

I became friendly with Ernie Banks of the Chicago Cubs back in the early 1960s. He was my son's hero as well as mine. Ernie told me to bring Richard to a Dodger game about an hour before game time so he could meet him in the Chicago dugout—give him a ball and a bat.

When we arrived, I told Ernie that Richard knew everything about him.

"Like what?" asked Ernie.

"1-31-31," answered the twelve-year-old Richard.

"1-31-31?" asked Ernie, puzzled.

Since Richard had memorized every statistic from his baseball card, he replied—"The date of your birth on top of the card—1-31-31!"

Ernie and I have met each other on rare occasions at golf tournaments, airports, and other places—and "1-31-31" has become our password.

Recently, I made an appearance at Wrigley Field to throw out the first pitch. When I arrived at the park, I asked if Ernie was on the premises. (I hadn't seen him for several years.) Yes, he was in the dining room. "Go over to him," I advised a young man, "and whisper 1-31-31 in his ear."

In two minutes my old friend and I were embracing. He knew the password.

And he still thinks it's a great day to play two!

MONTY HALL, a native Canadian, began the American game show Let's Make a Deal *in 1963. It ran on all three major U.S. television networks for twenty-three years.*

In 1970 Ernie Banks hit his 500th homer. The Cub captain celebrates at the Friendly Confines.

MILO HAMILTON

◆ ◆ ◆

To me, baseball is ingrained with growing up in the Depression. People hung on to the game when they had little else. I'll never forget my dad and his friends talking baseball at the cigar store. My mom used to buy bread a day late to save a penny, then give me the penny for licorice or other candy. One year—1938— I saved 35 cents to buy my first *Spalding Guide*. It was the year after Ducky Medwick won the Triple Crown, and his picture was on the cover. I became a big Medwick fan: It's funny how things stay with you for life.

In Iowa, every little country school district had a team. Families'd bring food to the games and we'd eat by the car. It was really the start of tailgating. Baseball was affordable. There'd be no admission, but we'd pass collection in the seventh inning to buy balls and bats. That was our entertainment back then, and why not? In a sense, baseball has been us all along.

You look at Civil War photos, and there are companies playing a form of baseball. Then the war ended, and baseball spread from the Eastern Seaboard across the land. By the start of the twentieth century, you can almost trace hardship by the people who dominated the game—first, farm kids and players from Southern mill towns, then the Irish, Italians, then blacks and Hispanics. Baseball was their ladder to a better life.

I got into baseball in 1945 with Armed Forces Radio. I did other things—music, news—but knew the game was for me. How many people years later can say they can't wait to get to work each day? Why do I love it? You don't have to be a hulking guy to play it. Football,

Iowan Bob Feller struck out a record 18 batters in one game—when he was only nineteen. In 1940 he tossed the A.L.'s first opening day no-hitter. Many consider him baseball's fastest pitcher.

you'd better be 300 pounds; basketball, a giant. Baseball's for any size. Too, it wears well. I've done other sports, but can't imagine calling a football or basketball game each day. I do in baseball—counting exhibitions, 200 games a year. Then there's the camaraderie. When a guy retires, what does he miss? Not the game, but the clubhouse, the guys you travel with—your friends.

I love baseball's unpredictability. I'll be calling a game with my radio partner, and something happens

⬥⬥⬥

…Grown men playing a kids' game with short pants.

⬥⬥⬥

that'll make me say, "You ever see that before?" He laughs, "No." Between us we've been calling games for maybe seventy years. Plus memory. One game will trigger another, which leads to a story, then another. When I entered the Baseball Hall of Fame in 1992, my favorite player was there, Stan Musial, and manager, Al Lopez. So was Bob Feller. Both of us came from Iowa, and we started talking about the 1930s and Depression, and I began thinking about my mom and dad.

Ultimately, the families of Hall of Famers were taken by bus to the induction ceremonies. The players and other inductees were taken to a special room. All of a sudden I see Brooks Robinson and Johnny Bench asking for autographs. It was wonderful—they were like twelve-year-olds. That's the baseball I grew up with: Grown men playing a kids' game with short pants.

MILO HAMILTON began calling big league ball in 1953 with the St. Louis Browns. Since 1985, he has been the Voice of the Houston Astros.

MARVIN HAMLISCH
⬥ ⬥ ⬥

Baseball has been an enduring constant in my life. As a child, I enrolled at the Juilliard School of Music. Once a year every Juilliard student took an examination in his or her proficiency at their instrument. The test would determine whether you kept your scholarship for the following year. In my case, it was an absolute must, since my parents couldn't afford the tuition. The exam took place in front of the people they called the Jury. (Has a nice ring to it: like "convicted on all counts.")

I'd usually begin the day of the exam by throwing up. And that was the high point of the day. (It never got any better in the fourteen years I attended Juilliard.) My mother would give me nothing but weak chamomile tea, or I would sip shot glasses of Maalox. I would think about the hours after the exam when I'd be able to join my friends and play baseball. There would be no further need to protect my hands. The summer would come, and I'd be free till September.

Years later, my wife looked at me and said: "Marvin, it's time you knew that you're made up of more than your work. You never had a normal childhood, and you never knew what it meant to be happy when you were young. Tell me the truth: What was the one thing you really loved when you were growing up?"

"I was a baseball freak since I was a kid."

"Marvin, who did you root for?"

"It was the Yankees all the way."

Three weeks later I woke up to find a handsome brochure on my desk. Could it possibly say what I think it says: "Yankee Fantasy Camp." The whole thing had been arranged. It was a done deal; I was registered. Yankee Fantasy Camp is a place where *mature men* go to have their dreams come true. They go to Florida and play baseball with the stars of their youth— Mickey Mantle and Whitey Ford and the rest. One of the first musicals I saw as a teenager was *Damn Yankees*. In it the manager says, "A long-ball hitter, that's what we need. I'd sell my soul for a long-ball hitter."

So there I go—the kid who had been called "Fingers" Hamlisch. The kid who wanted to catch a fastball but couldn't, for fear of ending his musical career, was on his way to Florida, wife in hand, like a scene out of *Field of Dreams*. And I'm doing all the

things I never had done as a child. Because, back then, as the kids were whipping the ball around the infield, I was home practicing the scales. And I'm thinking I might be meeting that great contemporary philosopher, Yogi Berra, who once said, "You can observe a lot by watching." And one of the things I'm observing is that the *players and coaches are nervous* and keep telling me: "Listen, Marv, if a ball's hit to you on a line and you don't think you can handle it, don't hurt your hands, don't break the hands that feed you—let it go." And I'm thinking: Are you kidding? I've been waiting for this all my life.

So armed with Mineral Ice and Ben-Gay, I started to play ball. A real jock. Pride of the Yankees. All these famous former baseball stars are telling me, "I'll never forget the night I saw *Chorus Line,*" and I'm saying to them, "I'll never forget the catch you made against the Red Sox."

The great moment came for me in a game in which I got a single off Whitey Ford. It was unbelievable. Mickey Mantle was umpiring at second base. The next batter came up and hit a single, and I should have gone to third base, but I

Whitey Ford had a century-best .690 winning percentage. The Chairman of the Board holds the World Series record for wins, losses, starts, opening game starts, and Ks.

So remember, folks, if you ever come across the highly regarded best-seller "Famous Jewish Sports Legends," look under "H" for Hamlisch.

as the audience is applauding, before you turn around, you push a button and you can see the game's score, and then you take your bow. I had the ability to more or less continuously know what the score was.

In 1996, the Yankees lost the first two games. In Game 3, they finally grabbed the lead. I was going crazy. I'm even prouder that it didn't affect my work. "The Way We Were" stayed a ballad. I did not make it go fast. When you're up on the stage, you're conducting. And when you look at the beeper you're a fan.

MARVIN HAMLISCH, admitted to the Juilliard School of Music at age seven, is a renowned pianist, conductor, and composer.

stopped at second. The coach kept signaling me to make the turn and take third. But I stayed at second. When the inning was over, John Blanchard, the coach, stormed over to me: "Why the hell did you stop at second? Why didn't you take third? Weren't you watching the damn sign?"

"I'll tell you the truth," I said. "I couldn't. I couldn't leave second base. How could I? It's not every day I get the chance to talk to Mickey Mantle." So remember, folks, if you ever come across the highly regarded best-seller *Famous Jewish Sports Legends,* look under "H" for Hamlisch.

Postscript. Since then my love for the game, if anything, has grown. In 1996, the Yankees got in the World Series. My problem was that I was conducting the Pittsburgh Symphony Pops. Throughout the Series I'd be out of town, and conducting during the games. I had to devise a way to check in during the show. So I bought a beeper, which gives you sports scores, the market, CNN, and so forth. But you can't have it go *beep* during the concert, so I had the beeper deactivated. I'm proud of my solution. Before each piece, I placed the beeper on the lectern, where it sat next to the music as I performed. What you do is, just

John Blanchard, one of three catchers (with Yogi Berra and Elston Howard) to hit more than 20 homers for the 1961 Yankees.

ERNIE HARWELL

◆ ◆ ◆

I had a couple of speaking engagements in the winter of 1954, and one day I just thought I'd sit down and jot out some notes on baseball. They came together in a poem, "The Game for All America," and it was finished after several days of polishing. The *Sporting News* printed it in their 1955 opening day issue, and ran it through 1962. It's been translated into six different languages. I hope it expresses what people feel for the game.

Baseball is President Eisenhower tossing out the first ball of the season; and a pudgy schoolboy playing catch with his dad on a Mississippi farm.

It's the big league pitcher who sings in nightclubs. And the Hollywood singer who pitches to the Giants in spring training.

A tall, thin man waving a scorecard from his dugout—that's baseball. So is the big, fat guy with a bulbous nose running out one of his 714 home runs with mincing steps.

It's America, this baseball. A reissued newsreel of boyhood dreams. Dreams lost somewhere between boy and man. It's the Bronx cheer and the Baltimore farewell. The left field screen in Boston, the right field dump at Nashville's Sulphur Dell, the open stands in San Francisco, the dusty, wind-swept diamond at Albuquerque. And a rock home plate and a chicken wire backstop—anywhere.

There's a man in Mobile who remembers a triple he saw Honus Wagner hit in Pittsburgh forty-six years ago. That's baseball. So is the scout reporting that a sixteen-year-old sandlot pitcher in Cheyenne is the "new Walter Johnson."

It's a wizened little man shouting insults from the safety of his bleacher seat. And a big, smiling first baseman playfully tousling the hair of a youngster

President Eisenhower, throwing out the first ball at the Senators' 1953 opener. Bystanders include future Presidents Johnson (far left) and Nixon (center) and managers Bucky Harris and Casey Stengel.

outside the players' gate.

Baseball is a spirited race of man against man, reflex against reflex. A game of inches. Every skill is measured. Every heroic, every failing is seen and cheered—or booed. And then becomes a statistic.

In baseball, democracy shines its clearest. Here the only race that matters is the race to the bag. The creed is the rulebook. Color is something to distinguish one team's uniform from another.

Baseball is Sir Alexander Fleming, discoverer of penicillin, asking his Brooklyn hosts to explain Dodger signals. It's player Moe Berg speaking seven languages and working crossword puzzles in Sanskrit. It's a scramble in the box seats for a foul—and a $125 suit ruined. A man barking into a hot microphone about a cool beer, that's baseball. So is the sportswriter telling a .383 hitter how to stride, and a 20-victory pitcher trying to write his impressions of the World Series.

Baseball is a ballet without music. Drama without

words. A carnival without kewpie dolls.

A housewife in California couldn't tell you the color of her husband's eyes, but she knows that Yogi Berra is hitting .337, has brown eyes, and used to love to eat bananas with mustard. That's baseball. So is the bright sanctity of Cooperstown's Hall of Fame. And the former big leaguer, who is playing out the string in a Class B loop.

Baseball is continuity. Pitch to pitch. Inning to inning. Game to game. Series to series. Season to season.

It's rain, rain, rain splattering on a puddled tarpaulin as thousands sit in damp disappointment. And the click of typewriters and telegraph keys in the press box—like so many awakened crickets. Baseball is a cocky batboy. The old-timer whose batting average increases every time he tells it. A lady celebrating a home team rally by mauling her husband with a rolled-up scorecard.

Baseball is the cool, clear eyes of Rogers Hornsby, the flashing spikes of Ty Cobb, an overaged pixie named Rabbit Maranville, and Jackie Robinson testifying before a congressional hearing.

Baseball? It's just a game—as simple as a ball and a bat. Yet as complex as the American spirit it symbolizes. It's a sport, business—and sometimes even religion.

Baseball is Tradition in flannel knickerbockers. And Chagrin in being picked off base. It is Dignity in the blue serge of an umpire running the game by rule of thumb. It is Humor, holding its sides when an errant puppy eludes two groundskeepers and the fastest outfielder. And Pathos, dragging itself off the field after being knocked from the box.

Nicknames are baseball. Names like Zeke and Pie and Kiki and Home Run and Cracker

The irrepressible Willie Mays smacked 660 homers, won 11 Gold Gloves, and was named to a record-tying 24 All-Star games. Willie, it was once said, is where triples go to die.

and Dizzy and Daffy.

Baseball is a sweaty, steaming dressing room where hopes and feelings are as naked as the men themselves. It's a dugout with spike-scarred flooring. And shadows across an empty ballpark. It's the endless list of names in box scores, abbreviated almost beyond recognition.

The holdout is baseball. He wants 55 grand or he won't turn a muscle. But it's also the youngster who hitchhikes from South Dakota to Florida just for a tryout.

Arguments, Casey at the Bat, old cigarette cards, photographs, Take Me Out to the Ball Game—all of them are baseball.

Baseball is a rookie—his experience no bigger than the lump in his throat—trying to begin fulfillment of a dream. It's a veteran, too—a tired old man of thirty-five, hoping his aching muscles can drag him through another sweltering August and September.

For nine innings, baseball is the story of David and Goliath, of Samson, Cinderella, Paul Bunyan, Homer's Iliad and the Count of Monte Cristo.

Willie Mays making a brilliant World Series catch. And then going home to Harlem to play stickball in the street with his teenage pals—that's baseball. So is the husky voice of a doomed Lou Gehrig saying, "I'm the luckiest guy in the world."

Baseball is cigar smoke, roasted peanuts, the *Sporting News,* winter trades, "Down in front," and the seventh-inning stretch. Sore arms, broken bats, a no-hitter, and the strains of "The Star-Spangled Banner."

Baseball is a highly paid Brooklyn catcher telling the nation's business leaders: "You have to be a man to be a big leaguer, but you have to have a lot of little boy in you, too."

This is a game for America, this baseball!

A game for boys and for men.

ERNIE HARWELL is the only man to broadcast big league ball in seven decades. Since 1960 he has been the Voice of the Detroit Tigers.

JOHN HAVLICEK

◆ ◆ ◆

I never knew his first name, but his gas station was called Cocky Pyles. It was the center of the town where I grew up, Lansing, Ohio, about sixty miles west of Pittsburgh, in the early 1950s. Cocky's was our universe. Guys pumped gas, ate candy, just sort of sat around. You'd get a Coke for a nickel, and put peanuts in your drink. Maybe we had too much time on our hands. Anyway, baseball was its hub. This was before TV, and we'd hang on baseball on the radio. That is, when we weren't throwing bottle caps. You know, throw it a certain way—single. Screw it up—double

When (Leroy) Satchel Paige, forty-two, debuted in 1948, he had already won hundreds of games in the Negro Leagues.

or home run. I just loved the game. So did my family, and all of my friends.

The Pirates were kind of lousy back then, so we followed the Indians. I can't name a starting lineup now, but I can remember the entire Cleveland lineup, say, of 1951. I mean, Jim Hegan, Luke Easter, Bobby Avila, Dale Mitchell. And the pitchers—man, Lemon, Garcia, Wynn. No wonder my grandfather got so involved. He'd be listening at Cocky's, and if they were losing he'd get up and walk along the railroad tracks. Too nervous to listen, just walked, worried. Maybe by the time he got back they'd be ahead.

Every year we took the three-and-a-half hour trip to Municipal Stadium for a doubleheader. What a day. My mom packed potato salad, fried chicken, and you could actually take it into the ball-park. They'd never let you do that now: Gotta make concession sales. But up those two-laners we went, get there, and you unpack your food. You talk about memories. How about Ted Williams hitting six in a row in the seats in batting

Phil Niekro celebrates his election to the Hall of Fame. Knucksie won a record 121 games after turning forty.

practice. Or Satchel Paige. We were there for a game he pitched for the Browns. Rhythmic windup, *different* windups. He'd throw that blooper pitch. A lot of panache. I also saw the Homestead Grays when they came through town. Everybody in Lansing worked in the mines, and every mine and town had a team. A couple of my uncles played the Grays and the House of David. Man, baseball was in my blood.

And not just mine. Try this on for size. Two hundred people in Lansing: How about five professional athletes from our town? Bill Jobko went to Ohio State, then played for the pro football Rams, Vikings, and Falcons. Johnny Blatnik was with the Phillies, and had his career hurt by the war. All Joe Niekro did was win 221 games. And what about my dear friend Phil Niekro. Two Hall of Famers—me in basketball and Phil in baseball. One day Phil was a high school freshman at a time Bill Mazeroski was a senior. They pitched in a district game, and Maz beat him—Phil's only loss in high school. Mostly Maz played shortstop. One of my uncles played on a semipro miners team at second. He used to say, tongue in cheek, that he was so good Mazeroski couldn't dislodge him. Imagine, one of the great second basemen! Thank goodness Maz is now in Cooperstown.

I played baseball in high school and could have signed for the bigs. There wasn't any draft, so teams sent out bird-dog scouts to see if you were any good. Five teams wanted me: Pirates, Orioles, Indians, Yankees, and Giants. I remember going to a tryout at Forbes Field. Phil Niekro signed for $500 at a tryout camp. Here's a story that tells a lot. He was cut at nineteen, and it killed him. He didn't want to go back to the mines. Worse, he didn't want to disappoint his dad. So he comes into the manager's office, crying. "I can't be cut. I can't go home. My father will be devastated." Phil says he'll shine shoes, cut grass, clean bases, anything to stay with the club. The manager agreed. All Phil did was win more than 300 games.

I don't want to toot my horn, but I was all-state in high school football, baseball, and basketball. I played baseball in the American Legion and then at Ohio State. There I had my most embarrassing moment. In high school, there aren't any fences. You leg out homers. One Friday afternoon in college we were supposed to play Indiana, but the game got rained out so we had a tripleheader Saturday.

The first game began at 9:00 A.M. Man, by the third game we're tired and we're stealing signs. At the plate, I knew what was coming. This one at-bat I hit it hard. The thing was, I didn't know where it went—just out there, somewhere—so I'm tearing around the bases. It's like high school, except that this drive went *over* the fence. I get to third and the coach said, "It's outta here!" I love baseball, but it keeps you humble. Never got to show my home run trot.

JOHN HAVLICEK starred in basketball at Ohio State, was drafted by the Cleveland Browns, and instead joined the Boston Celtics. In 1983, Hondo was elected to the Basketball Hall of Fame.

ED HEARN

◆ ◆ ◆

In 1986, after eight trying years in the minor leagues, I realized my childhood dream of playing Major League Baseball. In my rookie season with the New York Mets, we captured the World Series with a dramatic come-from-behind victory. A year later, I was traded to Kansas City. My future seemed set as the starting catcher. Just a couple of average years and I would be expecting to reap the rewards of a lucrative professional career.

Instead, I suffered a serious shoulder injury and spent the next three years fighting to come back, only to have to walk away from the game I loved. Yet little did I know, the physical obstacles that awaited me were far more devastating than the shoulder that caused my athletic demise.

Less than six months after my baseball career ended, I was diagnosed with three potentially life-threatening health conditions. Once a strong, vibrant professional athlete, I was reduced to a man who could barely care for himself. Yet I hung on, and used these physical challenges to make what many have called "one of baseball's most incredible comebacks." Never giving up is what baseball means to me.

After three life-saving kidney transplants, months of dialysis, a successful bout with cancer, the aid of a breathing machine each night, a costly IV treatment once a month, and up to fifty pills a day, the curves life threw me have been transformed into a platform of inspiration.

It took the thrill of being a major league player.

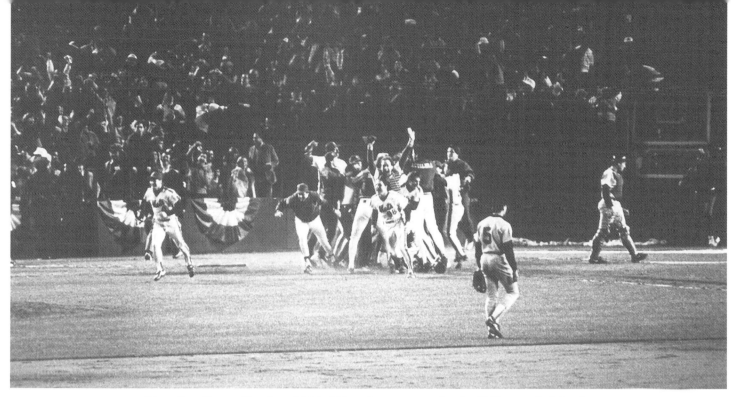

Shea Stadium, October 1986: Miracle, or metaphysical? Down 5–3 in the 10th inning, with two out and two strikes, the Mets win Game 6.

It took the wicked curves that once made me feel as if this game of life was more than I was ready to handle. It took the great depths of discouragement, despair, and selfish contemplation of the most desperate of acts—a loaded .357 Magnum pistol. On the other hand, it also took faith and a sometimes gut-wrenching desire to climb above the wall of self-pity and mediocrity. It took, most importantly, a wonderful wife and an invigorating young son. And, unbelievably, a new player in the game of life has evolved.

Even though I was so tired of swinging at what seemed to be one curve after another, the real game plan, my true destiny, began to reveal itself one fall day in 1992 at a local Rotary luncheon. Following a speech I had reluctantly agreed to, a man who worked with professional speakers planted in my mind a very important seed of encouragement. A couple of years later, through the crusty, often bitter memories of the past and the daily struggle against long-term chronic health challenges, that seed finally began to blossom.

Today, some ten years after life's curves seemed to have me headed for the bench, I am back in "the line-up." As an author and professional speaker who travels around the country, it is now my privilege to use these unique circumstances to inspire and encourage my fellow man. I have the privilege to instill hope in those who have lost their faith in life. I can inspire my fellow man to discover the goodness within him and to share it with the world. I encourage leaders to have integrity and ethics, to lead with compassion and understanding. I teach employees to be responsible for their actions, have pride in their work, and treat fellow employees with kindness and respect. I tell children that they are unique and special; that with perseverance, persistence, and courage they can fulfill their dreams.

Far be it from my game plan for life, but it is awesome to be back in the batter's box contributing in a far greater way than I ever thought possible—better than any 70-home-run season or making the All-Star team.

Many people may not understand the sincerity in my words when I discuss the work I now do away from the park. But the truth is, I look forward to speaking to a group of people more than I ever looked forward to playing in a big league game. When we celebrated winning the World Series, then took part in a ticker tape parade and went to the White House to meet President Reagan, I thought that was the ultimate. Nothing I'd do would surpass that for fulfillment. But you never know what you're capable of until situations force you to strive beyond what you ever thought possible.

Even if I played in the big leagues another ten years, maybe earned another World Series ring or two, I can honestly say I would not be impacting people's lives the way I do now. I do treasure the time I spent in baseball. I still have many of my major league highlights at home on videotape. Occasionally, I'll pull them out to watch. But as nice as those memories are, they don't compare to the satisfaction I get from public speaking. I am paid to talk, but the greatest paychecks are emotional.

When people come up to you after a speech and say thanks for lifting them up, or express their gratitude for touching their lives in some way, you can't put a price on that.

I once thought there was nothing more important than becoming the next Johnny Bench. Life proved me wrong.

I once thought there was nothing sweeter than winning the World Series. Life proved me wrong.

I once thought all my medical problems and the adversities that accompanied them served no real purpose. Life proved me wrong.

More than a decade ago, I was on top of the baseball world with the '86 Mets. Who knows if I'll even be here in another decade?

But I know this: I'm alive, and I'm going to keep swinging for the fences regardless of life's curves.

ED HEARN, a catcher for the Mets in 1986 and the Royals in 1987 and 1988, is a speaker for the Bottom of the Ninth Foundation.

PHILIP R. HOCHBERG
◆ ◆ ◆

At the baseball stadium you hear a voice speaking over the public address system. That's me—or used to be. In fact, whenever someone learns about it for the first time, they invariably seem to point to those unseen "speakers in the sky" and say, "You mean, that's you I hear..."

I was the public address announcer of the Washington Senators from 1962 through 1968. I joined the football Redskins in '62, and was their PA announcer for thirty-eight years. I love baseball—it's so different from other sports. In other sports, the PA announcer gives information to the crowd after something has happened. In baseball, you're introducing someone. It's a more traditional, calmer approach—like the game.

I broke in through a March '62 audition. The Senators were moving into new D.C. Stadium, but there were only five or six guys trying out for the PA position. I was the best of a bad lot, only twenty-one years old, and a little scared. I remember thinking, "I hope the Senators don't think they've made a

The 1962 All-Star Game in Washington, D.C.

mistake." Doing public address work isn't brain surgery—but neither was I Bob Sheppard. It helped that there wasn't much scrutiny: I could learn my craft. A couple years ago the *Washington Post* did a big story on the Orioles' Rex Barney's successor. That wasn't true in my time. Plus, I was in graduate school and then law school. I could use the $20 a game. I used to try to do my law school class preparation while announcing the game. I soon realized that I wasn't doing a good job on either.

Our Senators clubs were, to put it charitably, not the scourge of the American League. We finished last in 1962, liked it, and kept finishing last each year. Losing, you remember amusing incidents, not great plays: There weren't many, at least by the Senators. Nor did we draw much, except when the Yankees came to town. So many of the memories, for some reason, seem to deal with them. One night in early 1962, Roger Maris came to bat. He'd hit 61 homers the year before, and the big crowd pumped me. So I said: "Batting third, the right fielder, number 9, Roger Maris"—and I elongated "Maris," gave it great bombast, like many public address people do today. I find those theatrics distasteful now—and to his credit, Bob Addie, dean of the Washington press corps, found them repugnant then. Hearing me, Bob marched over to where I was and said, "Roger Maris? Roger Maris?"—he stretched out the syllables, imitating me—"You introduce him like you would anyone else." Everyone heard him. I was embarrassed. But it brought me down to an even keel.

Baseball is less spectacle than daily fact. You're interested in the game, inhale its atmosphere, but from time to time don't devote full attention. Once again against the Yankees I missed a batter. I announced, "Batting ninth, the pitcher, number 23, Ralph Terry." Only one problem: Leadoff batter Bobby Richardson was up. It seemed like everyone in the stadium (except me) knew who was up. And it drew a crowd noise that I had never heard before—and thankfully never heard

since. Then there was the 1962 All-Star Game at D.C. Stadium. The introductions were prepared by the Senators' front office, and they left out a player. I introduced the entire American League team, and Elston Howard was still in the dugout. Lessons learned, the hard way.

Maybe this was our unconscious revenge against the Yankees for their tyranny over the years. In 1983, I did the Cracker Jack Old-Timers Baseball Classic in Washington. Dividing duties with a colleague—there were so many players entering and leaving the game—I did the American League. When I introduced, "Number 5, the Yankee Clipper, Joe DiMaggio," I—literally—got chills down my spine. That didn't happen with the 1960s Senators, but it often can with baseball.

In a way, baseball is like the presidency—names change, but not the institution. I've done PA of many presidential inaugural parades, but never an opening game. For years, my predecessor, Charlie Brotman, had done Washington's season opener. In 1962, he said to the club, "You know, this may be too much for a rookie. You'd better let me do it." He ended up doing every presidential opener while I was the Senators' PA voice. I didn't mind. Baseball is bigger than all of us—including mikemen you hear but seldom see.

PHILIP R. HOCHBERG, of the Washington, D.C., firm of Verner, Liipfert, Bernhard, McPherson, and Hand, specializes in broadcasting and cable television.

PAT HUGHES

◆ ◆ ◆

Baseball lost a lot of fans in the strike of 1994–95. One thing that brought back a lot of them was the great home run race of 1998 between Mark McGwire and Sammy Sosa. In the end, each broke Roger Maris's single-season home record of 61. The Cubs' Sosa smacked 66, while the Cardinals' McGwire belted the unfathomable total of 70.

I am the Chicago Cubs' radio play-by-play man on WGN. My partner is color announcer Ron Santo, a former slugger who starred for the Cubbies back in the 1960s and 1970s. I work every day, so I had the pleasure of witnessing Sosa's magnificent MVP season. Oh, by the way, Sammy also led the Cubs into the playoffs in 1998.

What baseball means to me is how exciting, dramatic, and just plain fun an extraordinary season like '98 can be. I never wanted the games to end that year. Each day America was at the vortex of a once-in-

September 8, 1998: Mark McGwire and Sammy Sosa embrace after Big Mac's 62nd homer.

a-lifetime thrill.

Is the Cubs–Cardinals rivalry baseball's greatest? Or is it the Yankees–Red Sox, or maybe Giants–Dodgers? Certainly, these are the top three. The Cubs and Cardinals battle in two of America's favorite playgrounds— Wrigley Field and Busch Stadium. Regarding the Cubs' notorious losing history, I tell people that if you have to endure a miserable season, Wrigley is the place to do it. What a great place to watch a game!

Busch Stadium, too, is always filled with loyal and knowledgeable fans. In recent years, many new high-tech, fan-friendly parks have sprung up from coast to coast. Know what? None of them can compare with the atmosphere of Wrigley on a sunny afternoon, or Busch on a warm summer night. Those two venues enhanced the excitement of 1998.

In St. Louis, lots of Cubs fans are always there to cheer when Sosa hits a long one. In Chicago, you should hear how noisy it gets when McGwire launches one over the bleachers onto Waveland Avenue. I have to smile when I see a man and a woman holding hands at either park: one wearing a blue Cubs shirt and the other a red Cardinals cap. I bet they have some lively dinner table discussions!

Unlike 1961, when Maris broke Babe Ruth's record on the season's final day, it became apparent

It might be! Sport's Jackie Gleason.
It could be! A half-century calling baseball. It is!
A life worth retelling. Harry Caray.

that both Sosa and McGwire would surpass Maris's 61. But when, who would get there first, and who would end up with the most? Daily the pressure rose—the crowds, the reporters, the history, the drama.

I enjoy writing. But unlike writers, a broadcaster can't go back and edit his mistakes. This concept becomes terrifyingly clear when you are announcing moments of potentially great historical significance. You agonize over how you should call a moment. What words should I use, in what sequence, and what inflection is the most proper? You know if you get too excited, you'll ruin the moment. Sleep is lost.

In 1974, Milo Hamilton made the classic call of Henry Aaron's 715th home run. He told me, "It's okay to plan a few words, but you have to sound extemporaneous." That's how I felt as both approached Maris's record.

The Cubs had experienced a magic journey that year, replete with historical achievements. For example, Sosa cracked 20 homers in June, the most ever by a man in a single month. Therefore the two words that kept bouncing around in my head were "magic" and "history." I decided to try and use them if I could on a big moment.

By coincidence, McGwire broke Maris's record

against the Cubs in St. Louis the night of September 8, 1998. I vividly recall the moment. Steve Trachsel pitching for the Cubs. McGwire had grounded out his first time up. The second time up, Trachsel's first pitch was a sinking fastball low and in. The gigantic redhead swung and drilled a low liner to deep left. This wasn't a typical soaring McGwire home run that was almost as high as it was far. But I knew with his awesome power, even a line drive could clear the outfield wall. My call on WGN radio: "McGwire drives one to deep left!—this could be!—it's a home run! Number 62 for Mark McGwire!" Pause. "A slice of history and a magical moment in St. Louis! A line drive home run to left for Mark McGwire of the St. Louis Cardinals!"

Thank goodness the words tumbled out in the proper order. What an unbelievably exciting moment for a broadcaster! ESPN-TV played my radio call over and over. Radio stations across the land replayed the historic moment—I heard from many old friends in the days that followed.

Next came the topper. McGwire ran over to the box seats to hug members of the Maris family—it was incredible, people were crying, I had tears in my eyes. Then Sosa came running in from right field and jumped into Big Mac's arms. It was one of the best scenes I have ever witnessed at a major league park. What sportsmanship, respect, friendship, and joy the two men shared!

Later that week, Sammy himself hit number 60, then 61 and 62. Earlier in the year the great Cubs Voices Harry Caray and Jack Brickhouse had died. How they both would have loved that 1998 season! I wanted to pay tribute to both of them somehow. So after I called Sosa's 65th home run, I said, "Holy Cow! and Hey-hey! for Harry and Jack." ("Holy Cow" was Harry's pet phrase and Jack's call of a Cubs homer often included "Hey-hey!") It was that kind of family feeling.

As I write the Cubs are in first place with a five-game lead over the—guess who?—Cardinals. Sosa is still cranking out homers for the Cubs, and so is McGwire for the Cardinals. Baseball is thriving in Chicago and St. Louis, and across America. Will there be a pennant race this year for the Cubs and Cards? It looks like it. Will there be another great Sosa-McGwire home run chase? Probably not this season. Maybe never again. But they gave us a classic in 1998 and reminded us all just how easy it is to fall in love with baseball over and over and over again.

PAT HUGHES has been the radio Voice of the Chicago Cubs since 1996. Previously he broadcast for the Milwaukee Brewers.

KAY BAILEY HUTCHISON
◆ ◆ ◆

My first heroes were baseball players—not Joe DiMaggio nor Mickey Mantle. They were George Orgeron and Larry Bulaich, Little League players in La Marque, Texas.

In our small town, the Little League stadium was the social center. Our summers consisted of games on weekdays (and nine-cent movies on Saturdays). Cheering wildly, munching snow cones, and taking losses very hard were part of growing up in the golden years.

In later years, it was a real hero to whom I turned when I was State Treasurer of Texas. I wanted to do a public service announcement for the state's unclaimed property auction—so I asked Nolan Ryan to help. He and I did the public service spot on the home field of the Texas Rangers. The spot was an instant hit—thanks to the great popularity of Nolan Ryan—a role model on and off the field.

Now I still love to cheer wildly—for the Texas Longhorns, Texas Rangers, and Houston Astros.

To reach The Ballpark in Arlington, you leave the Nolan Ryan Expressway for the Rangers' home. Number 34 struck out 5,714 batters during an amazing career.

Baseball *is* America's sport.

KAY BAILEY HUTCHISON, the great-great-grand-daughter of Charles S. Taylor, among Texas's earliest settlers, is the first woman to represent Texas in the U.S. Senate.

DICK IRVIN

◆ ◆ ◆

In 1946, I was a fourteen-year-old kid living in western Canada. But my dad was the coach of the Montreal Canadiens, who that spring won the Stanley Cup—one of twenty-four. Hockey was, and is,

a religion in Montreal, and back then the season ended in early April. As hockey stopped, baseball began— which brings me to a man who that year was as big a hero as any Canadien.

In 1946 Jackie Robinson played his only year with the International League Montreal Royals. Branch Rickey had signed him the previous October—perfect man, perfect town. He knew that a black player would be accepted far more easily in Montreal than in the States, where segregation existed. This way Robinson could prepare for the majors—which he entered in '47 and where he became a star.

The first time I saw Robinson play was at Wrigley Field in 1947. But by then I felt I'd seen him—because of what I heard in '46. He won the batting title, and

"Luck is the residue of design," said Branch Rickey. He invented the farm system and integrated baseball, and he pressured the major leagues to expand.

the Royals the Little World Series. Nobody batted an eye in Montreal about his being black. Once fans rushed him for autographs after a home game at Delormier Stadium. One writer said: "It was the only time where white fans were chasing a black guy, and everybody was happy."

What Jackie endured around the league, of course, was not the tolerance of Montreal. It was tough, but so was he—we can't imagine what he felt. The last time I saw him was in 1972, the year he died. I was emceeing a dinner in Montreal that Jackie attended. I was shocked at his condition, diabetes, he could barely see. Robinson got up and talked for three minutes, totally spontaneous, about his year in Montreal, his friends there, the street he lived on. You could hear a pin drop.

The gods in Montreal are named Morenz, Richard, Beliveau, Lafleur. But a deity that year played baseball, too.

DICK IRVIN buoyed CBC's Hockey Night in Canada *for thirty-three years. The Foster Hewitt Award recipient for broadcast excellence has also written many best-selling books.*

MONTE IRVIN

♦ ♦ ♦

Baseball to me means everything good—it means America. When I was growing up baseball was king. Today it's still enormously profitable and popular—but in the 1920s and 1930s basketball was minor. There was barely an NFL. Golf wasn't much. Every grade school, high school, and college played baseball. Every city and county had teams. On every playground you played softball or baseball. It was everyone's dream to have a bat and a ball.

Back then we didn't have Little League—didn't need it. Our playing was a weeding-out process. I liked that you didn't have to be big, just skillful. People thought more of you if you were a baseball player. When school got out we played in the independent and summer leagues. I remember: Each Sunday a buddy picked me up at 10:00 A.M. He was older, had a car, and like me was already dressed in uniform. We drove forty-five minutes to Paterson, New Jersey, where people would be gathered at East Side Park. We'd play one, maybe two games, and wouldn't get home till nine o'clock. A full day of baseball—and we still wanted more!

Why did we love it? It's the physical and cerebral, doing something well, executing. You knew you weren't going to make a ton of money. But you could get, say, $15 to $25 a week for playing. Work a job on the side, and you'd make more than the average guy. The only thing I regret is that you couldn't aspire then to organized ball because of the color barrier. In 1936, our coach took us to Yankee Stadium to see the Yankees.

Otherwise, we saw the Negro Leagues. Each week the Negro Leagues came into my home, East Orange. On Sunday I'd go to Ruppert Stadium in Newark to see the Newark Eagles. They dressed well, played smartly, we'd try to pattern ourselves after Josh Gibson, Sam Bankhead, Oscar Charleston. That's when I learned: It matters how players conduct themselves.

A lot, of course, has changed since then. I started in the major leagues in 1949. Salaries were tiny compared with now. Today you can play one, two, five years, and quit. You don't have to worry about finances for the rest of your life. Another difference: When I grew up, people dressed up for a game. The ladies had on nice dresses, men hats and suits.

Afterward you'd go out to dinner. Today, anything goes. We didn't have AstroTurf. Kids now have all sorts of electronic stuff. If we had a radio, that was big! Plus, players now don't know adversity. Many lives have been fairly easy. Ours weren't.

If I had any advice to players today, it would be to be more grateful, dedicated, and thankful for when you came along. You can earn money for your family, then do what you want after a career. Show a little more emotion, be kinder to the fans, to the children. It's their game—just like when I was growing up.

MONTE IRVIN starred in the Negro Leagues before joining the New York Giants in 1949. He was inducted into Cooperstown in 1973.

Before a renovation in the mid-1970s, Yankee Stadium fused a facade, triple tiers, short foul lines, Death Valley, in-play flagpole, and monuments in center field.

DAN JANSEN

◆ ◆ ◆

I was ten, maybe twelve years old. My friend and I always went to the ballpark—County Stadium in Milwaukee—early in hopes of getting a ball during batting practice.

We were in the right field bleachers and a group of four or five of the Brewers were playing pepper near the fence. One of them accidentally popped one up over the fence and I caught it!

They wanted to continue playing but had no other balls with them. One of the players came over to the fence and told me he would give the ball to me when they were finished if I would give it back to him now.

I threw the ball to him, much to the ridicule of the

Paul Molitor (above and, in a typical pose, opposite) averaged .306 over 21 seasons. "I never was that strong," he said, "but I valued consistency." Molitor retired with 3,319 hits.

twenty or so other kids that now crowded around. They all told me I would never get the ball back.

I began to believe all the kids and spent the next fifteen minutes thinking I had just thrown back what would probably be my only chance of ever getting a ball.

As their pepper game ended, I stood near the fence in the crowd of kids. The player came over, scanned the crowd until he saw me, pointed me out, and threw me the ball!

To this day I have never forgotten that one day at the ballpark, nor have I forgotten the player who kept his word: Paul Molitor.

DAN JANSEN overcame adversity in the 1988 and 1994 Winter Olympics to win the 1994 1,000 meter speedskating race in a world record 1:12.43.

S. CHARLES JETER

♦ ♦ ♦

Baseball is in the blood, if not the genes. I loved it as a child. I grew up in Alabama, then spent my last year in high school in Nashville. I was lucky: Unlike now, it was okay to be a good-field, no-hit shortstop! I went to college at Fisk University, and some scouts briefly looked at me. Always I followed black players in the major leagues—Robinson, Campanella, Irvin. They were role models, I tried to emulate them. My league was the National: They had most of the great black players. Then they'd play the Yankees in October and get beat. I kid Derek that I soon became a Yankee-hater! That changed, of course, when they drafted him

I get asked if I pushed Derek into baseball. The answer is no: I just wanted him to be involved. He played basketball, soccer, and football growing up in Kalamazoo. Where I perhaps helped was that I'd played baseball, I knew the game, and I'd share my experiences. I'd talk about shortstop, where to play hitters, how to throw from the hole—and above all, the intangibles in which baseball is so rich.

To me, baseball is a lot about attitude—not getting too up or down, enjoy each game, then forget it and go on. If you do well, enjoy it. If you don't, review the game, learn from your mistakes, but don't let it burden you. Derek was very good in high school. Then he'd go to tryout camps around the country and see players with enormous talent. To me a lot of things matter more than talent: work, education, never being satisfied. The intangibles have made Derek what he is.

Friends say, "Do you know, Charles, that you're the only father in the world today to have your son play shortstop for the New York Yankees?" Shortstop is a vital position, and the Yankees are sport's glamour team. I'm glad that his first love, which is my first love, allows him to earn a good living. But what I'm even prouder of is how he plays the game, all out, with a respect for the game, his teammates, managers, and coaches, and how he carries himself off the field. That's what matters most.

In high school Derek had maybe twenty-five games a year. I'd live and die with every at-bat. Now, with 162 games each season, I'm a little calmer. He's going to have good games, bad games, make some errors, get some hits. I try to keep an equilibrium, which isn't easy. I'm pretty good at Yankee Stadium. My wife says, "You keep more of an even keel at the park than watching the game at home!" You never stop trying—Derek to be a better player, and me to be a better dad.

DR. S. CHARLES JETER manages his son's business affairs and is the Vice President of Derek Jeter's charitable Turn 2 Foundation. Previously, he had a private clinic practice.

July 21, 1957: Members of the Flatbush Faithful vie for a foul ball at Ebbets Field.

Derek Jeter became the 1996 A.L. Rookie of the Year. His Yanks won the World Series four of his first five full years.

ROGER KAHN

◆ ◆ ◆

Good baseball and great poetry have been the passions of my life. Each is as fresh and radiant today as when I was a boy.

ROGER KAHN is the author of The Era, Games We Used to Play, *and the celebrated* The Boys of Summer.

LARRY KING

◆ ◆ ◆

Baseball is in the fabric of the American soul. The cliché goes: Baseball is as American as apple pie. I say more so. You can buy apple pie anywhere, but baseball is still a kid and his father shagging fly balls on a June afternoon at the park.

I grew up in Brooklyn and the Dodgers were my life. I didn't have much money, but as often as I could, I paid my 50 cents to sit in the center field bleachers and watch the Bums play their crazy game.

I was there in 1947 when Jackie Robinson played in his first game against the then-Boston Braves. (I would later in life interview Jackie on five occasions, including just a few months before he died.) I think he embodied all that the game lacked and then gained. It took too long for an African-American to play in the majors, but when it happened he was the right choice. He had dignity, leadership qualities, and was one damn fine player.

I remember more about baseball games than any other instances in any other sport. I forget a hockey game as soon as it's over, but enjoy it while it's happening. I can still see Michael Jordan's shot in Utah—one of the crowning moments in basketball history—but that's about it in my basketball memory bank. I can see flashes of some pro football games, but that's all they are—flashes. But I remember hundreds of baseball games.

I remember remarkable fielding and stupid errors, heroic clutch hitting and failure when it counted. I remember how ballplayers walked and ran and stood in the batter's box, or on the pitcher's mound. Whenever I go to

Brooklyn, USA: Dodger fans gather more than twelve hours before the ticket office opens for Game 3 of the 1949 World Series.

a game, I cannot tell you when I'll be home. No other sport makes that happen.

Baseball is the core of what sport is about. As Babe Ruth so eloquently said, "Baseball was, is, and always will be to me the best game in the world."

LARRY KING has interviewed more than 40,000 guests, including the Dalai Lama, Mikhail Gorbachev, Nelson Mandela, and seven U.S. Presidents.

MOONLIGHT GRAHAM

Graham, Archibald Wright

B. Nov. 9, 1876, Fayetteville, N.C.
D. Aug. 25, 1965, Chisholm, Minn.

YEAR	1905	BB	0
TEAM	NY N	SO	0
GAMES	1	SB	0
BA	—	PINCH HIT AB	0
SA	—	PINCH HIT H	0
AB	0	PO	0
H	0	A	0
2B	0	E	0
3B	0	DP	0
HR	0	TC/G	0.0
HR%	—	FA	.000
R	0	G by POS	OF-1
RBI	0		

"If you build it, they will come":
Moonlight Graham's actual statistics.

W.P. KINSELLA

◆ ◆ ◆

I am attracted by the open-endedness of the game. Other sports are twice enclosed, first by time limits, then by rigid playing boundaries. There is no time limit on a baseball game, and on a true baseball field the foul lines diverge forever, eventually taking in a good part of the universe. This makes for myth and for larger-than-life characters, which is what interests a writer of magic realism such as myself. In hockey, basketball, or football it doesn't matter how wonderful the players are—they are confined to a tiny playing surface and there is little possibility for magic. I have been able to bring players back from the dead and have an outfielder run from Iowa to New Mexico chasing a fly ball, making baseball much more conducive to wizardry than other sports.

W. P. KINSELLA wrote the award-winning novel Shoeless Joe *in 1982. It was later adapted into the classic film* Field of Dreams.

PAUL KIRK

◆ ◆ ◆

Baseball is the unique unifier of the ages. It allows little boys to dream of their manhood and old men to dream of their boyhood. I can't imagine a greater gift.

PAUL KIRK, the former Chairman and Treasurer of the Democratic National Committee, is Co-Chairman of the Commission on Presidential Debates.

Baseball as meritocracy: Only skill counts, not age or size.

CHARLES C. KOONES

◆ ◆ ◆

Now that I live in Los Angeles I've taken on a National League coloration. But when I think of baseball I think simply of shortstop to third base for the Baltimore Orioles. I grew up in Washington, and the Senators left town when I was a kid. So we were forced to look down the road for our baseball. That meant the Orioles—and short to third.

All my role models played there. Mark Belanger. Cal Ripken, Jr. Brooks, of course. To me it meant the game. There's something about a hard shot to the left side. Little time to react. The fielder having to make a dazzling play. It's drama, entertainment, and nobody did it better than my idols on the O's.

Baseball is a working man's sport. Belanger and Ripken brought a working-man effort. Every day, day in and day out, there they were—diving, throwing, robbing sure base hits. With Brooks, especially, there was also that approachability. I've got two autographs I treasure still today.

Where I work is an amazing place—celebrities all the time. But none are more big league than my heroes growing up. What a great title for a movie: *Short to Third*.

CHARLES C. KOONES is Group Vice President and Publisher of Variety, Inc., the worldwide leader in entertainment business information.

The Human Vacuum Cleaner. "Brooks Robinson played a simple game," said broadcaster Chuck Thompson. "Hit it to him and he'd catch it—on grass, artificial turf, a marsh, a swamp."

LEONARD KOPPETT

◆ ◆ ◆

Contributing to a book called *What Baseball Means to Me* means, first of all, that I must take that title as a question. What *does* it mean to *me*? The answer, which comes immediately, has two parts;

1. A lot.
2. Different things at different times.

When I was an immigrant child, having come to New York from Russia at the age of five, it was the essential and dominant feature of my Americanization. This was in the late 1920s and early 1930s, and no other sport generated such ubiquitous comment nor carried comparable prestige. With other kids, we played street versions of baseball (including stoopball and stickball). Among American adults it was an endless topic of conversation. Reading daily newspapers (there were twelve to choose from in New York at that time) provided the main opportunity to learn the new (English) language and practice arithmetic. The very fact that this subject was a complete mystery to my parents and their fellow Russians naturally made it that much more attractive as a means of self-differentiation.

And the fact that our apartment house was just one block up from Yankee Stadium didn't hurt.

The next phase, also typical of my age group, was fandom. You picked a team to root for (in this case, of course, the Yankees) and through that, spread your awareness to all opponents and, in due course, to much of the game's history. One became, simultaneously, a Yankee and a baseball fan. The older you got, into the teenage years, the more immersed you became in the lore and continuity of this endlessly unfolding yet thoroughly comprehensible (to a child) activity.

Exposed in those years to so many Yankee, Giant, and Dodger games, and free of any illusion about my own athletic potential, I had become a dedicated follower well before reaching high school. Among life's manifold pleasures, the ballpark was a unique experience, not yet diluted by radio or television availability. It glowed for all the trite (but powerful) reasons: green grass, sunshine, hot dogs, echoing

No big leaguer has hit a fair ball completely out of Yankee Stadium, though Mickey Mantle came closest. Here he extends Don Larsen's 1956 perfect game.

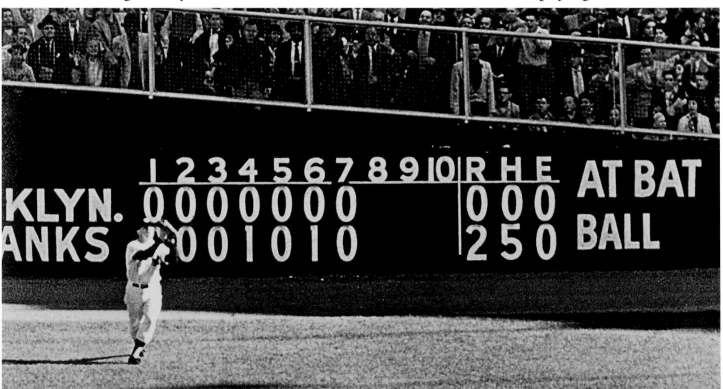

sounds, suspense and excitement, unfettered right to scream and yell, and (long before ABC appropriated the phrase) the vicarious thrill of victory and agony of defeat. And on all the many more days of non-attendance, merely finding out what happened could provide that pleasure to my imagination.

No other activity had as direct an effect on one's daily mood. Your team won, it was a good day; it lost, it was a bad day. Whatever else was going on, that undercurrent of feeling could not be escaped.

By the time I entered college, I knew I would never give up this addiction, and had figured out how to handle it. Whatever I'd do for a living, I would have to spend enormous amounts of time and money on ball games, leaving little room for other enjoyments. But if my gainful employment could be tied to the ball games, there would be plenty of opportunity to do everything else in my nonworking time.

My course to a baseball-writing career was set.

Once I became a professional (after returning from the Army), I outgrew fandom very quickly. Now my job was to *understand* what I was trying to describe. My fan experience had given me sufficient background on the historical level, but now I had to learn not merely who won, but why, and how, and what were the ball-field (and off-field) realities being lived by the people I wrote about. Rooting became irrelevant (because, among other things, as time went on, some good guy was losing as often as some bad guy was winning); comprehension became paramount.

So I became a serious (but never solemn) "student of the game"—and discovered that this was much more fun, more stimulating, more fascinating, more complex, and more satisfying than mere fandom had ever been.

What, then, does baseball mean to me now and for the last fifty years?

It means what medicine means to a doctor, physics to a physicist, music to a musician, or what any professional field means to those who practice it. Where it fits in American culture, philosophically and psychologically, I leave to those who labor in those areas. For me it's simply the most intricate, interesting, varied, and self-renewing game I know, and beyond the game on the field itself, its structure, history, and population are equally fascinating.

Each day, as I keep learning a little more about it, I enjoy it more. I can imagine a world without baseball, but can't imagine wanting to live in one.

LEONARD KOPPETT has written half a dozen books about his favorite sport, including The Thinking Man's Guide to Baseball. *He received the Hall of Fame's J.G. Taylor Spink Award in 1992.*

BOWIE KUHN

◆ ◆ ◆

Baseball's charm is the simple fact that there is nothing quite like it. The word "unique" is misused almost invariably but not when applied to baseball. It is unique: indisputably and dramatically a world unto itself. Surrounded by what too often is dull and compulsive conformity, baseball has always been unembarrassedly different.

In some form or another older than American history, baseball is rich in lore, fable, tradition, and storytelling. The great preacher, Norman Vincent Peale, while sitting with me at Yankee Stadium once told me that the game was like the Bible because of the stories that poured forth in such prodigal joy from its people. He was right. I will never forget my young children sitting around the feet of Casey Stengel and Ducky Medwick in Cooperstown's Otesaga Hotel devouring their stories and pleading for more of which there could never be enough. It was like the blind Homer reciting the folktales of ancient Greece.

Casey Stengel's 1949–60 Yankees won 10 pennants and seven World Series.
His 1962 Mets lost 120 games. The Ol' Perfessor also spawned his own language: Stengelese.

There was also something magical about the architecture of the old ballparks that impressed the young and imprinted green memories on their minds indelibly. For me it was Griffith Stadium in Washington and Forbes Field in Pittsburgh where I first saw American and National League games. The expectant walk up the tunnels gave as its fulfillment the breathtaking pastureland of the largest ballparks in major league America. Happily, new parks in professional ball are reverting to the architectural magic that gripped my early imagination.

Of course, the look and mechanics of a ball game are like no other game with the possible exception of an aged ancestor called cricket. Alexander Cartwright's rules of the diamond game written in the era of Tippecanoe, Tyler, and Taylor were unique. While most other games, then and now, are content to move an object to and fro on a rectangle, usually in a considerable crowd of athletes, baseball's shape and individuality of its players are singularly its own. Even the marvelous Native American game of lacrosse was carved into the rectangular pattern.

The greatest danger to the game today is that it might fall into some kind of conformity with the entertainment world in which it competes. It should celebrate and not be afraid of its differentness, its transcendentalism. A modern Rip Van Winkle, falling asleep for a century, would awake and say, "Ah, yes, I know this game."

BOWIE KUHN has loved baseball since working the Griffith Stadium scoreboard as a boy. He served as the commissioner of Major League Baseball from 1969 to 1984.

EMERIL LAGASSE

◆ ◆ ◆

When it comes to ballpark food, I'm a soft drink and hot dog and beer kind of guy. Give me some Fenway Franks with golden mustard, maybe a hamburger, French fries, that's heaven. Today you go to some parks, they've got the sushi, regional foods, trying to be hip. Forget it. My dad and my uncles drank beer at the park when I was a kid. Today so do I. That's baseball. Memories and tradition. Put me at the ballpark, man, I'm at home.

I grew up in a little town outside Boston, Fall River. Fact is, I played in the same place, Maplewood Park, with Red Sox catcher Russ Gibson, across from his house. I'd come home each day from school and practice pitching, thirty-five, forty minutes, play stickball, Little League, city league, made a couple all-star teams. It's hard to say what baseball meant to me. Sure, I had school and music. Later on I started to cook. But always there was baseball—my anchor, it's America. You'd read about it all winter, wait for spring to come. Opening day was my best day of the year.

I'll admit I was a baseball junkie. I loved Ted Williams. But the guy I really admired was Carl Yastrzemski, number 8, my hero. I took pride in knowing every position and player, how many wins, homers, average, really into it. I was a big Red Sox fan, and remember '67, the Impossible Dream, the devastation of Tony C. But my mother's brother was a die-hard Yankee fan! Talk about family arguments! Every year he'd go to opening day at Yankee Stadium. I'd go to Fenway eight, ten times a year. Today I spend a lot of time in New York and really respect and admire the Yankee management. Just don't tell my Sox buddies back home.

What does baseball mean to me? It molded me. I remember learning from my dad a respect for the game. It's America's sport, its pastime. It taught me about leadership and responsibility. I didn't realize it at the time, but it was shaping me, maturing me. So much of this country—past and present—is wrapped up

You can't beat food at the ballpark.

"Buy me some peanuts and cracker jacks." A vendor peddles at Chicago's South Side Park in 1905.

it was difficult for me to see the ball. It was the bottom of the last inning. If we got them out, we would win. I heard the crack of the bat and saw a fuzzy object coming toward me. I put my glove over my face to protect it. The ball stuck in my glove. I was the big hero, even though I hadn't really seen what was going on.

FRANKIE LAINE has made 21 Gold Records. His hits include the theme song for the TV show Rawhide *and title track for the popular movie* Blazing Saddles.

This ball got away.

in that little white ball. So when you're at the ballpark, skip the elegant stuff, have a hot dog, and inhale the game. And when you hear me say "Bam" on my show, just think of it as Yaz going long.

EMERIL LAGASSE, America's best-known chef, began working in a Portuguese bakery at age twelve.

FRANKIE LAINE

◆ ◆ ◆

I was ten and we had a game against our chief rival. I played center field, back as far as possible. I was very nearsighted, and

JULIUS LaROSA

♦ ♦ ♦

I was born in Brooklyn ten years before Pee Wee Reese—my first idol—came up from Louisville to play shortstop for the Brooklyn Dodgers. It was late in the 1940 season. The following year we win the first pennant in twenty-one years! I was a Dodger fan until O'Malley broke my heart, along with millions of other Brooklyn Dodger fans, when he took them away from us. My heart was with Reese and Hodges and Campy and Snider and the rest—unfortunately, it was never the same again.

My saddest moment: When I discovered the empty coffee can in which I kept my baseball cards was lost during a move from our apartment in Brooklyn to a home in Mount Vernon, New York. (No, we didn't move there because Ralph Branca lived there!)

Second saddest moment: Yep! Bobby Thomson's homer in 1951.

Happiest moment: When my Uncle Tony—who would have been the best uncle in the world...except that he was a Giant fan!—home on furlough, took me to see my first World Series game. It was 1943, the Yanks against the Cardinals. I don't remember who won—I just remember being there. (But I do remember telling Uncle Tony I'd been in Yankee Stadium once before; that my father, his brother, had taken me to see Bobby Feller pitch against Atley Donald, who had a pretty good fastball himself.)

Another special moment: Sometime in the mid-1950s I met Whitlow Wyatt, who'd won 22 games in '41 and was now the Phillies' pitching coach. I ask him what the name Phil Masi means to him. He smiles and says, "That bum! We were in Boston. Two outs in the bottom of the ninth and he breaks up my no-hitter with a lousy base hit!" Then he smiles and says, "Julius, you're a real baseball fan, aren't you!"

And one more! Sometime in the early 1970s, the

I was a Dodger fan until O'Malley broke my heart, along with millions of other Brooklyn Dodger fans, when he took them away from us.

Mets ask me to do the National Anthem before the Old-Timers Game; this one saluting players who at one time or another during their careers played with either the Giants or the Dodgers. I was thrilled! (When it comes to big leaguers I'm a thirteen-year-old—well, I used to be, anyway!) They asked, too, if I would sing a couple of songs at the dinner following the game. I did, including this parody of the great Rodgers and Hammerstein hit "My Favorite Things."

Hearn, Kerr, and Willie, and Irvin and Westrum,
Good manners demand that I say Bobby Thomson,
Hermanski and Amoros, Abrams and Loes,
Erskine and Walker—how Rube's stomach shows!

Now for some real names!

Joe Pignatano, Gionfriddo, Cimoli,
Branca and Maglie, Lombardi and Cookie,
Lavagetto, Camilli, Furillo—my bums!
Roy Campanella...could they bang the drums!

Joe DiMaggio, Joe DiMaggio, it would have been
*   so sweet...*

If you had played in Brooklyn, instead of New York,
My life would have been...complete!

If you can take another parody, to the tune of "Hello, Dolly," I sang:

Hello, Pee Wee, well, hello, Pee Wee,
You were my first hero back when I was ten!
And then there's Pete Reiser, oh, that Pete Reiser,
You were something, you were special, you could do it all!
I know that you remember, but do they remember,
On that day that Mickey Owen dropped the ball,
You hit a homer, in your first World Series!
You should have been the hero that day,
To me you were the hero that day
And pity the ones who never saw you play!

Reiser came up and hugged me when I finished, whispering in my ear, "I wish [Branch] Rickey could have heard that!"

Campy once said, "You have to be a man to play baseball, but you gotta have a lotta little boy in you, too." I collect Social Security now, but every time I sing the Anthem, and meet some of the players before or after the game—I'm a little boy again.

JULIUS LaROSA's musical career began in 1950 when he joined the U.S. Navy Band. He still signs letters, "Good field, no hit."

From 1940 to 1942 and 1946 to 1958, Pee Wee Reese led with his bat—and with his heart. He was inducted into the Hall of Fame in 1984.

JACK LARSON

♦ ♦ ♦

The keepsakes of my Los Angeles boyhood are all involved with baseball. My dad was a thwarted professional player. His best friend, Hughie McMullen, became a major league switch-hitter. I was raised by them to be a ballplayer. I have three Louisville Sluggers, presents from Hughie of increasing length as I grew up, with my name burned into each. I have two baseballs signed by World Series teams and various mitts from small to larger. I have my dad's prized tiny golden baseball engraved "Geo. E. Larson Champions" that his L.A. team won in the 1930s in a workman's league. Best of all is a page in my *Baby's Year Book* that testifies to our love of baseball. Written in my dad's hand, dated March 28, seven weeks after I was born, under the caption "Baby's First Outing," is this: "Jack Edward's first outing was to see a ball game at Wrigley Field played by Los Angeles and the Chicago Cubs. Chicago winning, 10–1. [Charlie] Root pitched for the Cubs, [Norman] Plitt for the Angels." That would be L.A.'s old Wrigley Field owned by the chewing gum Wrigley who owned the Cubs and the Angels as well as Catalina Island, where both clubs had their winter quarters.

Hugh McMullen played for Cincinnati in 1929. In four seasons he batted .176 with 19 hits and 6 RBIs.

My dad, who felt he couldn't rely on baseball for his livelihood, had become an iceman in East L.A. Big, honest Hughie, who was childless until later in life, took his chance on baseball and played for the New York Giants, Washington Senators, and finally Cincinnati Reds, before he was traded to the minor leagues. My first memory of him is as a catcher for Oakland up the coast from L.A.

Off-season when Hughie was home, he and my dad had me practice catching, throwing, and batting like other kids on

Wrigley Field in Los Angeles, 1949: A minor league bandbox, with power alleys 345 feet from the plate. It hosted TV's **Home Run Derby** *in the 1959–60 offseason.*

the block practiced the piano or violin. Those kids didn't turn out to be violinists or pianists and I didn't turn out to be a ballplayer, either. But I tried. In grammar school (there were no Little Leagues then), I played shortstop on our team, just like my dad. Sometime just before World War II my teammates took nicknames after our big league heroes: Billy became Gomez, Harry was DiMaggio, and I was called Pee Wee (after Pee Wee Reese or maybe because I was small for my grade, having skipped two grades in school).

Then came the war and our world changed. My dad went into the armed forces along with all the other men of draftable age, ballplayers, teachers, and truckers alike. There wasn't any more baseball for a while. The stadiums were closed, the cities of California were in blackouts at night, mothers and older sisters started working at the local war plants, and we kids helped the war effort with after-school paper drives and collecting used metal and rubber for recycling into tanks and tires. At war's end, Hughie's baseball days were over and, not having made a lot of money in the game, he became a truck driver like my dad. He hauled gasoline while my dad switched from ice to wholesale milk delivery. They had given up on their baseball dreams for me. It was not my talent.

With the rise of Little League, Hughie, who with his wife had adopted a baby girl, didn't get involved. My dad, however, coached one Little League team after another until just before he died. When the Dodgers moved to L.A., my dad was in the bliss of the Elysian fields when his team was winning in their stadium on Elysian Park Avenue. The last time I saw Hughie, just before his death, was at my dad's funeral. I followed the strong old man as he slipped away amid the monuments of Forest Lawn to sob over the loss of his best friend.

What does baseball mean to me? It means my boyhood, our love of the game, and those I so loved.

JACK LARSON is a playwright, actor, and film producer who played legendary cub reporter Jimmy Olson in the 1950s The Adventures of Superman.

DAN LEBATARD

◆ ◆ ◆

What does this sport mean to me? This question, unlike the baseball itself, isn't the easiest thing in the world to get your hands around. I'm a thirty-two-year-old Yankee fan from South Florida, so baseball to me isn't black and white nostalgia or families gathered around a crackling radio or Hemingway's old fisherman romanticizing about the Great DiMaggio. I'm a member of the ESPN Generation, so baseball is:

Lee Smith, moseying in from the bullpen.
Ivan Rodriguez, coming out of the crouch.
Billy Martin, launched from the dugout as if by
    catapult.
Ken Griffey, Sr., reaching into the crib and passing
    down that swing to his son.
Greg Maddux versus Tony Gwynn.
Randy Johnson versus John Kruk.
Nolan Ryan versus anyone.
But especially versus Robin Ventura.
Andruw Jones, center field.
Mike Piazza, opposite field.
Barry Bonds, anywhere on the field.
Triples.
Rookies.
Plays at the plate.
A shortstop and second baseman partaking in ballet
    with second base as the stage.
The sheer delight and discovery on a child's face when
    he learns it's okay to throw the peanut shells right
    on the floor.
Cal Ripken, punching in every day.
Roger Clemens, punching out every fifth.
Oscar Gamble's Afro.
Don Sutton's perm.
Jay Buhner's bald.

Jim Leyland's mind.
Maddux's eyes.
Doug Rader's nose.
Rollie Fingers's mustache.
Mickey Rivers's mouth.
Vin Scully's voice.
Kevin Brown's snarl.
Carlos Delgado's smile.
Jason Giambi's scruff.
And Don Zimmer's entire face.
Rickey Henderson, running.
Rickey Henderson, trotting.

Rickey Henderson, walking.
Questioning the manager after the game.
Sitting in the dugout next to him before it.
Limping Kirk Gibson, rounding the bases while
    looking like he's trying to start a lawnmower.
Joe Carter, rounding the bases without ever touching
    the ground.
The pure and perfect happiness on Edgar
    Renteria's face.
Sammy Sosa's little hop when he knows, literally
    jumping for joy.
Reggie, swinging and connecting.
And Reggie swinging and missing, too.
Harry Caray's home run call.

Even on a pop-up to second.

Roger Clemens, bringing it.

Rafael Palmeiro, swinging it.

The Yankees, ringing it.

The team of Randy Johnson, Ken Griffey, and A-Rod
    never winning anything.

And the team with John Shelby, Mickey Hatcher,
    and Mike Marshall in the middle of its lineup
    winning it all.

Pinstripes.

And, yes, Houston's uniforms, too.

Those caps the we-are-family Pirates wore.

Beer here!

A mint-condition collection of Dave Winfield
    baseball cards.

The delivery Dan Quisenberry says he found in his flaw.

Mo Vaughn's neck.

Frank Thomas's shoulders.

Charles Johnson's chest.

Kirby Puckett's heart.

Pedro Martinez's arm.

Ellis Valentine's, too.

Jose Canseco's biceps.

Mark McGwire's forearms.

Gary Sheffield's wrists.

Tom Glavine's palm.

Mike Scott's split fingers.

And whatever goop was at the end of Gaylord Perry's.

Here's to Felipe Alou's gut feeling!

And to not feeling Tommy Lasorda's!

The 1997 Florida Marlins, the best team money
    could rent.

The first time you walk into Wrigley Field.

John Olerud's grace.

Omar Vizquel's range.

Will Clark's swing.

John Kruk's quotes.

Chipper Jones's drawl.

Lenny Dykstra's spit.

Even Bobby Valentine's ego.

Jeffrey "Penitentiary Face" Leonard, one flap down.

The 3-1 pitch to Mike Schmidt...

Or Paul Molitor...

Or Rod Carew...

The 0-2 pitch by Bert Blyleven...

Or Steve Carlton...

Or David Cone...

And Donnie Moore delivers to Dave Henderson...

I don't believe what I just saw...

Ground ball to Buckner...

Don Baylor.

The player, not the manager.

Mike Hargrove.

The manager, not the player.

He's pitching to Jack Clark?

He's walking Bonds intentionally with the bases
    loaded?

Anxious Rob Dibble throwing up blood in the bullpen.

Angry Rob Dibble throwing fire upon emerging
    from it.

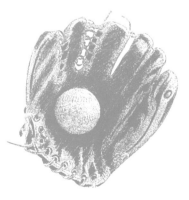

Bo Jackson off Rick
 Reuschel.
Colorado's pitchers, praying.
Carlton Fisk, begging.
And Manny Ramirez, so
 good he need not do either.
Deion Sanders, first to third.
Ken Caminiti, third to first.
Who let the dogs out?
Okay, that one, not so much.
Pascual Perez, losing his directions.
Lou Piniella, losing his temper.
George Brett, losing his mind.
Spring training.
Game 7.
Opening day.
The Green Monster.
New ballparks.
Old ones, too.
Luis Tiant's hips.
Kent Tekulve's side.
Bartolo Colon's rump.
Johnny Bench's thighs.
Kenny Lofton's hamstrings.
Andre Dawson's knees.
Mark McGwire's feats.
And, finally, take me out to the
 ball game, still.

DAN LeBATARD, an award-winning
Miami Herald *sports columnist,*
writes essays for ESPN Television,
has a weekly show on
ESPN Radio, and is a
contributing writer to
ESPN The Magazine.

Ten times Joe Carter
knocked in 100 runs. He
won the 1993 World
Series for Toronto with a
three-run homer in the
last inning of Game 6.

ELMORE LEONARD

♦ ♦ ♦

When I was a boy in Detroit there was no organized baseball for ten-year-olds. However, we did collect Blue Valley Butter cartons and mailed them in to the company—in answer to an offering they made—in return for blue-and-yellow baseball caps. I went to Blessed Sacrament, a Catholic school. The only team we played was known as the Harmon Street Gang. They didn't have uniforms, but stole all their equipment from Sears.

ELMORE LEONARD is perhaps America's leading crime fiction writer. Many of this thirty-five novels like Get Shorty *and* Out of Sight *have been adopted for film.*

Yankee Stadium, June 8, 1969: Mickey Mantle's number 7 is retired. "Now I know," said Mantle of the ovation, "how Lou Gehrig felt."

The madding crowd: Players converge in St. Bernadette's Little League, Brooklyn, 1960.

MICHAEL LEVINE

♦ ♦ ♦

It felt like the official coronation of the American dream, that sunny day in September 1965. More than 50,000 disciples convened on Yankee Stadium, a mass pilgrimage gathering in the Holy Land to honor the great Mickey Mantle. In 1965, things were simpler. Baseball was America. Mickey Mantle was God. And New York—brimming with power, teeming with optimism—was the Holy Land. The greatest of all—the man who, before his knee injuries, could outrun a fly ball—Mickey Mantle—was being mass-worshipped as only a New Yorker of that time could possibly understand.

I remember clutching my ticket to Mickey Mantle Fan Appreciation Day tightly in my eleven-year-old palm like it was a prescription for spiritual transcendence. I was sailing like a kite, floating through the faceless, nameless crowd, knowing that I, in this early autumn dream, would catch a glimpse of the American deity. Sportswriters of the day had made Mantle out to be someone that, in later years, I found he wasn't. But something about the canonization of this great ballplayer from Commerce, Oklahoma, was real to me. Scores would crowd around him after the game, no doubt, hoping to touch his clothing, or better yet, those amazing switch-hitter hands.

Taking our seats in Yankee Stadium, white banners professing endless love and allegiance to the Mick rippled in the warm afternoon breeze. Puerile adolescents in baseball caps wiggled in their seats. Middle-aged men smelling of Aqua Velva rubbed their clean-shaven chins thoughtfully and folded their arms. Their wives, hair covered in brightly colored scarves, fiddled with their handbags. But what I remember most was Mantle. There he stood, the lengthening shadows of late summer stretching out before his broad shoulders; his all-American good looks and affable smile resonated throughout the stadium. His spectacular career was nearing an end. But standing there in his Yankee pinstripes, a mighty phantasm of the American dream, he became immortal in my young mind.

When I look back on it, I can't grasp the innocence and optimism of it all. Was it merely a beautiful boyhood dream? In 1965, we had just left Camelot; we were still living a pre-Vietnam vision. We were still Marilyn Monroe, JFK, and Jackie; we were Mickey Mantle and his Yanks. We were baseball; we were America; and we were the greatest. Nothing could stop us. Sometimes I still wake in the middle of the night, hearing his amiable Oklahoma drawl echoing across the field, and the crack of his bat beckoning young boys of that day to fall to their knees and grown men to tears.

MICHAEL LEVINE heads a leading entertainment public relations firm.

The Stadium. Mantle's best year was 1956: He hit 52 homers, with 130 RBIs and a .353 average. "Healthy," said Mel Allen, "he was the best I ever saw."

Roy Campanella was a three-time MVP for the Brooklyn Dodgers.

HAL LINDEN

◆ ◆ ◆

I grew up not far from Yankee Stadium. I still remember my first game. My cousin took me, and we sat in deep left field, looking over Tommy Henrich's shoulder. The irony is that I was a *Dodger* fan, living in the *Bronx*. I think that's the definition of a life-threatening situation. How do you explain it? Maybe I was a troubled kid. Actually, the Yankees were a little dull. The Dodgers were more exciting—even as they broke your heart.

It was a long trip from the Bronx to Ebbets Field, but I knew it inch by inch long before I saw it—where Pee Wee played, or Campy, or Pete Reiser hit the wall, where the right field scoreboard was, or that sign,

"Hit Sign, Win Suit!" They were as familiar as any member of your family.

I remember, too, the great games—Cookie Lavagetto ending Bill Bevens's no-hitter: That happened when I was in high school. Or the Thomson homer, in college: It created a kind of numbness. Or Podres's winning our only World Series after so many tries. But what sticks is how baseball pervaded our time—especially on radio. You'd hear a game come at you from a dozen different directions.

Remember "FOB"? That meant the bases were Full of Brooklyns. Red Barber taught me that—even to a Dodger fan in the Bronx. Life-threatening? Life-enhancing. That's what baseball meant to me.

HAL LINDEN, who starred in television's Barney Miller, *is an actor, singer, and musician. He has earned one Broadway Tony and two TV Emmy Awards.*

PATTI LUPONE

◆ ◆ ◆

I had the honor of singing the national anthem in Cooperstown for the 1999 Hall of Fame induction class. That weekend, while standing in the lobby of the Otesaga Hotel to check in, my husband spotted the great Buck O'Neil.

We had met Mr. O'Neil a year earlier at umpire Bob Motley's home in Kansas City. We walked over, said hello, and talked briefly. We were getting ready to leave when our son Josh asked Buck if he would please sign a ball (even though this was frowned upon in the hotel).

Mr. O'Neil said he would sign it for Josh on one condition—he had to catch it first. Buck told Josh to back up twelve to fifteen feet and he would toss it to him there in the lobby. The look of concentration on our son's face to catch that baseball is still vivid in our

Buck O'Neil (in his playing days, above, and, left, in retirement) played and managed in the Negro Leagues. From 1948 to 1955, his Kansas City Monarchs won five pennants and two Black World Series. Later, as a Cub scout, O'Neil signed Ernie Banks and Lou Brock. In 1962 he became the major leagues' first black coach.

minds. That day was surely one of the most memorable baseball moments in our family's life, and one of the many things we love about baseball.

Oh, by the way, he caught it.

PATTI LuPONE is equally at ease at recordings, film, TV, or the dramatic stage. Credits include Patti LuPone on Broadway, Sunset Boulevard, *and* Matters of the Heart.

JEFFREY LYONS

◆ ◆ ◆

Baseball is one of the best ways ever devised to try, albeit in vain, to control time and escape from the continual ticking of the clock that is the measure of our lives. Yet, ironically, it is the sport most steeped in tradition through the constant summoning of numbers and events in the past for endless comparisons with the present.

Former Red Sox manager Jimy Williams said the aim of baseball is "to play in cold weather twice." Its arrival in the throes of winter, with pitchers and catchers reporting to training camps, is the first sign of the inevitable renewal of nature, the promise of warm weather, blue skies, and the day-to-day events that chronicle the seasons. Spin a radio dial in a car on a rural road late at night during the season and you can hear three, four, maybe five or six different games; you are listening to the sounds of an American summer. It is the only game where men of nearly every size and description can be and have been stars; every game is different, every pitch brings the possibility of something happening for the first time.

People who don't understand the game bemoan the fact that "it's boring, nothing happens. It moves so slowly." These are the people who demand instant gratification and only sports where nothing is happening just below the surface. In fact, in a baseball game something is usually happening at any given moment, be it physical or psychological. You just have to know where to look. Is an infielder playing in, are the outfielders shaded this way or that, is the catcher calling for a breaking pitch, does the manager have confidence in the rookie he is sending up in a clutch situation, is a sign being stolen, did the catcher get crossed up, is the bench deep enough for the late innings? Baseball minds want to know.

If you play poorly in a football game, you have to wait a week to redeem yourself. In baseball, redemption can come later in the game or, at the latest, the next day or two. It is the only human endeavor, furthermore, in which a 70 percent failure rate is the benchmark of a star. As Ted Williams, who set the standard, said: "Hitting a baseball is the hardest thing in sports to do." No other sport lends itself to trivia like baseball. From obscure

Ty Cobb had 4,191 hits, averaged .367, won 12 batting titles, and stole a then-best 892 bases.

I remember meeting Ty Cobb at Yankee Stadium a month or so before he died in 1961—frail, uncharacteristically modest, perhaps aware the end was near.

Fast Pitch softball player that I would become—I'm seen trying to catch the ball. I remember later in the game marveling at Robinson's pigeon-toed way of running, as he stole second and scored: the most exciting player of modern baseball.

I remember meeting Ty Cobb at Yankee Stadium a month or so before he died in 1961—frail, uncharacteristically modest, perhaps aware the end was near. I knew Joe DiMaggio. He was a friend of my father's and visited our home many times. He once summoned us to the stage at a card show, gave me a friendly shove,

hometowns of players (Red Jacket, Arkansas; Big Cabin, Oklahoma; Ribnick, Czechoslovakia) to colorful nicknames ("The Grey Eagle," "Old Aches and Pains," "Old Scrap Iron," "The Big Train," "Twinkletoes") and endless other eccentricities. It is, furthermore, a game of constantly changing equations and situations, a day-to-day progression of highs and lows, triumphs and failures, errors and great plays.

There is no clock; there is really no out-of-bounds since foul territory can be part of the outcome. While basketball may have a few expressions like "downtown" or "sky hook," and football some, baseball has an endless array of expressions: "Baltimore chop," "Texas Leaguer," "can of corn," "Uncle Charlie," "dinger," "tater," and "stepping in the bucket," to name a few. They are part of the lexicon of American English.

The first game I remember attending was at the Polo Grounds around 1949. We were sitting in restaurateur Toots Shor's third base box. Jackie Robinson was at bat for Brooklyn and hit a towering foul ball. The newspaper showed my mother trying to protect me from the ball, which was coming down over our seats, while—future high school and Central Park

Bob Feller led the A.L. in strikeouts seven times and threw a record-tying twelve one-hitters.

and took my then-nine-year-old son aside and spent ten minutes telling him what I was like at his age.

I met and interviewed my other baseball hero, Carl Yastrzemski, in the Red Sox dressing room that star-crossed year of 1978. I've become a close friend of former Red Sox manager and major league infielder Joe Morgan, and met Mickey Mantle on many occasions. Yogi Berra knew my father and recalled him fondly for me. Indeed, my father was the only journalist on the scene of the infamous 1957 fight at the Copacabana nightclub. Stan Musial knew him, and I was an acquaintance of Hank Greenberg. I still see Bob Feller in Cleveland when I'm in town to see the Red Sox face the Tribe. Bill White, the great former first baseman, longtime Yankee announcer, and National League President, is a friend. These and the other major leaguers I've known—Jim Bouton, Ken Harrelson, Art Shamsky, Jerry Remy, Dave Campbell, Bobby Murcer, James Timothy McCarver, Keith Hernandez, Bob Montgomery, Tom Seaver, Fran Healy, Steve Lyons, Rick Cerone, and many others are cherished friendships.

I often wonder what ballplayers would be doing if there were no baseball. I also wonder what life would be like. It is not a pleasant thought. There is a line in a movie called *D.A.R.Y.L.* in which Michael McKean says to a boy: "The first thing you have to know is that all life begins and ends with baseball." Aside from family and career, it sure does.

JEFFREY LYONS is a WNBC-TV, New York, film and theater critic and host of the PBS series Sneak Preview.

The Georgia Peach at the Yankees' 1958 Old-Timers Game. A 1950 writers' poll named him the first half-century's greatest player.

JOHNNY MAJORS

◆ ◆ ◆

I grew up in Lynchburg, Tennessee, a town of about 400 people that is best known for its Jack Daniel's distillery. My mother, father, and six of us kids lived in one side of the house that my grandmother owned, and she lived in the other side. I was the oldest. The first five of us were close in age, so I always had someone to play with. The side yard was our favorite playground, even though it was small. This is where we would play our pickup baseball, football, hide-and-seek, or whatever the game of the day was. Our father coached the high school sports and was influential with our sports interest. For that reason, we changed with the seasons. My grandmother used to caution us about not wearing out the grass on our side of the yard. Of course, that was to no avail.

Our youngest brother was too small to hit the ball, so we would roll it on the ground to him just so we could have another person to play with. We did the same with our only sister. Anything for a game! People in Lynchburg have often wondered how we grew up to be adults, because they couldn't count the times they had seen a Majors kid run across the highway and back to retrieve a stray ball.

One of the real thrills was being able to play across the street in Miss Mattie Bob's vacant lot. She rarely let us play there, so it was a treat. It was fenced in, and we had our own big-time ballpark. Across the street from her lot was a service station. It was

Family affair, 1960: Bob Bossard, son of the White Sox then-groundskeeper, slides into Sherman Lollar.

a major feat to hit the ball across the street and onto the roof of the garage. I will never forget the first time I did it. I was nine, and I felt like I was Joe DiMaggio.

We had to drive many miles to see a major sports event. Virtually every year, my father would pile us all in the car and take us to see the Nashville Vols, a Double-A team. We always arrived well before the teams came on the field. My father wanted to see it all—how the players warmed up, how they used their gloves, how they ran. I think this helped us appreciate the various games that we loved even more. We never left any game early, either. We stayed until the final out and even watched the players walk off the field. This influenced me very much.

Every time I go to any game, I get there well ahead of time. I want to see it all as well. The most embarrassing recollection that I have in baseball happened when I was ten. We were playing a pickup game in Fayetteville, Tennessee, which was a bigger town. My father was the coach. We didn't have uniforms, but Fayetteville did. It was the bottom of the seventh inning. I was pitching and had a man on third. I asked the third base coach how many outs there were, and I understood him to say two. The batter hit the ball to me and I threw to first base, getting the runner out. The man on third scored. I thought the inning was over, so I began to run off the field. But there was only one out. I cried because they won the game as a result of my mistake.

JOHNNY MAJORS has won one national college football title (University of Pittsburgh, 1976) and two Coach of the Year awards.

DAVID MARANISS

◆ ◆ ◆

When I think of baseball, two lines of thought rush forward in my mind about family and childhood freedom. They seem contradictory on the surface, yet are deeply conjoined in my memory and are part of the same sensibility. Baseball enjoyed a singular place in the Maraniss family, not just as a sport, but as a means of communication. Through baseball I could speak to my father, and he could speak to me, and through baseball all of us, my parents and brothers and sisters and I, could pass our familiar love back and forth, telling and retelling stories and myths that bound us together.

Perhaps it was baseball that made us a family in the first place. It brought my father, a lanky dark-haired kid from Coney Island with a sweet left-handed swing, out to the University of Michigan, where he met my mother, a Midwestern blonde. Baseball was part of the birth rite as well. The family story goes that when my little sister was born, my father was at Briggs Stadium in Detroit with my older brother and sister, sitting in the center field bleachers, watching the Tigers take a 4–1 lead over the Red Sox into the late innings. The Red Sox get the bases loaded and Ted Williams steps to the plate and my dad is out there screaming, "Walk him! Walk him!" but the Tigers don't walk him, and the next thing you know the ball is screaming off his bat and out into the bleachers and the Tigers lose again.

I've heard that story a thousand times, and never tire of the telling. It is part of the family lore, existing in that comforting world between myth and reality, right next to the story about how when I was two years old my father held me in his arms as he listened to the radio broadcast of the 1951 cross-town playoff, Dodgers versus Giants, and reacted to Bobby Thomson's home run by dropping me to the floor in disgust as though I were his suddenly useless baseball mitt—an act that I later interpreted as love of baseball, not abuse of son.

Baseball means my mother accompanying my son to three straight Milwaukee Brewers games in the middle of another desultory season, without complaint. Baseball means my dad sitting on a little side porch in his boxer shorts and T-shirt on a late-spring evening, listening to Harvey Haddix spin a perfect game into extra innings, yet marveling more at Lew Burdette somehow carrying a 12-hit shutout. Baseball means my grandmother sitting on her couch in the house on the farm outside Ann Arbor, listening to the soothing crackle of Ernie Harwell describing Don Wert fielding the ball and firing across the diamond to first-sacker Norman Cash. Baseball means my son at age seven perfectly mimicking the chicken flap of Joe Morgan at the plate and the swift seamless stroke of Paul Molitor.

Yet for all these family connections, there is another aspect that shapes a different value in my life—independence. When I was a kid in Madison, Wisconsin, we played baseball all summer with absolutely no interference from adults. We saw our parents as little as possible, and we never brooded about whether they were ignoring us or not giving us quality time, and they never seemed to worry about whether we were safe. There was no Little League in Madison, no overbearing fathers reliving their childhoods, no loud-mouthed mothers harping at the umpires. In the city recreation league, we coached our own teams and rode to the games at Wingra or Vilas together not in an SUV but in a raucous line of wide-wheeled, one-speed bikes.

That, finally, is what baseball means to me—more than the green grass, the crack of the bat, the buzz of the crowd at a major league ballpark, the somnolent lull between pitches, more than any of that, I think of a group of kids pedaling toward the diamond on a summer morning, their gloves flapping against the handlebars, free and easy.

DAVID MARANISS is a longtime Washington Post *political writer and associate editor and author of the best-selling* First in His Class: A Biography of Bill Clinton *and* When Pride Still Mattered: A Biography of Vince Lombardi.

On May 26, 1959, Harvey Haddix pitched a perfect game over the first 12 innings, retiring the first 36 Braves—but he lost, 1–0, in the 13th inning.

JUAN MARICHAL

◆ ◆ ◆

Every day I thank God for the life I've lived—for baseball. I love the game. I'm going to die a fan. I was born one—because even as a kid I thought of baseball players like gods. I wanted to be a player at an early age. At that time I didn't know anything about the major leagues, or Hall of Fame. My dream was to someday be included on the national team of my country, the Dominican Republic.

Each morning I'd leave home real early for school and stop halfway to play baseball. Sometimes I'd get to school late. Sometimes I wouldn't make it at all! When

Sandy Koufax won three Cy Young Awards and hurled four no-hitters. He entered Cooperstown in 1972.

my mother found out, she was very upset. "What are you going to do when you grow up?" she said. "A person without an education has a hard time to survive." She was right. I don't have much of an education. But maybe I knew something that my mother didn't.

I'd say, "I'm going to be a major league baseball player. Every time you hear about me on radio and television you'll be happy and proud."

She said, "Happy and proud can't buy anything. What are you going to do?" Play baseball. I knew it, even then.

Today you see a lot of kids in my country wanting to be a big leaguer—Alex Rodriguez, Manny Ramirez, Sammy Sosa, Vladimir Guerrero—not because of the money, but because they love the game. This is one reason Sammy, Pedro Martinez, they give 150 percent—which is what they should. I tell players that they represent our country—and the game.

Take Ted Williams. Sitting next to him was a big thrill for me. Or Willie Mays playing behind me in center field. What counts is how you act—on the field, and off. That's especially true with today's Hispanic influx. When I was little, Bombo Ramos was my idol. The day I saw him pitch, I switched to the mound from shortstop. People's eyes are on you. It matters if you behave.

I think back on facing Mickey Mantle in the All-Star Game and 1962 World Series. Or facing Sandy Koufax. Or the night in '63 when I beat Warren Spahn, 1–0, in 16 innings. They don't make games like that anymore. Family, kids, grandkids, and maybe someday, great-grandkids—I'm a happy man. I owe it all to baseball. That's what the game means to me.

JUAN MARICHAL forged a 243-142 lifetime record. He was inducted into the Hall of Fame in 1983.

PEDRO MARTINEZ

◆ ◆ ◆

Baseball means everything to me—my job, my pride, my family. As a professional, I take it seriously. As a player, I can't remember when I didn't love the game. In the Dominican Republic, it's a path to a better time—a way out of poverty, to give back to people who helped you. Baseball is my passion and my way of life.

In the Dominican you come by it naturally. Everybody plays baseball. It's the number one sport. You

don't have to wait till the weather warms. Every day you're out pitching, hitting, hoping. Baseball is about practice and dedication. I learned that as a kid—and developed physical skill. You build up your body—and what you know about the game.

I know the game. My dad played baseball professionally, and my uncles, brothers, and cousins. We have fifteen members of my family for whom baseball's how we live. That's one reason I wanted to pitch in Boston. People think of their long streak since winning a World Series. I think of how they're the most faithful fans alive.

Every day *they're* out there supporting you—giving everything they have. That's the only way to play baseball—and to love it, too.

PEDRO MARTINEZ is already among baseball's all-time great pitchers. The Red Sox ace has won two Cy Young Awards and was MVP of the 1999 All-Star Game.

Martinez joined Boston in 1998. A year later he struck out a franchise-record 17 in one game.

EUGENE McCARTHY

◆ ◆ ◆

Baseball is different games. The difference is not accidental, but essential, even metaphysical. First, baseball has a singular and distinctive relationship to time. Only baseball is called a "past-time." Baseball is above or outside of time. Football, basketball, hockey, and soccer are divided into measured halves, quarters, and periods. They are controlled, even dominated, by time. Not so for baseball, which either controls, dominates, or ignores time. Theoretically, an inning can go on

forever. The same is true of a game. Interruptions generally are limited to acts of God, such as rain, normal darkness, or failure of the lighting system. These acts are declared to be what they are by the umpire. If, for any reason, a game must be halted, time is not "taken out." Umpires do not look at their watches as do referees. Rather, time is "called." Again, theoretically forever, by the umpire, possibly for eternity.

Baseball is also played in a unique spatial frame. Other games are played inside defined and measured areas: rectangular or nearly rectangular fields, rinks, or floors. Not so with baseball, which is played within the lines of a projection from home plate, starting from the point of a 90

Bill Klem, a.k.a. The Old Arbitrator, was an N.L. umpire from 1905 to 1940. "I never made a wrong call," he said, "at least in my heart."

> *One occasionally hears the cry "fire the referee," but one seldom hears the cry "kill the referee." That demand is reserved for umpires, and with good reason. Umpires have to be dealt with absolutely, for their powers are absolute.*

degree angle and extending to infinity. Baseballs never absolutely go out-of-bounds. They are either "fair" or "foul," with the umpire standing by to settle disputes.

One occasionally hears the cry "fire the referee," but one seldom hears the cry "kill the referee." That demand is reserved for umpires, and with good reason. Umpires have to be dealt with absolutely, for their powers are absolute. Referees are called, or appointed, to make judgments. Umpires, by contrast, exist and act in their own right. They are not asked to make judgments. They make them.

The power of the umpire is inherent in word and tradition, a fact that seems unknown to baseball owners, sportswriters, even by umpires, who should know the origin of their power. The name, "umpire," is basically theological. It is derived from the Old French word "nom-père," meaning "one who is with-out père," literally without father or superior. "Refuse not," the medieval divines warned, "the umpeership and judgments of the Holy Ghoste."

Knowledge of the theological and metaphysical roots of the game did not help me hit a good inside curveball from a right-handed pitcher. The game is the same whether played in Enron Field, or Yankee Stadium, or as described by Robert Fitzgerald in his poem "Cobb Would Have Caught It":

> In sunburnt parks where Sundays lie
> Or the wide wastes beyond the cities
> Teams in grey deploy through sunlight.
> Innings and afternoons, Fly lost in sunset.
> Throwing arm gone bad. There's your ball game.
> Cool reek of the field. Reek of companions.

EUGENE McCARTHY served as U.S. Senator (Minnesota) from 1949 to 1971 and in 1968 vied for the Democratic presidential candidacy. That fall he covered the World Series for Life *magazine.*

TIM McCARVER
◆ ◆ ◆

What does baseball mean to me? What has it done *to* me, physically, and *for* me, cerebrally? It gives you an ability to show passion, which, in turn, allows your personality and depth to show. It is central to my life.

I say *to* me, physically. I kid Bob Gibson about my thumb. I caught Bob and other big league pitchers for twenty-one years. It left my left thumb twisted and torn. Fastballs and sliders are the jackhammers of the catcher's life. I can manipulate my thumb in many ways of which I'm not proud. It gets real sore on cold mornings—sort of a USS *Arizona* memorial to the craft.

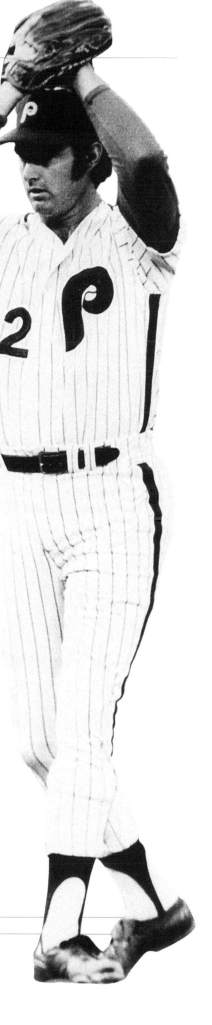

On the other hand, the game is ingrained. I went into baseball a very young and innocent man two weeks out of high school in 1959. I came out of playing much wiser, if sorer, and knowing much more about life through travel—a long trip from Memphis. I often think about what I'd have done if I hadn't played baseball. I surmise I would have gone to college, played football, and been finished athletically by age twenty-five. What then? Perhaps law school, but thanks to baseball, today I can't imagine a life of working nine to five. I have never looked back.

Ironically, football was my first love. Long ago baseball became my final love. What does it mean? First, fascinating people on the field. Where would you find another Bob Gibson? Another Steve Carlton?—vocal *or* silent. Many athletes care deeply about life and society. It irks me that baseball folks are often thought to be one-dimensional. Their concerns extend to culture, music, reading, medicine. Your experience from time spent on the road helps form your philosophy of life. Time spent at the park forms steadfast friends for life.

What does baseball mean? It's my life professionally, and personally. Do I regret spending time away from my family? Sure. But what's new about that? There is something about the game that seduces you, a narcotic. You ask yourself, *When* do I walk away? *How* do I walk away? *Do* I walk away? I haven't for forty-two years. Even those who do almost always come back. The only ones who don't aren't welcomed. For the rest, it's your home.

Why do we stay? Part of it is immediate reaction: You get so used to reaction from crowds that you miss it, need it, seek it in an almost infantile way. It's in the blood, the genes. I find that I have to vacation almost immediately after the season ends because if I don't I spend too much time thinking about the game. What was fun becomes obsession. Travel to other parts of the world energizes and refreshes me. It allows for greater appreciation for a life like no other.

It comes down to a void: Baseball fills it. People ask why? As a broadcaster part of the fun is finding a different way to describe the same thing. But every once in a while you'll see a game or a play that shocks you. "Gosh, I've never seen that." Part of it is how the game reflects you—playing, or announcing. Take Nomar Garciaparra. See him play, and you know the man—the passion, the *joie de vivre*. Or Derek Jeter. He's understated, pulls down the curtain. When he smiles a little, he smiles a lot.

People ask if baseball has changed. Not a lot. I know I'm in the minority.

Steve "Lefty" Carlton won 329 games and four Cy Young Awards. He struck out 4,136, including a then-record 19 in one game.

Players still react as human beings in ways not always admirable. In the 2000 World Series, when Roger Clemens threw a bat at Mike Piazza, I thought of myself in 1962 at Triple-A Atlanta. I was frustrated and slammed the bat down near the dugout. It bounced up and landed in the lap of a thirteen-year-old kid. I was horrified, thinking I could have injured him. The father reacted in a way both kind and wonderful. "We understand. Don't worry about it." Decency like that stays with you forever.

One thing in baseball that has changed is its niche. It is a healthy outlet, more vital than when I was growing up in the 1950s because, unlike then, other outlets today can be demonic. Drugs, violence, offensive lifestyles—we didn't have those then. That makes baseball even more important now. Currently, my business is television, but I keep telling people that ratings only reflect part of baseball's lure. Look at attendance. When Roger Maris hit his 61st homer in 1961, breaking Babe Ruth's record, only 23,000 watched at Yankee Stadium. Today the Yankees regularly draw three million people yearly. Think of the daily buzz about the game. Or what it means to the country. No other sport comes close.

A while back I read Richard Ben Cramer's book *Joe DiMaggio: The Hero's Life*. It talks about how, say, in 1940, second-generation immigrants came to know America through baseball. People would talk about the '27 Yankees, a great team that they'd never seen. Baseball was their ticket to becoming an American. It's the same today. What an experience: A Pakistani cab driver in New York wearing a Yankee cap talking about Paul O'Neill. I look at my left thumb, what the game has done to me. But what it's done for me is so monumentally more.

TIM McCARVER played big league ball from 1959 to 1980—one of seven in our modern day to span four decades. He now broadcasts for Fox Television.

JAMES M. McPHERSON

◆ ◆ ◆

Long before I was a professional historian, I was a baseball player. In high school I played second base and was captain of the team my senior year in a medium-size high school in mid-1950s Minnesota. We drilled endlessly on the double play, and my outstanding memory from those years was a 2–1 victory over our archrival for the conference championship, which ended in a game-saving double play in which I was the pivot man leaping high to

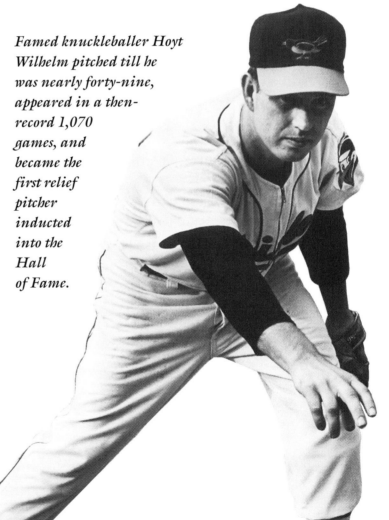

Famed knuckleballer Hoyt Wilhelm pitched till he was nearly forty-nine, appeared in a then-record 1,070 games, and became the first relief pitcher inducted into the Hall of Fame.

avoid the runner trying to take me out.

I played college ball for a year but then became absorbed in academic work to prepare for graduate school and my career. During my graduate-student years at Johns Hopkins in Baltimore, I resumed my interest in baseball—this time as a spectator.

We lived close to the old Memorial Stadium and walked over there many afternoons and evenings to watch the Orioles. It was inexpensive entertainment for impecunious graduate students—$1.50 for an upper-deck seat behind home plate. I saw several famous players in action—Mickey Mantle, Ted Williams, Roger Maris, Brooks Robinson, and others. I saw Maris hit a couple of home runs in his record-breaking year [1961] and saw Williams hit one of his last homers before retirement. My favorite memories, though, are of watching ancient Hoyt Wilhelm come in as a late-inning reliever and befuddle hitters—and sometimes his own catcher—with his own incomparable knuckleball.

Because the Orioles inevitably trailed the Yankees in those years [1959–62], I acquired an anti-Yankee bias that has never left me. When the Yankees played the Pirates in the memorable 1960 World Series, I had a bet with a graduate-student friend (who sometimes annoyed me with his professions of superior baseball wisdom) that the Pirates would win. The loser of the bet had to write twenty times on a classroom blackboard: "I am a baseball ignoramus." When the Yankees won the sixth game, 12 0, my phone rang insistently but I refused to answer because I knew it was my friend calling me to gloat.

I had the last laugh, however, when Bill Mazeroski hit his famous homer. It was the most satisfactory World Series I ever experienced.

JAMES M. McPHERSON, America's foremost Civil War historian, won a Pulitzer Prize in 1988 for Battle Cry of Freedom: The Civil War Era.

ROBERT MERRILL

◆ ◆ ◆

I'm seventy-five years old. What a gift! Baseball makes me feel like a child! I played baseball as a kid in Brooklyn with a fellow named Tommy Holmes for a church team. We both got between $5 and $10 a game and I could see he had that big league swing. Me? I didn't dream of singing thirty-two years for the Metropolitan Opera. I wanted to be a pitcher. The problem is I had a forty-mile-per-hour fastball. Holmes'd kid me. "You're lucky you got a voice."

Years later I was touring Ohio in the spring. I sang *The Barber of Seville* in this huge auditorium. Afterward we had a reception and I hear this guy say, "Hey, Merrill, you've got a hell of a voice, but I didn't understand a word." I turned around—it was George Steinbrenner. He said, "I just bought the Yanks, and I want you to sing the National Anthem." That's how it began—my singing for the Yankees—actually, my return to the game.

As a kid I threw the out-curve, and in-curve, and drop—a slider. My hero was the Yanks' Red Ruffing. He had this great windup, would pick his left leg up, and keep it hard in the air. I said, "I'm going to pitch like him." So I did one day in Coney Island, picked up that leg, and fell right on my ass. It's a good thing Joe DiMaggio didn't know that. He became a very good friend. One year I was singing in his hometown, San Francisco. I went to his family's restaurant on the water. His relatives started talking about him and soon he arrived. I asked for his autograph. He said, "Give me yours first." Talk about a thrill.

Thurman Munson. "Baseball just reminded me of a stallion running free,"
said the 1969–79 Yankee catcher. "There was a freedom to the game."

Joe didn't open up with many people, but he did when we sat in Steinbrenner's box. He'd talk about the good old days. One day we got to reminiscing. I'd left the Met by then, and he the Yankees. I said, "Why'd you leave?" He said, "Well, I'll tell you. They offered me $100,000, and I was tempted 'cause I liked the money. But some of those young pitchers, I didn't see the ball as well. I just didn't enjoy putting on a uniform anymore." He paused, then said, "Why'd you leave the Met?" I said, "I just didn't enjoy putting on my costume anymore." People yelled, "Bravo," but I wasn't happy. It's that pride you have. We didn't want people saying, "Jeez, I remember him when."

Baseball is such a people sport. Once I grabbed Joe's arm as I was walking toward the mound to sing. "C'mon," I said, "you can sing the Anthem in Italian." Another Italian was another good friend, Billy Martin. Once Steinbrenner said to me before an Old-Timers Game, "Get your ass down there and manage the team." They gave me Thurman Munson's pants, but I didn't have a jersey. Martin was managing the Yanks, and he'd worn number 1 as a player. As a gag someone gave him the uniform 1 1/2. Billy put it in his office. So he yells, "Hey, Merrill, put this on." He never got it back. I hope the Yankees retire it someday!

Seriously, every time I go to Yankee Stadium I go to Monument Valley, where real numbers are retired. Forget the Met—this is a real thrill! That baseball feeling never leaves you. I still remember the first World Series game I sang at in the 1970s. I got out there, not scared, but butterflies, and just stood there and gazed around. This is what I wanted to do, where I was born to sing. That year the Yankees won the Series, and in the off season I'm sitting with DiMaggio and George. "Okay," Steinbrenner told an aide, "come on in." They brought in Series rings for Joe and me. Joe was like a kid. He just kept looking at it.

The Yankee catcher was Thurman Munson. I never knew what he was thinking. One Series game I go out to sing and he says, "Don't blow the words." Next night I go past him by the plate. "Don't blow the game," I told him, "ya bum, ya." I'll never forget the night he died flying his plane [1979]. Steinbrenner told me, "That god-damned plane, I offered to buy it for him." We had a service for him at St. Patrick's Cathedral, then a night at the Stadium. I was there with [Terence] Cardinal Cooke and sang "The Lord's Prayer" and "Ave Maria." The players were wiping their eyes. I have a picture of that in my living room.

People? For years baseball wanted me to sing at induction day at Cooperstown. I said, "Not till Phil Rizzuto gets in." Finally, he makes it and I'm going to sing. Phil was so anxious. The night before we're both at the Otesaga Hotel and I get a call from his daughter. "Mr. Merrill, Phil's so nervous, he's losing his voice." I say, "Meet me downstairs." I gave her some cough drops. We drive to the induction and Phil's sweating. Sure enough, I sing the Anthem, Phil gets up, and he's wonderful. Later he says, "Where do I get those drops?"

Phil Rizzuto was inducted into the Hall of Fame in 1994.

A final Yankee, of course, was Mantle, interesting guy, didn't say much. One day he came up and said, sheepishly, "Mr. Merrill." I say, "What's this Merrill stuff? It's Bob." He says, "My wife loves music. And one of my sons loves opera. Would you send him one of your records?" I sent him a recording of arias I'd done at the Metropolitan. Several weeks later he said, "My son loves that." You don't forget a moment like that.

Memories? I was once asked to throw out the first ball. I got thirty feet from the plate and one-hopped it. The Met didn't make me as nervous. I was on the committee that brought the Cracker Jack Classic back to Washington. That first year of '82 I'm coaching third base and Luke Appling hits a liner between the outfielders. I gave him the slide sign, and he belly-flops into the base. Safe! Then it hits me. He's seventy-five years old! Later Luke hit a home run. Talk about the noise! I still have autographed baseballs of every old-timer that played in that game. No review from the *New York Times* ever meant as much.

ROBERT MERRILL has sung from the greatest opera houses to Broadway, records, and television. In 1993, he received the National Medal of the Arts.

RAY MEYER

◆ ◆ ◆

I've always loved baseball. As a youngster I played ten times as much baseball as I did basketball. I played in Wrigley Field and in Comiskey Park. I remember vividly playing for the State Championship at the Cubs' park. Phil Cavarretta pitched against us. I played second base for the A.B.C. (American Boys Commonwealth). We won, 7–2. During the game, Mr. Landis, the Commissioner of Baseball, came into our dugout and I stood up and gave him my seat for pictures. I was the only player left out of the photo. I couldn't find my socks that day and Mr. Landis asked why I wasn't wearing any. I told him I was playing Notre Dame style— that's how they dressed then. At that time I never believed I would enroll there.

At our awards banquet, Babe Ruth and Lou Gehrig stopped by and gave out the awards. What a thrill that was!

When I was in seventh grade, the church I attended built a little gym for basketball. It was there that I started to play the game. When summer rolled around I went back to baseball. I went to St. Patrick's

High School and they didn't have a baseball team. Consequently, I devoted myself to basketball. It gave me an opportunity to receive a scholarship to Notre Dame. There I played freshman baseball and fully intended to play every year. In my sophomore year I injured my knee and had surgery. I never played baseball again. It was then that I turned from player to fan. I never lost interest.

After graduation I became a basketball coach, and had the opportunity to meet some of the greatest players and managers. We became friends and I cherish their friendships. While coaching the College All-Stars against the Harlem Globetrotters we played in Arizona while some major leaguers were in spring training. Ted Williams was there and I wanted to see him bat. I drove over to the ballpark and I brought a movie camera with me. I took pictures of Williams batting and I marveled at his swing. It was beautiful!

One year with the All-Stars we were playing the Trotters in the Boston Garden. I heard someone calling, "Coach, coach." It was Moose Skowron in the stands

Kenesaw Mountain Landis, baseball's first commissioner (1920–44). **Current Biography** *called him "the only successful dictator in United States history."*

and I motioned for him to come down to the bench. He did and brought Yogi Berra with him.

Bill Veeck was a great friend. I spent many hours with him and loved him. One night I was attending a banquet with him right after DePaul lost the first game of the season by about 18 points to UCLA. Bill was sympathetic and he told me it looks like I am going to have a long year. I told him we were going to have a good year. It was the first time we could match up to them man-for-man. That year we went to the Final Four! After we lost to Indiana State I met Bill at another banquet. He told me he won a lot of money on our ball club. I questioned him and he remarked, "You told me you were going to be good."

I threw out the first pitch for the Sox and Cubs. I sang "Take Me Out to the Ball Game" during the seventh-inning stretch of a Cubs game. It was the same day Sammy Sosa hit his 60th home run in 1998. I have so many fond memories.

I attend the ballpark whenever I am able and I watch on TV. The World Series is always special. I watched the longest game in World Series history in 2000— four hours and fifty-one minutes—and enjoyed every minute of it. Baseball affords me a great amount of enjoyment. I love baseball and I always will.

RAY MEYER coached DePaul University's basketball team from 1942 to 1984. He had thirty-seven winning years, a 1945 NIT title, two Final Four berths, and a 724-354 record.

ROBERT H. MICHEL

◆ ◆ ◆

Baseball is a game of moments and memory. I can still remember as a young boy in Peoria painting screens out in the yard listening to Bob Elson's description of the Cubs–Pirates game in which Gabby Hartnett hit that twilight home run to win that very critical game in the last of the ninth. [September 28, 1938: The Cubs won the pennant over Pittsburgh by two games.] Oh, those Cubs. The last time they played in the World Series ['45], against Detroit, I was still overseas at the conclusion of World War II, sweating out another boat trip to America. There was a five-hour time lag, so we listened to those games via the Armed Forces Radio well into the early hours of the next morning. Unfortunately, as the record shows, the Cubs lost the Series and we have been losing all too many games and series since then. Doesn't matter. I'll be

"People have told me they didn't know the ball was in the bleachers," Gabby Hartnett said of 1938's "homer in the gloaming." "Maybe I was the only one who did."

a die-hard Cub fan for the rest of my life. My father wouldn't have understood—but my mother would.

Many times I was asked during my lengthy time in politics for my most embarrassing moment. I always referred to my being a softball pitcher for White Grade School in Peoria. One afternoon my father came by the ballpark where we were playing and told me I had to go work in the garden. Neither the coach nor my team-mates understood why a father would take his star pitching son from a crucial game just to work in the garden. Actually, they were Depression days—and my father, being a French immigrant, didn't grasp what baseball meant to his son.

My mother, though, was a different story. She was an ardent Cub fan, listening to the radio broadcasts while quilting in her sewing room. When I returned home from school she would give me the results of the game. She would have liked me to pitch that day. What's more, she'd like that I still love baseball.

ROBERT H. MICHEL served as a U.S. Congressman from Illinois from 1956 to 1999 and as Minority Leader from 1981 to 1995. He also helped found the Emil Verban Society of Chicago Cubs fans.

JON MILLER

◆ ◆ ◆

I grew up in Half Moon Bay, near San Francisco, and was a Giants fan. In 2001, I got to broadcast Barry Bonds's monumental season. It took me back to the first year I really followed the game—1961. Like most kids, I remember the initiation well. I read baseball, listening to games on the radio with Russ Hodges, played the board game Strat-O-Matic. All the while I kept bugging my father to attend a game at Candlestick Park. Finally, he relented. In April of 1962,

It's human nature to think players always hustled when we were young. They haven't changed: We have.

he and my godfather, Keith Allen, took me to my, and their, first big league game. It had quite an effect.

Nineteen sixty-two was some season. The Yankees won another pennant. The Dodgers lost Sandy Koufax in mid-season and still won 102 regular-season games. Don Drysdale went 25-9. Maury Wills stole 104 bases. My Giants had great names—Willie Mays, Orlando Cepeda, Willie McCovey, Felipe Alou—an exciting team, hit homers, drew big crowds. Sometimes I wonder if I'd so love the game if I'd grown up in a bad market, boring team, anonymous players. Thankfully, I lucked out. Sixty-two was my rite of passage—my coming of age as a baseball fan.

Most kids never forget their first game. We're younger, more impressionable, things seem more vivid. I was no different. That April game the Giants had *19* runs on *12* hits and no errors. The Dodgers got *8* runs on *15* hits and *3* errors. That's some line score. Dodger pitchers walked 10. Billy O'Dell threw a 15-hit complete game. Mays, Alou, and Jim Davenport homered. The attendance was 32,189—a big crowd on an early-season night. Other than that I don't remember a thing. Just kidding.

Everyone wanted to see the Dodgers—so we got into a big traffic jam on the Bay Shore Freeway. We hadn't bought tickets, so I stood in line listening to the first inning on radio. The Giants loaded the bases against Stan Williams, and didn't score. Finally, we got in our seats in the second inning. From then it's like stop-action—a game in frames. It's funny what sticks with you four decades later.

First of all, it was cold. We sat in the upper deck, first base side, section 19, reserved seats, and at one point I picked up the binoculars and had no feeling in my hands. Even at that point I had priorities. I looked out at Mays. Then came the exciting part. I looked over at the Giants' broadcast booth and saw Russ Hodges, whom I was listening to on a transistor radio. Soon,

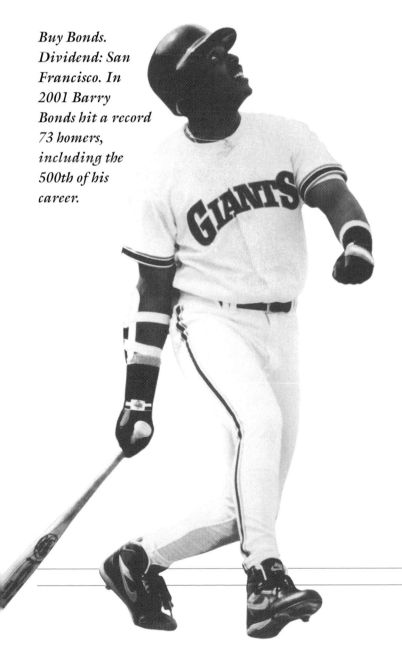

Buy Bonds. Dividend: San Francisco. In 2001 Barry Bonds hit a record 73 homers, including the 500th of his career.

I was looking at him say what was I hearing.

I remember being thrilled that I could follow other games by looking at my scorebook and then the scoreboard, where they listed scores and pitchers. I remember Felipe Alou, who always hustled, hit a sure double play ball. He stopped running, then sped up when Junior Gilliam threw wildly to first. My dad said, "Look at that, he didn't run." I still think of that when people say today's players aren't as old-school as guys, say, four decades ago. It's human nature to think players always hustled when we were young. They haven't changed: We have.

My first game is when my dad taught me to keep score. Pretty soon I was keeping score at home. That night my scorebook was pretty full: The Giants led, 19–3, going into the ninth, at which point O'Dell started to get lit up. Alvin Dark, their manager, got Jim Duffalo up in the bullpen, whereupon O'Dell finished. I know this because a guy doing research on microfilm at San Francisco's public archives heard me talk about the game—and sent me the game account by writer Bob Stevens.

After the game Dark was asked if he minded having to rouse the bullpen. He said, "No, Billy was just trying to throw strikes. I knew he wasn't tired because he had *only* thrown *150* pitches." Only 150 pitches! Actually, Stevens wrote the real number—165. That's what starters were expected to do before the rise of relievers. Before the game the Giants had had a contest and asked fans to predict the final score, who'd be the winning and losing pitchers, and whether anyone would pitch a complete game. The closest anyone came was predicting O'Dell's complete game and a 7–5 Giants win. In baseball, you never know.

Sixty-two was proof of that. The Giants were four games out with seven left. In the fall, they'd play at day—that cold again—and the Dodgers'd play at night. That whole last week I'd listen to Russ and Lon Simmons do their game, then re-create the Dodger game at night. I even found that I could get KFI out of Los Angeles and hear Vin Scully. What a climax: Giants keep winning, Dodgers keep losing, Russ and Vinnie doing the same game at night!

That final day the Dodgers led by one, but lost to St. Louis, 2–1, on Gene Oliver's home run. Mays's 47th homer beat Houston, 1–0. The Giants game ended first, and the crowd at Candlestick sat there listening to Russ's re-creation from Los Angeles. I was listening by radio, and on the final out—a pop to the Cardinals' Julian Javier—you thought Candlestick would fall down.

The Giants, of course, won the playoff and then lost the Series to the Yankees. But I remember a postscript from the final regular day. The 49ers were playing football that afternoon at Kezar Stadium, where thousands were listening to the Giants game by radio. The players would break the huddle, and the crowd would go nuts. The 49ers wondered what was going on. In baseball, it's always something—one reason I love it. Especially since that first incredible game.

JON MILLER has broadcast for Oakland, Texas, Boston, Baltimore, and since 1997 San Francisco. He also announces baseball on ESPN.

BILLY MILLS

◆ ◆ ◆

As an eleven-year-old boy, I tried out for the Little League team on the Pine Ridge Indian Reservation. After a few weeks of practice, we were issued our uniforms. When the coach gave me mine, I enthusiastically placed the pants at my waist to see if they fit. My eyes caught a glimpse of the outside of the left pant leg. It was covered with rust from the belt loop all the way down to the bottom.

No matter how hard I tried to get the coach to give me another uniform, it appeared I was destined for the rust-covered pants. Unwilling to accept this destiny, I went to my dad for advice.

My mother died when I was seven. By this time, Dad had become my mother and father as well as my friend and mentor. I knew he would console me. I watched with joy as Dad squeezed lemon juice all over the rust stain and began to rinse it with water. Magically, he soon produced the most beautiful baseball uniform I had ever seen.

My talent for baseball never did match my desire to play the game or the professional look of my uniform. It didn't help that my glove never, ever allowed the ball to enter. The fact I was the worst player on the team became apparent not only to me, but to the coaching staff and other players. Just the same, we had a wonderful experience and we all enjoyed the companionship.

I remember one thing Dad told me: "You will find your desire in sports, drama, music, dance, the arts, or

Ace and/or fashion plate: A Little Leaguer begins his throw.

academics. I am glad you are playing baseball, son."

Just before the next season, my father died from a stroke. A few days after the funeral, my cousin Butch and I were sitting on the porch steps at my home listening to the sounds of two meadowlarks calling one another. I sensed Butch was trying to ease my pain from the loss of my father. He said, with compassion, "Although you can't play baseball very well, I bet you do something famous in sports."

Shocked, but sensing his sincerity, I asked, "Why do you say that?"

He responded, "All the great athletes I've read about had to overcome hardships. They were either poor or orphaned and people made fun of them. All three of these things have happened to you, Billy."

As those words echoed through my mind, I thought about what my father had told me about finding your desire. This sparked my exit from baseball, and distance running became my passion. My enjoyment of baseball today is watching my grandson Alex play Little League.

BILLY MILLS's 10,000 meter victory defined the 1964 Tokyo Olympics. He is the only American ever to win that event.

In 1998 Sammy Sosa hit 66 homers—and raised money for hurricane victims in the Dominican Republic. Its president gave him the nation's highest medal.

OMAR MINAYA

◆ ◆ ◆

What does baseball mean to me? Things that start when you're young and end when you're old. When you come here from another country, baseball combines a unique place in the fabric of society with freedom and hope— a way of showing expression, what you are, what you do. You grow older—and in my case, enter baseball as a livelihood. Then baseball becomes a job and means the best and worst in people: the best, kindness and generosity; the worst, baseball's ugly history of racism. There is no doubt that baseball is more a reflection of America than any other sport, for better or ill. You see that inside the game, and never forget.

The fan, of course, doesn't see that conflict. What he sees are players of every size and shape. So he connects, develops an affinity. What baseball means to him is romance—a feeling that baseball is life. For players it's a big *part* of life. Then we get older and a strange thing happens. We refind that romance of our youth— baseball as hope, innocence, a transcendent experience. Think of the symmetry: freedom as a kid, hard knocks later, still later a belief that the game is good. No other sport goes full circle. That's what baseball means to me.

OMAR MINAYA, born in the Dominican Republic, played in the minor leagues and Italy. He is Senior Assistant General Manager and International Scouting Director of the New York Mets.

GEORGE J. MITCHELL

◆ ◆ ◆

During the baseball season, the first thing I do in the morning is to check the box score of the previous day's Red Sox game. Then I check out the other box scores, and the standings. On those rare days when the Red Sox are in first place, I know it's going to be a good day all around.

When I was growing up in Maine, I knew the batting average and power stats of every Sox starter long before I knew the names of my state's senators. So with me, and with all of my family, rooting for the Sox is a lifelong tradition.

One of the toughest things about returning to chair the peace negotiations in Northern Ireland one year was that I missed the playoffs. That was really painful at the time. But after the Sox were beaten by the Yankees, I was glad to have been in Ireland. It would have been more painful to watch.

My hope is that my life lasts long enough to see the Red Sox win a World Series. But I'm sixty-seven and haunted by the thought that Pedro Martinez pitches only once every five days. However, as I write this the Sox are in first place. The starting pitching is

*Fenway Park opened on April 20, 1912—
the same month that the **Titanic** sank. Baseball's
oldest park features a 37-foot-high wall, hand-operated
scoreboard, sparse foul turf, and long-suffering fans.*

holding up well. And the bullpen is showing signs
of returning to last year's form—miracle of miracles—
as among the best in the league.

Am I dreaming? Am I once more kidding
myself? No. I think this is it. This is the year they
go all the way.

I know I've said the same thing each spring for
sixty years. But isn't baseball, and life, about hope?

*GEORGE J. MITCHELL served as U.S. Senator (Maine)
from 1980 to 1995. Later, chairing peace negotiations in
Northern Ireland, he helped fashion a historic accord.*

**As a child, said Bart Giamatti, "I knew that
Fenway...was on the level of Mount Olympus, the
Pyramid at Giza...the czar's winter palace, and
the Louvre—except, of course, that it was better."**

REG MURPHY

◆ ◆ ◆

Hank Aaron walked to the plate and Atlanta held its breath. April 8, 1974. He had reached the magic number: 714. Now he needed one more home run to become the all-time home run leader. Baseball fans chant, pound the floor, scream at umpires and opposing pitchers. They love their heroes and despise the visitors, making their alliances known to everyone. But now the great circle of humans in the oddly shaped Atlanta Stadium fell as silent as worshippers at a shrine. Aaron swung and bat met ball. In that supercharged atmosphere, the collision sounded like an axe hitting hardwood. The crowd roared because it knew...Aaron had the record. Tommy Nobis, the burly and suddenly exuberant Atlanta Falcons linebacker, was standing immediately behind me. He brought both hands down on my collar-

bone with such joyful enthusiasm that I believed it shattered. The pain lasted as Aaron jogged toward home, but it was as nothing compared to the wave of joy that infected a stadium crowd gone suddenly wild. We could breathe again.

REG MURPHY published or edited the Atlanta Constitution, San Francisco Examiner, *and* Baltimore Sun. *In 1996, he was named President of the National Geographic Society.*

April 8, 1974: Hank Aaron hits number 715 to pass Babe Ruth. He retired with a record 755.

A reminder that the term "fan" stems from "fanatic": A man reproaches Leo Durocher near third base at the Polo Grounds.

TY MURRAY

◆ ◆ ◆

I remember being the only seven-year-old in Little League who truly chewed real tobacco. I also remember all the neighborhood kids meeting at my house to play. We even had a home plate umpire who would wear a construction hat we got from a friend's dad. He wired on some wire mesh for a face mask and then stood behind a piece of plywood to call balls and strikes. We were all best of friends and we played every week, but I never remember when it didn't end in a fistfight over the rules or a call that we couldn't agree on. I'm glad we have all learned how to deal with controversy better over the years.

TY MURRAY began riding calves at age two. Ultimately, he became six-time professional Rodeo Cowboy Association World Champion All-Around Cowboy.

PHIL MUSHNICK

◆ ◆ ◆

Whew! That was a close call. Twice in recent years the St. Louis Cardinals have almost made the World Series against my Yankees. In 1996 and 2000 the Braves and Mets, respectively, beat them in the League Championship Series. Until then, for a few days it looked as if I'd have to relive the fall of 1964, the last time the Cards played the Yankees in the Series. Or, as Lisa Simpson said, "Why do I get the feeling that someday I'll be describing this to a psychiatrist?"

October, 1964. It was the best of times, it was the worst of times.

I was twelve. Mel Stottlemyre had come up in midseason to go 9-3, the Yanks were where they belonged, and I hadn't yet heard of the SATs.

And I'll always remember the Cards–Yanks Series as the one I don't remember.

There was a problem in 1964. A big problem. My bar mitzvah was eight months away and the only thing I knew of Hebrew was that it hurt my throat. Hebrew School was cutting into my baseball time and my parents had long ago rejected my idea to renounce my Judaism until I turned fourteen.

I was several months into daily, after-school Hebrew classes, and already the other boys in my class could chant a blue streak while I faked it, mumbling things such as, "No batter, no batter."

Some of these kids were good. One kid was named Tuvey Lipson. I always thought that his first name was Tuvey, until I found out that it was David. Tuvey was his Hebrew name. How could I compete with a kid who went by his Hebrew name?

But that's nothing. There was a kid in the class named Charlie Polotti. He was half Italian, half Jewish. He was a lot better at Hebrew, too. I couldn't even compete in Hebrew School with a kid named Polotti!

Yankee Stadium, July 21, 1965: Forget the Designated Hitter. Pitcher Mel Stottlemyre completes an inside-the-park grand slam.

Anyway, Game 1 was in St. Louis on a Wednesday afternoon. As the opening neared, I was forced to choose between my religion and my God—baseball.

Besides, aren't the very first words in the Book of Genesis about baseball? "In the big inning..." And wasn't the Yankees' star center fielder named Mickey Mandel?

But the choice was not mine. I was going to Hebrew School, by parental decree. My father, a pragmatic son of the Depression, was a man of few words, blazing blue eyes, and a firm hand that would, from time to time, make me wish I hadn't insisted on getting in the last word.

"You'll never make a living from sports," was his standard response to spending all my time in pursuit of sports. Of course, he was right.

The trip from Junior High School 27 to Hebrew School was no joy ride. Two city buses—don't lose that transfer slip—then a long walk to Congregation Aguduth Achim Anshe Chesed, which, roughly translated, means "No Pepper Games."

But the walk *did* bring me past Tommy Curatore's Soda Shop. Ahhh, Tommy's! Home of the nickel fountain soda. Flavors in every color of the rainbow. Seltzer, plus two steady pushes on the syrup pump. Stir, don't shake. Heaven.

Game 1, October 7, 1964. At approximately 3:40 P.M. en route to Hebrew School, I was drawn to Tommy's, not for a soda, but for the TV with the rabbit ears antenna that would sit atop a kitchen chair near the back of the long, narrow shop.

I sat at the fountain, milking my nickel soda, swiveling to watch the game; watching the Yanks blow a 4–2 lead. As Whitey Ford was being replaced in the

sixth by Al Downing, it was time to go to Hebrew School. Better late than never.

I took my seat in Hebrew class, where Tuvey Lipson and Charlie Polotti already were going to town. The Yanks and Cards would have to finish the game without me. "No batter, no batter."

Things went downhill from there. My beloved Yanks lost the opener, then lost the series in seven games—and I only saw two of them. The memory void, so help me, still lingers and still bothers me.

Then began a twelve-year malaise for the Yanks, living in what used to be known as "the second division." In May, by the time my bar mitzvah rolled around, the Bombers were en route to a sixth-place finish.

I didn't fare any better. On May 15, 1965, the

Stottlemyre won 20 games three times and retired in 1974 with a 2.97 ERA.

Yanks beat the Orioles, but I butchered my bar mitzvah. First time anyone can recall a *haftorah* chanted in what sounded like pig latin.

At the ceremony's conclusion, as is the custom, the congregation presented me with my very own prayer book. Usually, a warm, personal inscription is added to the inside cover; something about the wonderful job the bar mitzvah boy did and how proud the synagogue is to have the young man as one of its members—hopefully for many years to come.

The inscription in mine was very short, and written in Hebrew. Translated, I think it means, "And don't come back."

That's what I remember about the last time the Cardinals played the Yankees in the World Series. Seems like only yesterday. Or a million years ago. Or somewhere in between. The '96 Braves and 2000 Mets put those tortured memories on hold. But I'll never forget the '64 Series, mostly for what I don't remember.

PHIL MUSHNICK is the TV Guide *sports critic. He also writes a regular column for the* New York Post.

Briggs Stadium, 1958: Boston's Sammy White tries to nab Billy Martin's pop near the screen.

LEROY NEIMAN

◆ ◆ ◆

It's the little gestures in baseball that count and serve to explain in a special way "What baseball means to me"—like courtesy.

Home plate action often permits players to extend courtesies that few sports provide, including baseball. Baseball players vary, of course. Let's cite a batter–pitcher relationship around home plate, for example.

A batter hits a long foul fly ball to the outfield and takes off for first base in case it turns fair. Meanwhile, some catchers will pick up the discarded bat and then present it to the batter upon his return to the plate.

Some don't.

Some batters will hit a towering pop foul back of home plate and the catcher throws off his mask and goes for the ball only to have it drop onto the screen. Meanwhile, the batter has picked up the mask and will then hand it to the catcher as he returns to his position behind the plate.

Others don't.

Like baseball, like life.

LEROY NEIMAN has been chosen Outstanding Sports Artist in America by the Amateur Athletic Union and given the Olympic Artist of the Century Award.

Murray Kempton, the late newspaper sage, was a baseball fan who once said something about politics that applies to baseball. "I don't think of myself as a Democrat as much as I am a fan of Adlai Stevenson," he said. For most of my life, I have been first a fan of Ted Williams, then a fan of baseball.

Teddy Ball Game was not likely madly for Adlai, but his politics remain irrelevant. In the Fenway Park press box in 1977, Roger Angell advised two nonsportswriters, Mike Barnicle and me, not to inquire about the political or social beliefs of ballplayers. "They are what they do," he said.

But Ted Williams has always defied categorization. My boyhood admiration of the graceful swing of number 9 was not much upset by revelations that he cussed and fussed. I once witnessed his gesture to grandstand boo-birds that the Boston papers tactfully called "a French salute."

As an adult, I met him at a charity event. He growled, "Ah, a knight of the keyboard!" inquired about Cliff Keane, a needling *Globe* sportswriter he respected, and cheerfully told stories about Willie Tasby and others.

A hero in World War II and in the Korean War, Williams was also heroic on July 25, 1966, the day he entered the Hall of Fame. He said, "I hope that someday the names of Satchel Paige and Josh Gibson in some way can be added as a symbol of the great Negro players that are not here only because they were not given a chance."

This was a political statement by any standard, proving that stereotyping Ted Williams is as hard as striking him out. That day, he also praised Willie Mays, who had just surpassed Ted's career home run total.

The new Hall of Famer also offered an American credo that not only

In 1965 Satchel Paige, 59, blanked Boston for three innings. "Don't look back," he said. "Something might be gaining on you."

confirmed my youthful hero worship, but explained much more. Baseball gave him, Ted Williams said at Cooperstown, the chance "not just to be as good as someone else, but to be better than someone else. This is the nature of man and the name of the game."

MARTIN F. NOLAN, a Boston Globe *reporter, Washington Bureau Chief, Editorial Page Editor, and now Associate Editor, has been a Pulitzer Prize finalist for editorial writing and commentary.*

Josh Gibson of the Homestead Grays and Pittsburgh Crawfords was called the Black Babe Ruth.

DAN PASTORINI

◆ ◆ ◆

When I was growing up, Willie Mays was my hero. My dad called me "Willie" to his dying day. I couldn't get enough of the game—still can't. Baseball players are unique in their personalities. They're loosey-goosey, they razz you, carefree, nothing bothers them. Even today I regret not playing it after I was drafted by the Mets in 1967. I wonder what might have happened. As it is, it introduced me to a larger world.

As a kid in Southern California I had a good arm, so I pitched in Little League. But I never liked it that much. I've always been a hitting kind of guy. Give me the bigger bats and scores: Guess I'm like most fans. That's why I was glad when I got shifted to shortstop in high school. Lots of action, you're in on plays. Later I moved to center field, then right, which I didn't like: too boring. But as I said: Baseball led to a wider stage. Alaska, summer of my freshman year, 1968.

Talk about baseball heaven. I played on the Alaska Goldpanners against teams like Omaha and Yakima, Washington. We toured Japan for two weeks. Man, I didn't know such a place existed. If it hadn't been for my baseball scholarship, I wouldn't have gone to college (Santa Clara University), which means I wouldn't have played football and been drafted by the pros. Ironically, baseball made everything else possible. But it's not what I remember. In baseball you remember the guys, and plays.

How's this for our Alaska team? Bob Gallagher, my teammate, later went to the majors. So did Bob Boone, Jim Barr, and Dave Kingman—teammates all. We never lost a series, and I had the best summer of my life hitting— .311. Then I came home and got introduced to the slider. Mr. Slider ended my career. I remember turning to the umpire and saying, "Is that legal?" What shouldn't have been was Kingman. Talk about wild: One day he

North Toward Alaska: Game not called on account of snow.

pitched batting practice and threw a ball behind my head. I walked away shaking. Another time he hit a ball 'bout 600 feet. A missile launcher didn't go that far.

Football's like war. Baseball's more gentle. You remember the exceptions. One day Santa Clara is playing USC. They stick me in right field. I'm bored to death. A big All-America named Bill Seinsoth's at second base when a single is hit toward me. Seinsoth's slow, gets about two steps past third by the time I throw home, and the catcher nabs him. Next thing I know a fight breaks out, guys brawling right and left, I'm near the bottom of the pile, and Rod Dedeaux, USC's famous coach, is taking a shot at me. That I could understand. What I never got is why the 1967

Mets wanted to give me so much money to sign.

I got drafted real low, something like 656th, because they knew I wanted to play football. Then the Mets started waving money on the off chance I'd sign: They'd seen my arm and wanted to make me a pitcher. There's that problem again: I wanted to *hit!* So I play football, *get* hit by mad-dog linebackers, and here I am. Still wondering if I should have gone the other way about three decades ago.

DAN PASTORINI was an NFL quarterback for twelve years. Retiring in 1983, he turned to drag racing, becoming the third man to break the 270-mile-per-hour barrier in a top fuel dragster.

ROBERT PIERPOINT

◆ ◆ ◆

Like most kids growing up in Southern California, I played baseball in grammar school. But no one ever taught me the finer points of the game, or even of the basics. So the first time I played in junior high school I made some stupid errors. The razzing I got was so

Willie Mays's "Say Hey" became his moniker.

traumatic that I quickly gave up the game and turned to tennis.

During the ten years I served abroad as a foreign correspondent for CBS I was totally out of touch with American sports. Soccer was the big thing. But when I ended up in Washington covering the White House, baseball once again came into my view. I went to a couple of games of the old Washington Senators. Then they disappeared toward Texas and I turned back to tennis. I even played a few matches on the White House courts, and thought baseball was out of my life forever.

But with our kids grown and gone, I retired and we moved back to California. We settled in the San Francisco area just in time to catch the renaissance of the Giants. It had been a long dry spell for them since the winning ways of Willie Mays and his teammates. But under Dusty Baker they became a rejuvenated team, rekindling our interest in baseball.

With the time to watch and a good team to follow, we became Giant fans, and began to learn the wonderful nuances of baseball. Dusty won the National League's Manager of the Year award three times. He and his team won our hearts back to the great American game of baseball! P.S. I still play tennis.

ROBERT PIERPOINT served as CBS TV's White House and diplomatic correspondent from 1957 to 1979. He then became a regular contributor to Sunday Morning with Charles Kuralt.

MADELYN PILKINGTON

◆ ◆ ◆

It's said that you love baseball more as you get older. I'm writing on behalf of millions of Americans who believe this to be true—and I should know. I turned 100 years old last year.

I'm like many people who are past retirement: I plan each day around baseball games on television. We didn't have TV when I started following baseball in the 1940s. The game hooked me because of its hitting and action. No team better showed that than my favorite team, the Yankees—McCarthy through Torre, DiMaggio to Bernie Williams. I used to work in New York, and would go to Yankee Stadium with friends from the office. Not much has changed. Baseball was a highlight of *that* day, too.

The Yankees have won more World Series than any team. But I remember one Series they lost. Our family was living in Pittsburgh in 1960 when the Pirates won on Bill Mazeroski's famous homer. The city went crazy—confetti, dancing, a torch-light parade, people eighty acting eight! Baseball does that to you—makes you feel young. Unless you were a Yankee fan: Maz made me feel old!

Today I live in Charlotte, and follow the Braves on WTBS. They're the South's team, and I like their manager, Bobby Cox. He reminds me of great Yankee managers like Casey Stengel and Yogi Berra. The only difference is that Bobby speaks English. I especially like interleague play since now I can see my two favorite teams play each other in the regular season.

Looking back, baseball is like a ribbon running through the years. So much has changed. This wonderful game has not. It's an old friend that never lets you down. I'd like to write more, but can't. The Braves are on in a couple minutes.

MADELYN PILKINGTON hopes for another Braves–Yankees World Series—with a different end than 1996 and '99.

Braves manager Bobby Cox played for the 1968–69 Yankees. In the 1996 and 1999 World Series, he faced New York manager Joe Torre, who once played for Atlanta.

DAVID PLAUT

◆ ◆ ◆

I make my living producing features and videos for NFL Films. Pro football is a terrific sport by the Nielsen TV ratings and all other polling data. But before I ever felt the pull of the pigskin, I was a baseball fan—and it's hard to forget your affection for a first love.

Geography played a critical role. I was born and raised in Cincinnati—a baseball town of the highest pedigree. This was B.B. (before the Bengals)—or much of any other big-time sports except for a few NCAA basketball titles from the Cincinnati Bearcats. So all year 'round— even in winter's icy grip—the talk was about the Reds.

Plus my dad worked for WSAI, the team's flagship radio station. He would constantly bring home Reds souvenirs and old scorecards for his toddler's toy box. Yes, the same station that helped fans stuff the ballot box in the 1957 All-Star Game voting process—the infamous scandal where seven—count 'em—*seven* Reds made the National League starting lineup (and for the record those "magnificent seven" were catcher Ed Bailey, infielders Johnny Temple, Roy McMillan, and Don Hoak, and outfielders Gus Bell, Frank Robinson, and Wally Post).

It was a crime so heinous that Major League Baseball yanked Bell and Post from the batting order, then shut down all fan voting participation for more than a decade. My pop wasn't—and still isn't—ashamed of any of it. In fact, he looks back upon his employer's polling fraud with devilish pride.

Frank Robinson was the first man to become MVP in each league and the first black to manage a major league team.

In 1957, I was a little too young to appreciate the depths of such larceny, but I sure liked the Reds logo—the baseball head with the nineteenth-century cap and handlebar mustache. It was a symbol sadly discarded when the facial-hair-hating Bob Howsam became team general manager in the late 1960s. I wish they'd bring the little fella back. My folks eventually gave me a bobbin' head doll of the mustachioed Red as a birthday gift. When it finally shattered a few years ago, my sainted wife scoured local hobby shops around Philadelphia where we now live and eventually found a replacement. She still refuses to tell me how much it cost, but whatever the amount it was money well spent.

My biggest thrill from baseball occurred the day I attended my first game at Crosley Field, circa spring 1961. The defending world champion Pittsburgh Pirates clobbered the Reds but I didn't care. My eyes drank in the looming black scoreboard and Crosley's unique tilting terrace at the warning track. My nose sniffed out the intoxicating aromatic blend of peanuts, grass, grilled hot dogs, and Burger Beer (proud sponsor of all Reds broadcasts back then).

That same afternoon, I opened my first-ever pack of baseball cards and experienced another epiphany: '61 Topps number 25—the treasured group photo of Bell, Robinson, and Vada Pinson entitled "Reds' Heavy Artillery." Forty years later I still have that card, protected from harmful elements in an airtight glass holder, sitting on my desk, adjacent to a family photograph. It remains the Hope Diamond of all my diamond artifacts.

DAVID PLAUT is an Emmy Award–winning producer with NFL Films, book critic for USA Today's Baseball Weekly, *and author of four books.*

Bank One Ballpark, home of the Arizona Diamondbacks. It features a pool, Jacuzzi, and retractable roof.

DAN QUAYLE

◆ ◆ ◆

My baseball roots go back to youth. I started playing Little League when I was seven or eight—first in Huntington (Indiana), then after we moved to Phoenix. I really wanted to play third base. The reason was because my grandfather, Robert Quayle, had been such a terrific third baseman that some big league scouts wanted to sign him. His dad, though, wouldn't let him because he thought it wrong to play professional baseball on Sunday. He went on to become a successful businessman. I knew he loved the game. I still remember him showing me his glove. To me, it had a magic property—and still does.

Now, about third: I just didn't have the arm. So I played second base. I remember nabbing a couple guys in a rundown—and it's a good thing: I had to earn my way into the lineup because I didn't knock the fences down. I wasn't that much of a hitter, but still got on base a lot. The reason was that I was so short: I turned it into an advantage! I had a tiny strike zone, and my manager more or less ordered me not to swing. It didn't matter, for I loved the game. It takes competition, teamwork, loyalty, and dedication. You learned what matters in life—and how tough, honest kids are the kind you wanted on your side.

What baseball means to me is passion. People know that I love to golf. Well, baseball has a lot of parallels. It's more of a team sport, but still accents the individual. Both stress power: It's astounding how far baseball players hit a golf ball. Even more, you've got to focus. Let your mind drift when the pitcher is about to throw—don't focus on whether, say, he'll throw a fastball or curve—and you'll be on the bench. You have to visualize.

What baseball means to me is variety: It combines lacrosse's tradition with cricket's erudition. The only thing the British don't like about cricket is that it can take three or four days to complete! A baseball game takes a couple hours. I like the sport's plots and drama. A couple years back I read George Will's insightful book *Men At Work*. It's got a whole section on the language of signs—how players, coaches, and managers communicate. When I'm at the park I try to intercept their language. So far, no luck. Maybe that's the way it should be: Big league ball is a world apart. It can be played by a precious few.

Finally, what I like about baseball are values—family. My dad was my assistant coach in Little League. I've been an assistant coach for my son's team. And today, I help out with my daughter's T-ball team. I sometimes think that T-ball would have helped me knock the fences down! Either way, its values unite our family—America's, and yours and mine—and have since the 1800s. Living in Phoenix, I go to as many Diamondback games as I can. You can imagine how I liked their 2001 title. Recently, I went to the BOB (Bank One Ballpark) with my daughter and son. We spent the whole night talking and enjoying one another's company. I can't think of a better way to spend an evening with people that you love.

DAN QUAYLE served as Congressman, U.S. Senator, and Vice President from 1989 to 1993.

ROB AND SALLY RAINS

◆ ◆ ◆

There is a magnet on our refrigerator that says, "We interrupt this marriage to bring you the baseball season." We both love and write about baseball. To us, it is as universal as marriage. Take Ichiro Suzuki as proof. (More on him shortly.)

The truth is, it was an interruption in the baseball season which let us get married. In 1980, Rob was a sportswriter covering the Cardinals for United Press International. Sally was working in the sports office at KMOX Radio. We were introduced by a mutual friend in the press box at Busch Stadium.

Because of work, there was little chance for us to date—until the two-month strike by the major league

players in 1981. That gave us plenty of time, and we decided to get married in February 1982, between the winter meetings and spring training. Our minister still has a copy of the program from the wedding, which listed the lineups for the white (bride) and gray (groom) teams. The reception was in the Stadium Club, down the concourse from where we met, and included entertainment from the organist at the park.

Since then, baseball has been a constant in our lives—no surprise, since Rob had been a huge fan since he was a young boy. In 1964, he tried to fake an illness in the third grade so he could go home from school to watch the World Series between the Cardinals and Yankees. Sadly, his mother saw through Rob's plan and said if he was sick he had to go to bed and couldn't watch the game. Rob says that was the day he decided

to become a sportswriter. One of his most treasured possessions is his baseball glove, a 1965 Ken Boyer MVP model from Rawlings.

Sally's first job was working in the concession stand at the Affton Athletic Association in St. Louis, the scene of dozens of baseball and softball games a night. Later at KMOX, during the strike, one of her jobs was to research and write re-creations of old games for Jack Buck and Mike Shannon to broadcast. Re-creations are an art form—like baseball itself.

In 1984, Rob left UPI to become the Cardinals' beat writer for the *St. Louis Globe-Democrat*. After the

In a sense, every yard is Backyard Park: Adults and kids play ball.

> *We have two boys, and when our second son was born, the doctor announced it was a boy by saying, "Now you have half the infield."*

paper folded in 1986, he spent five years covering the National League for *USA Today's Baseball Weekly*. Now back in St. Louis, Sally has co-authored baseball and softball coaching books—and deems her most important job driving our kids to their games, cheering them, and encouraging them on the drive back home. Rob co-hosts a radio talk show, *Talking Baseball*, with former major leaguer Andy Van Slyke, and writes books—his latest, *Baseball Samurais: Ichiro Suzuki and the Japanese Invasion.*

Universal? The book chronicles the arrival of Japanese star Suzuki into the majors, as well as all the other current Japanese stars. The stories about how Ichiro developed his skills through almost daily workouts with his father were strikingly similar to stories about other kids growing up in America who went on to major league success, or those from the Dominican Republic and other Latin American countries.

Fathers and sons, playing catch. The older generation passing the love of the game down to the next generation. It's been that way for years, not only in America but around the world. We have two boys, and when our second son, Mike, was born, the doctor announced it was a boy by saying, "Now you have half the infield."

One of our most vivid memories is bringing Mike home from the hospital, where his two-year-old brother,

B.J., was waiting with a question, "Mikey play baseball?" We informed him that Mike had to learn to walk before he could play baseball. B.J. nodded his head, turned, and walked out of the room. Two minutes later he was back with another question. "Mikey walk now?"

Of course it took a little longer, but B.J. soon had his brother playing baseball, and they are still at it. We have taken many road trips to attend major league and minor league games, and once B.J. won a free pizza in Harrisburg, Pennsylvania, by answering a trivia question correctly.

We might be the only family in St. Louis with a Wiffle ball field in our backyard, complete with a pitching mound, foul poles, and a name, Backyard Park. All of the neighborhood kids are out there almost every night, and often, Rob is with them.

We cried when we watched *Field of Dreams*, for the twelfth time. We can recite much of the movie from memory, and one of the most repeated lines is, "What's it got to do with baseball?" Around our house, the answer usually is "everything."

ROB and SALLY RAINS are still trying to convince the Cardinals to schedule a game at Backyard Park.

DAN RATHER

◆ ◆ ◆

Baseball is part of my earliest memories. When I was very young, my father used to take me to Sunday doubleheaders at Buff Stadium, home of the Buffs—the Houston Buffalos, a Double-A farm team for the St. Louis Cardinals.

Years later, I would do play-by-play of Buffalos games as part of my early broadcast career. But back then it was enough to walk into the ballpark and become enveloped by the sights, sounds, and smells within.

If you've seen the movie *Bull Durham,* you have

some idea of what old Buff Stadium was like. I remember being struck first by the improbably green outfield grass. Its freshly mown aroma competed with the smell of hot dogs and of bread from a bakery across the street from the park. I would have thought I'd forgotten the name of that bakery long ago, but the memory of that mixture of scents brings its sign back to my mind's eye—I think it was called Mrs. Baird's Bread.

Railroad tracks ran behind the center field fence— 404 feet deadaway—and the clanking and chugging of a freight train would punctuate the sounds of play and crowd at least once a game. For me, it only added to the romance of the place.

I couldn't tell you exactly what my dad and I talked about during those long, lazy summer Sundays in the stands. Baseball, sure some of that. But I imagine that most of our time was spent in the time-honored, silent communion between father and son—a ritual duplicated in the stands all around us.

One thing I *do* recall from that time is the way my father talked about Billy Dickey, the catcher then for the New York Yankees. Dickey had a great career, one that eventually took him to the Hall of Fame. I think my father liked and respected Dickey so much because he was a superb player, yes, but

also because he played *catcher*—the most blue-collar of positions. He squatted close to the earth and wore the "tools of ignorance," which my father explained was baseball talk for a catcher's gear. Like my father, he worked hard and with his hands.

Bill Dickey hit .313, made 11 All-Star teams, and helped win seven World Series. "Dickey isn't just a catcher," wrote Dan Daniel. "He's a ballclub."

What I knew was, I wanted to *be* Bill Dickey, even before I fully understood who he was and what he did.

Buff Stadium is no more. It was torn down years ago, and a furniture store now stands on the spot. So much has changed in baseball over the years, some good, some not so good. But enough has remained the same that, when I go to the ballpark, I can still close my eyes, absorb the sounds and smells, and remember what it was like so many years ago, sitting next to my father and wanting to be Bill Dickey. Sometimes, I even think I hear a freight train rumble past.

The thread that runs between summer days past and present. That's what baseball means to me.

DAN RATHER has covered the Kennedy assassination, Watergate, and the World Trade Center terrorist attack for the CBS-TV Network. Since 1981, he has anchored the CBS Evening News.

Dickey coached the Yankees in 1949–57 and 1960. Said successor Yogi Berra: "Bill is learning me his experience."

RICK REILLY

♦ ♦ ♦

The summer I was nine years old, five of us—the Cartin brothers, the Kawulok brothers, and I—would ride our bikes to Prairie Dog Field, which was our baseball park in Boulder, Colorado, back in the days when there actually were fences, instead of the dreaded multi-purpose field that can be turned into anything from a soccer pitch to a tai chi venue.

It was a wonderful field, and we played one game all summer—Home Run Derby. Past deepest center field, where no one could hit it, was a netted batting cage, and we decided on the first day of that summer that if anyone did crush

one into the net, the others had to pitch together and buy him a 39-cent Orange Slurpee at the nearby Kmart. Thirty-nine cents to us was a lot, and we never dreamed anyone could hit it, so it was a very safe bet.

That summer, every day, all we did was play Home Run Derby at Prairie Dog Field (162 games, yes, we were committed, we were obsessed, we were sick). Steve Kawulok kept stats as refined and as complete as those the Elias Sports Bureau puts out now: batting average, fielding average, home run percentage, home runs per at-bat. It was incredible.

I put out the weekly newsletter, which included drawings of us after hours in zoot suits at the local hot spot as though we were big leaguers dating Marilyn Monroe at the Brown Derby. But all summer, none of us hit one into the net in deepest center field. I was by far the smallest of the five and had no chance. I was lucky just to dink one over the left field corner near the foul pole. I think I hit maybe four or five homers all year. Finally, on the last day, one of us did.

It was a great moment. We rode our bikes immediately to the Kmart.

And I can still taste that Slurpee.

RICK REILLY, a Sports Illustrated *senior writer, has been voted National Sportswriter of the Year six times.*

There used to be a ballpark: Prairie Dog Field or the Polo Grounds, deserted by the Giants in 1957.

ANN W. RICHARDS

◆ ◆ ◆

What I know about baseball, you could put in a teacup. I have acquainted myself with such phrases as line drive, pop-up to center, and "from Tinker to Evers to Chance" to facilitate working crossword puzzles. My father once played in an exhibition game of donkey baseball—in which the players in the infield rode donkeys.

But baseball did not play a significant role in my life until I dated and eventually married a man who was a passionate Brooklyn Dodger fan. He loved the Dodgers and, in particular, he loved Jackie Robinson. I was not one of those women that tried to fake a knowledge of my sweetheart's passions. I was one that wanted to share them wholeheartedly. As a consequence, it was required that I should learn the Dodger batting order before we married. And I did.

The wedding was splendid. The honeymoon was enjoyable. But when I got home, I was astounded

"You throw like a girl!" Men would like to hit like this Lassie Leaguer in Worcester, Massachusetts, in 1962.

to learn that the Dodgers had changed the batting order. What possible good had it done to learn the old one if they were going to have a new one? I should have known then that it was just another "boy thing" and that men get meaning in their lives from changing batting orders.

My ex-husband probably still likes the Dodgers even though they moved to Los Angeles, but it is a mystery to me how any self-respecting Brooklyn Dodger fan could accept a move like that.

ANN W. RICHARDS was the 45th Governor of Texas, from 1991 to 1995—its first female chief executive in more than half a century. Previously she served two terms as State Treasurer.

PHIL RIZZUTO

◆ ◆ ◆

You never forget your first big league year. I went to the Yankee offices to sign my first player contract before going south in 1941, and was ushered into general manager Ed Barrow's office. I didn't know Barrow. I did know that the man in the frayed sweater, being shaved by a guy whom he kept calling Goulash, was Barrow. I sat silent until Goulash finished. Then the man who had just been shaved sat up and looked at me. "Young man, what is your trouble?" I told him I wanted more money. He shouted, "I give you this and no more. If okay, sign. If not, get the hell out of here." I signed. It's funny. Even the bat boy looked like a treetop on my rookie club. Red Ruffing, Bill Dickey, Joe DiMaggio looked like a forest. Nobody paid attention to me and I figured it was part of the initiation. But finally I began to worry that I'd done something wrong to deserve the ice treatment. Lefty Gomez looked like a nice guy, so

I told him I was worried. Lefty told me, "Relax, they're not snubbing you, they just haven't seen you yet."

PHIL RIZZUTO helped the Yankees win seven World Series between 1941 and 1955 playing shortstop. He was voted the A.L. MVP in 1950.

Vernon "Lefty" Gomez won 20 games four times. He once revealed the secret of success: "It's simple—clean living and a fast outfield."

EVAN ROBERTS

◆ ◆ ◆

Two weeks in 2000 separated the nirvana of my life from morbid hell. For the first time in my life, the New York Metropolitans reached the pinnacle—the World Series. Nothing could have been better. But two weeks later, my worst fear came true. Not that they lost the World Series, but the guys they lost to were their most hated rival—the team that shares our city—the hated New York Yankees.

After the Mets' Timo Perez retrieved Rick Wilkins's fly to clinch the playoffs, tears flew from my eyes. Nothing could surpass the feeling that came over me on that cool October night. The year before, the Mets left their heart and soul on the field and came up short against the Braves. Now, just one year later, I was experiencing the moment I had dreamed about.

Yeah, the Mets reached the Series in 1986, but I was only three years old and could not remember those events. So after years of struggle and ridicule, here I was at Shea Stadium celebrating my team in the Classic. There was one more hill to climb, but the feeling was indescribable. As Met players staged a victory jog around the warning track, I never envisioned that my worst fears would ultimately come true—or that their author would be that evil empire from the Bronx.

Two days later, when David Justice hit a dramatic home run to assure the Yankees a third straight trip to the Series, my first reaction was "bring it on." The Mets had easily disposed of the Cardinals in five games. Surely the Yankees, who barely survived the Mariners and Athletics, would be easy pickings.

In Game 1 I walked into Yankee Stadium with other Met fans expecting a cakewalk. We led into the ninth inning: Victory would show that the Mets were for real.

Enter reality. The Yankees tied the game. Three agonizing innings later the Mets crashed and burned. When Jose Vizcaino won with his run-producing single, I sprinted out of the stadium as quickly as possible. Defeat was bad enough. Dealing with Yankee fans was even worse. Then, again, I had taunted them throughout the game. Poetic justice in this most poetic of games.

The tide had turned. The Yanks took two of the next three games to come within 27 outs of a Subway clincher. Worst of all, if they won their third straight title they would celebrate in Queens. I was sure the Mets were going to win Game 5. During the game I pondered the sixth-game pitching matchup. Then came the ninth inning: The Yankees scored twice to break a tie. Mariano Rivera gracefully closed out the Series.

I will never forget the last out. Representing the tying run, Mike Piazza drove to deep center field, a drive I envisioned clearing the fence for an unbelievable homer. Then I saw it might not clear the fence—and envisioned Bernie Williams dropping it for a classic World Series blunder. I do not envision anymore. Bernie caught it, and Shea became Yankee Stadium Queens.

The Mets made the World Series: Nothing could be better. The Yankees beat them in the Series: Nothing could be worse. Two weeks, two sides. In baseball, you never know.

New York, New York: The 2000 Yankees celebrate after beating the Mets, four games to one, in the first Subway Series since 1956.

EVAN ROBERTS, eighteen, is America's youngest sports radio talk host. His weekly program, heard nationally on AAHS World Radio, was broadcast live from his bedroom so he could make school on time.

BROOKS ROBINSON

◆ ◆ ◆

I got married on October 8, 1960, and was driving to Lake Tahoe on my honeymoon when the Pirates and Yankees played their final game in the World Series. I'm in the mountains in Colorado and when I'm down in a valley I cannot hear the game, as the radio fades. When I'm on top of the mountain I get the game. So I stop on top of one of the mountains to hear the final inning when Maz hit his famous home run. What I remember is my wife of a few days sitting there shaking her head saying, "I can't believe this! You sitting here on top of this mountain listening to a game when we're on our honeymoon." At that point she realized she was married to baseball, too.

BROOKS ROBINSON is thought by many to be baseball's best all-time fielding third baseman. In 23 years with Baltimore, number 5 won a record 16 Gold Gloves. He was inducted into the Hall of Fame in 1983.

You can kiss it goodbye: Bill Mazeroski's blast against the Yankees wins Game 7 of the World Series, 10–9. Forbes Field, October 13, 1960.

A familiar sight: Beating the throw into third.

DIANN ROFFE-STEINROTTER

◆ ◆ ◆

Baseball, at heart, means learning it through your dad. When I was a little girl, I idolized my father. He was the more athletic of my parents, and he taught me the game. I grew up in Rochester, New York, maybe the country's best minor league city, and we'd go to games, hand in hand. Here's the problem: I loved to play sports, and wanted to play baseball. Here's a larger problem: I was a girl.

Only the boys played Little League baseball. So I neatly solved my quandary by playing Grasshopper Ball, which was even younger. I remember playing third base. But even more I remember how excited my father

was about me making the team. That excitement returned, years later, in 1994 after I'd won the Gold in the super giant slalom in Lillehammer. I'd been to big league stadia before, but never on the field, and here I was, at Busch Stadium, and the Cardinals were inviting me to throw out the first ball!

The boys were still doubting. The Cardinal catcher didn't know whether he should leave the plate and come toward the mound. He didn't have to. I threw a strike! You should have seen his face! I was so proud of myself, and grateful to my dad. You don't have to play the game to be part of the baseball family.

DIANN ROFFE-STEINROTTER was the youngest woman (seventeen) to take a Gold Medal at the World Alpine Championships. She won Olympic Silver and Gold Medals, respectively, at the 1992 and 1994 Winter Games.

TIM RUSSERT

◆ ◆ ◆

When I think of baseball, I remember September 6, 1995, a Wednesday, at Baltimore's Camden Yards. It was the night Cal Ripken broke Lou Gehrig's record for consecutive games played (2,130). There were no high fives or fancy strutting or commercial sponsorships, or tabloid hype—just one man playing baseball for the city he grew up in, not being recognized for running or throwing or hitting. This was different. It was about loyalty and discipline, perseverance, dedication. It was a most visible affirmation of the importance of everyone who gets up every day and does his or her job. It was the lesson of life for our children: Work hard and play by the rules. Example really *is* the best teacher. My son at my side, we cheered and applauded and nodded. We both realized that he understood what values are truly

September 6, 1995: Cal Ripken's final at-bat in the record-breaker. Note the "2,131" above the right field wall.

Baseball's Iron Man, Ripken won a World Series ring, passed Ernie Banks for most homers by a shortstop, and topped Lou Gehrig's 2,130 consecutive games.

important. For that magical moment between father and son, I am forever grateful.

Thank you, Cal Ripken, ballplayer and teacher extraordinaire.

TIM RUSSERT is the moderator of television's Meet the Press *and political analyst for* NBC Nightly News *and* Today. *He also hosts CNBC's* Tim Russert.

PAT SAJAK

◆ ◆ ◆

Growing up in Chicago in the 1950s and 1960s was unlike growing up anywhere else in the world, at least for a young baseball fan. It meant that you could come home after school, turn on the television, and watch—not cartoons or MTV or

Oprah or ads for the latest teen slasher movie—but Chicago Cubs home games from beautiful Wrigley Field.

It's hard to explain to those who are living in the *SportsCenter* era, but there was a time when televised baseball was rare, and televised *home* games were almost nonexistent, because owners thought no one would come to the games if they could see them on television for free. And yet there they were, home stand after home stand, the Cubbies on WGN, fighting valiantly to stay out of last place.

If you ever wonder how a team can finish last and set an attendance record (as they did in 1999) look no further than those sunny afternoons in Chicago decades ago. That's when lifelong loyalties were born. That's when you could see Ernie and Billy and Ron and hear Jack Brickhouse yell, "Hey-hey!" That's when you couldn't wait for a weekend or the end of the school year to actually see your heroes in person. I'm not sure whether the Wrigley family was visionary or lucky, but their decision to let us spend our youthful days with

their team instilled a passion that will never go away.

I was reminded of all that in August 1999, when I was invited to sing "Take Me Out to the Ball Game" during the seventh-inning stretch at Wrigley. Nothing had changed. It was a day game. It was being televised. The feelings were the same. At that moment, I was a young boy, coming home from school, turning on the TV and watching my heroes.

The Cubs lost that day, but it didn't matter. I knew I'd be back. In fact, I'd never left.

PAT SAJAK continues to roll 7 on television's top-rated syndicated series Wheel of Fortune.

RICHARD SANDOMIR

◆ ◆ ◆

Baseball is simply part of me, an instinct, a reflex, a strand of DNA, a battery that has never needed to be replaced. I suppose that other pursuits introduced to people as children are rejected through rebellion, or maturation, or replacement. Not me.

My fascination remains intact at the same nonfanatic level it began at. I love baseball, but I'm not about to call in to talk radio to vent my feelings about a trade I didn't like or wear Yankee regalia to a game as if Joe Torre were going to ask me to play.

And while I did well in elementary school, I recall absolutely nothing about second grade with my teacher, Killian Meyer, in 1964. But I vividly remember Ken Boyer's grand slam homer curling around the left field foul pole in Game 4 of the '64 World Series to beat the Yankees. I remember standing before my black and white TV, imitating my Yankees' batting stances, then made believe I was running the bases on my family's artificial living room turf. I can still do Mickey Mantle (there were differences between his right- and

Jack Brickhouse broadcast games for both Chicago teams. In 1948 he became baseball's first daily TV mikeman.

left-handed stances, but he still had that Walter Brennan trot no matter which side he hit from), Joe Pepitone, Clete Boyer, and Bobby Richardson.

Remember Mickey's grimace when he hit that home run against Barney Schultz in Game 3? I can still make that pained expression today.

Baseball just sticks to me. I doubt that I'm the most knowledgeable fan or sportswriter today. But I like what remains in my memory banks from the earliest years:

• The shard of paper on which Willie Mays signed an autograph for me.

• The photograph of Mantle on crutches, a cast on one of his legs, and arrows pointing to where he'd injured himself since 1951.

• Being able to imitate Mantle's elegant signature. (The two Ms are very different.)

• The mustard I got on my ear "speaking to the Babe" on the Hall of Fame telephones set up in the right field concourse at Yankee Stadium.

• My first Strat-O-Matic set of cards, and the 1927 Yankee Hall of Fame edition.

• Leaving Tom Seaver's 19-strikeout performance in 1970 before he even notched his 18th. I don't know why. I didn't drive and I didn't need to beat the traffic.

• Buying a magazine that compared the careers of Joe DiMaggio and Ted Williams from one of the souvenir stores under the overhead subway at Yankee Stadium.

• Cheering for the Yankees even in their dark post-1964 years, hoping that Horace Clarke and Jerry Kenney would once advance past mediocre. I knew Rich McKinney wouldn't. And to this day, I can still

imitate Stan Bahnsen's and Mel Stottlemyre's motions.

• Owning a hardcover copy of *Ball Four,* and reading it surreptitiously, as if I had done something wrong. I did the same thing with *The Godfather.* Both had lots of good parts.

My baseball battery gets recharged on a regular basis now, because I'm paid to watch sports and to talk to some of the people I used to watch play or call the games. And recently I compiled a collection of player memories of their first time at Yankee Stadium. One, from Stottlemyre, is the flip side of my being a six-year-old excited by his midseason 1964 summons from the minor leagues and his 9-3 rookie record. Mel told me that his debut game against the Chicago White Sox was his first visit to the Bronx.

He said: "We had a full house. I shut out

The Yankees' dressing room on opening day in 1965. The Bombers would finish below .500 that year—the first time since 1925.

everything and they didn't get to me. I was scared to death to come to the club. Growing up, I was a Yankee fan. I loved Mantle and Ford. To take away the fear, Elston Howard grabbed me right away and told me to pitch the way I always pitched. Mickey came over to say hello. I beat Ray Herbert, 7–3, went all the way, and Mickey hit a huge homer way up in the center field bleachers."

RICHARD SANDOMIR is the television sports and sports business columnist for the New York Times.

VIDAL SASSOON

◆ ◆ ◆

As a liberated limey, I must first say that I'm a fanatical football fan—the *real* football that's played with passion globally (where only the goalkeeper can use his hands). But I do have a touching story as it relates to baseball. I was invited to Yankee Stadium by a friend of long standing, sitting with 500 underprivileged youngsters who on that day were very privileged indeed. You see, the person who invited them and me created a foundation to do much good in the field of education. He actually went up to bat four times and had a very good day. Each time he hit the ball, these kids jumped up and down in their seats with elation! He has a joyous, giving heart. His name is David Winfield.

VIDAL SASSOON is a noted hairdresser. He founded the Center for the Study of Anti-Semitism and Related Bigotries at Hebrew University.

Dave Winfield bagged seven Gold Gloves, 465 homers, and 3,110 hits. The oldest man to garner 100 RBIs in a season entered Cooperstown in 2001.

Ebbets Field, the Cathedral of the Underdog from 1913 through 1957. Anything could happen here, and did.

DICK SCHAAP

◆ ◆ ◆

Growing up, I organized the Freeport, New York, Barons, who played in the Kiwanis League. Two years in a row, in the late 1940s, we won the New York State Championship, the first year playing the championship game in the Polo Grounds, the second year in Ebbets Field. I played briefly and without distinction at the Polo Grounds. I played most of the game and without distinction at Ebbets Field. But it still thrills me to say I played in those ballparks, even without distinction.

What I remember best about the Barons is one of our players who was the son of immigrant parents who barely spoke English. Each week, I would call his home to let him know when and where our next game was, and each week his mother would say to me, "Who's calling?" and I would say, "Dick Schaap," and she would say, "Big Shot?" and I would say, "No, Dick Schaap," and she would again say, "Big Shot?" Her son, whose English at the time was not much better than his mother's, was terrified when we went into New York to play a championship game. He was afraid that the tunnel under the East River would collapse and we would all be drowned.

Years later, I renewed acquaintances with that kid who could barely speak English. He had become an actor. He did Shakespeare in Louisville, Kentucky, and he had a small part in a Herb Gardner play on Broadway. I was delighted to see that one of us had made it to the big leagues.

DICK SCHAAP wrote thirty-three books, won six Emmy Awards, and hosted ESPN Magazine's The Sports Reporters *and ESPN Classic's* Schaap One on One. *He died in December 2001.*

JIM SCHMAKEL

◆ ◆ ◆

Friends don't get the meaning of a baseball equipment and clubhouse manager. What do you do? they say. What *don't* I do? Tiger General Manager Jim Campbell more than twenty years ago told me in October, "See you in spring training." My first five years with the club I had another job in the off season. Today it's so different. What do I do? We do everything.

Start with the locker room. We vacuum, clean the showers and rest room, dust, empty the garbage. If a pipe breaks, I have to call the maintenance man. You're responsible for the clothes the players wear—

In 2000 Detroit left Tiger Stadium for Comerica Park, which has a ferris wheel, carousel, dancing water fountains, and yawning alleys.

washing, cleaning, hanging them in the lockers. That Old English D on the Tiger uniform needs to look good. We make sure it does.

We're here to serve the players. We distribute mail, get tickets, arrange for baseball signings, take messages. When I started players'd arrive in the mid-afternoon for a night game. Today it's easier to get extra hitting—cages right under the stands—so they're up at ten, at the park by twelve, by two o'clock there are fifteen to twenty guys. It's their home away from home. That means food: We serve breakfast, lunch, and dinner. And thank God for our move from Tiger Stadium to Comerica Park. The old home dugout was on the third base side. The stadium kitchen was in the right field corner. I had to wheel their food right through the crowd! Forget that at today's "new old parks."

Take Camden Yards, Jacobs Field, Comerica. Visualize a football field—100 yards long, plus end zones, maybe 50 yards wide. That's how big the Tigers' new locker room is. Envision vacuuming it: You got maybe fifty people in there eating, drinking, watching TV, reading papers, being attended to by trainers. The Tigers used to have maybe four invitees a year. Now it's eighteen. Even more, the facilities are so much better—the whirlpool, the doctors—that the players *like* to come. That's another difference in what baseball's meant to me.

People don't realize what an equipment and clubhouse man does. Come spring training I'm at the park at 6:15 A.M. In the regular season I shop for food in the morning. Maybe I'm home three hours after a night game. One October, I charted how many hours I'd spent at the park that year—over 3,000. I stopped counting. On road trips I stay in Detroit to do paperwork, get food ready for their arrival home. In the off season I'll work nine to four, often with players—another change. The big money keeps 'em in shape all year. A final change: In the old days we sold T-shirts to players. They'd buy one or two. Now, with

A Tiger 25 feet long and 15 feet high with a raised paw guards Comerica's main entrance.

licensing, free stuff floods the clubhouse. "Hey, I need another T-shirt," a guy'll say. "No problem," I'll answer. You reach for what's come in the mail.

Why do you do it? Because baseball gets in your blood. What a way to spend your life. It's what I tell myself each day.

JIM SCHMAKEL grew up in Toledo, became the Tiger bat boy, and has been their equipment and clubhouse manager since August 1978.

WILLIAM SCHULZ

◆ ◆ ◆

It was June of 1957. I had just finished my freshman year of college and was about to start a summer job with the *New York Daily News*. The pay was low ($35 a week), the hours odd (usually 4:00 P.M. to midnight), the job description less than glamorous (copy boy). Yet it was the greatest summer of my life. To this day I marvel that I was *paid* to watch baseball five days or nights a week, to sit in the press box of Yankee Stadium, the Polo Grounds, and Ebbets Field, to eat free food and drink free beer, while writing the captions for Pulitzer Prize–winning photographers.

It was the last year that New York had three baseball teams, the Dodgers and Giants decamping at season's end for the greater riches of Los Angeles and San Francisco. But what teams they were:

The Yankees and Casey Stengel would run away with yet another American League pennant, their lineup featuring Mickey Mantle and Yogi Berra, Moose Skowron and Whitey Ford, Don Larsen and Elston Howard. The third-place Dodgers still transfixed their borough—Gil Hodges, Junior Gilliam, Pee Wee Reese, Carl Furillo, Duke Snider, Roy Campanella—and manager Walter Alston was in the fourth year of what would be a twenty-two-year string of one-year contracts. The Giants, managed by Bill Rigney, were in decline and would finish sixth. But they included the very players who had provided the greatest moment in baseball history six years earlier—Whitey Lockman, Don Mueller, and Bobby Thomson; and the rookie who was in the on-deck circle when Thomson hit the Shot Heard 'Round the World—the incomparable Willie Mays.

It was not just the hometown heroes I remember to this day.

Yogi Berra shows off the gifts he received on 1959's "Yogi Berra Day." The three-time MVP hit 358 homers, won 10 World Series, and was inducted into the Hall of Fame in 1972.

There was thirty-nine-year-old Ted Williams leading the Red Sox into Yankee Stadium in a year he would hit .388 and slug .731; Stan Musial, tormenting Dodger pitchers as always and hitting .351; Roy Sievers of the cellar-dwelling Washington Senators leading the league in home runs (42), RBIs (114), and total bases (331); Milwaukee's Warren Spahn adding another 21 wins to what would be a career total of 363, more than any other left-hander.

To this day I marvel that I was "paid" to watch baseball five days or nights a week...

And there were youngsters I could not possibly envision: the Dodgers' Sandy Koufax, a five-game winner who would be the greatest pitcher of his era; Henry Aaron, whose 44 home runs would help him years later shatter Babe Ruth's career record; the Detroit Tigers' Al Kaline, whose 3,000th hit (a double into the right field corner) I would see in Baltimore's Memorial Stadium seventeen years later.

Richie Ashburn, Enos Slaughter, Sandy Amoros, Early Wynn, Luis Aparicio, Gus Zernial, Jimmy Piersall, Lew Burdette, Frank Robinson, Ernie Banks—the names still run like poetry through my mind. These were just some of the players I was privileged to watch from the press box of three of

"If you can't imitate him," Yogi chimed, "don't copy him." At bat, no one could copy Berra.

the most fabled stadiums in baseball. In subsequent years, I would cover stories around the globe, interview Presidents and mobsters, help run the world's largest (and greatest) magazine. But never was there anything like the summer of '57.

WILLIAM SCHULZ is Executive Editor of Reader's Digest.

VIN SCULLY

◆ ◆ ◆

My love affair with baseball began strangely enough at a Chinese laundry in New York. The owner had posted the line score of Game 2 of the 1936 World Series in the window of his shop. The Yankees had pummeled the Giants, 18–4, and a little red-haired kid on the way home from school stopped to read it. I had only a vague idea of what was going on but I instinctively felt terrible for the losing team, and from that moment on became a fan. His love of the game led to the bleachers of the old Polo Grounds, grandstand seats courtesy of the Catholic Youth Organization and the Police Athletic League. Lifelong visions of blue cigarette smoke hanging like a gauze curtain over the infield, verdant green grass and sparkling uniforms, worshipping the players, and, above all, dreams. It led to the radio and television booth in Brooklyn's Ebbets Field as well as to press boxes all across America. This never-ending love affair provided me with the thrill of broadcasting twenty-five World Series, twelve All-Star Games, eighteen no-hitters, plus three perfect games, one of which was in the World Series.

What has baseball meant to me? Along with my family, it has been my life.

VIN SCULLY has won a Peabody Award, broadcast NBC's Game of the Week, *and been the Dodgers' Voice since 1950.*

At 22, Vin Scully announced his first big league game. He was ultimately voted "the most memorable personality" in Los Angeles Dodger history.

ALLAN H. (BUD) SELIG

◆ ◆ ◆

My earliest memories are about baseball. My mother, Marie, was an avid fan and she nurtured my interest in the game. As a young boy, I attended minor league games in Milwaukee and sometimes traveled to Chicago with my mother to watch the Cubs at Wrigley and the White Sox at Comiskey. Those were exciting days.

But my most exciting and memorable baseball trip occurred in 1949 when I was fifteen years old. My mother took me to New York to visit the three New York ballparks—Yankee Stadium, the Polo Grounds, and Ebbets Field. I remember the subway trips to the ballparks, the plush green fields, the stark whiteness of the foul lines, the smells of hot dogs and popcorn, and the crisp white uniforms worn by the home teams and the grays by the visitors.

As enthralling as it was to visit the Polo Grounds and Ebbets Field, attending a game at Yankee Stadium and having the opportunity to watch the graceful Joe DiMaggio patrol the vast center field in person was truly special.

I also got to see the great Jackie Robinson at Ebbets Field. I have always believed that Robinson's entry into the big leagues, ending the game's color barrier, was Major League Baseball's proudest moment. I was especially proud nearly fifty years later when I joined Jackie's wife, Rachel, and President Bill Clinton at Shea Stadium in New York to honor Jackie and the history he made. That night, Major League Baseball retired Jackie's number 42 in perpetuity, the first time such recognition was bestowed on an athlete.

But DiMaggio was my idol as a child and throughout my adult life. Years later, I had the good fortune to meet Joe on numerous occasions and developed a relationship with him. My admiration for him was as profound then as it was when I was a boy. He had an

Jackie and Rachel Robinson, with their dog Ricky, upon learning of the Brooklyn great's election to the Hall of Fame in 1962.

aura about him; being in his company was an event, bringing on an air of excitement, anticipation, and joy.

In that way, Joe DiMaggio personified the game of baseball. I was dedicated to my hero but I was enthralled by the game—its beauty, its strategy, its complexity, and above all, by its enduring history. That trip to New York, now so long ago, remains vivid and, as it turns out, is part of the courtship in the long love affair I've had for the game.

ALLAN H. (BUD) SELIG was born in Milwaukee, became the Brewers' owner in 1970, and was named baseball's ninth commissioner in 1998.

(Overleaf): "Where have you gone, Joe DiMaggio? A nation turns its lonely eyes to you."

WENDY SELIG-PRIEB

◆ ◆ ◆

Baseball is and always has been a very significant part of my life. My earliest memories are of listening to Cub games on the radio. My favorite players included Ernie Banks, Ron Santo, and Don Kessinger. We occasionally went to Wrigley Field for a game and I always hoped Leo Durocher would have an animated argument with the umpires! When I was ten years old my father and his partners brought Major League Baseball back to Milwaukee. My allegiance shifted immediately from the Cubs to the Brewers. While people often talk about how difficult it is to balance a family life with baseball, my experiences have proven otherwise.

If my father had been a history professor, as he wanted to be when he was in college, or an engineer, doctor, or lawyer, I probably would not have been particularly interested in going to the office with him. But because going to the office with my father meant going to the ballpark, I never turned down a chance to go with him. Not only did my father encourage us to be around, he also taught me about the game as well as the business. I remember, for example, in 1973 George Scott became the first $100,000 player for the Brewers, which was mind-boggling to me, a thirteen-year-old. I developed a special relationship with my father thanks to baseball and was able to learn about the business.

My husband, Laurel Prieb, grew up a Minnesota Twin fan and worked for the

Eight times Cecil Cooper hit over .300. Said manager Buck Rodgers: "He just goes out day after day and does the same thing."

Twins in various capacities for over fourteen years. Today we are both involved with the Brewers. A relationship that began with baseball as the common thread just culminated in our tenth wedding anniversary. The Brewers are a big part of our lives and we have seamlessly blended our personal and professional lives.

The great accomplishments and drama on the field made me a fan. I have so many recollections of favorite players and memorable games. At the top of that list is Cecil Cooper's game-winning hit in the 1982 League Championship Series. Near it is how in 1987 we started the season with a 13-game winning streak that included the club's only no-hitter, pitched by Juan Nieves against the Orioles. The streak also included an Easter Sunday in which we entered the bottom of the ninth down, 4–1, and won, 6–4, thanks to dramatic homers by Rob Deer and Dale Sveum. Robin Yount's 3,000th hit on September 9, 1992, also has to make the list. Each year it grows.

I chose baseball as my career when I recognized how important the game is to the quality of our lives. In college, I was a political science major and I knew I wanted to do something in which I could make a positive difference. I soon realized that is baseball's essence. So many things today divide us. Major League Baseball is one of those rare institutions that unite us. It crosses all socioeconomic, gender, and racial lines and provides us those important shared experiences that are essential to our sense of community. What does baseball mean to me? It means more each time I see a game.

WENDY SELIG-PRIEB is the President and Chief Executive Officer of the Milwaukee Brewers.

DONNA E. SHALALA

◆ ◆ ◆

I've had baseball fever as long as I can remember. I grew up in Cleveland where, win or lose, the Indians ruled. And I played in the girls' Pigtail Softball League where one of our coaches—George Steinbrenner—told us that if we worked hard, learned

Jim Thome hopes to help the Cleveland Indians win their first World Series since 1948.

Age may catch up with us.
But as long as we can
remember standing somewhere
on a baseball field ready
to catch the last out,
we remain forever young.

to throw overhand and slide, we would rule. He was right. That was many years ago, but my love for all things baseball has not diminished in the least. I still go to games, and a few years ago threw out the first pitch on opening day at Camden Yards in Baltimore. The Orioles jersey I wore that day hung in my office. As Secretary of Health and Human Services, I also teamed up with baseball legends like Joe Garagiola to get the message out to young ballplayers that if they smoke or chew tobacco their field of dreams may turn into a nightmare of serious illness or death. And that's really the point. For both players and fans, baseball has always been about holding on to our dreams. Age may catch up with us. But as long as we can remember standing somewhere on a baseball field ready to catch the last out, we remain forever young.

Dr. DONNA E. SHALALA served in the Peace Corps, taught, and wrote books, and served from 1993 to 2001 as Secretary of Health and Human Services. She is now President of the University of Miami (Florida).

CHARLIE SHEEN

◆ ◆ ◆

Baseball has always been a huge part of my life. I've attended games from spring training to the playoffs, from the All-Star Game to World Series. I've had roles in *Eight Men Out* and both *Major League* films (sorry about the second one). But the one moment that really stands out for me was a game on April 19, 1996, at Anaheim Stadium. It was the Angels against the Tigers, neither team had any postseason hopes, and I bought some seats in the left field bleachers for myself and a couple of friends. I did this because I wanted to do something I had never done before—I wanted to catch a home run ball. An empty glass cube sat on my mantel ready to

Charlie Sheen, as Oscar "Hap" Felsch, on deck in the 1988 film Eight Men Out.

Eight Men Out *actors play 1919 Black Sox (left to right) Arnold "Chick" Gandil,*
Fred McMullin, Charles "Swede" Risberg, and Oscar "Hap" Felsch.

house and display my prize.

Long story short, the only homer was hit to right. By the seventh-inning stretch, six balls had hit the left field wall in front of me, just out of grasp. It became apparent that I was being taunted and mocked by the Baseball Gods. And rightly so, I guess. I mean, who was I to attempt to cork the bat of fate? Like the old joke

goes, "How do you make God laugh?" The answer is, "Make a plan." I made a plan, and Baseball laughed at me. To this day I keep that empty cube on my mantel to remind me of the lesson I learned that day.

CHARLIE SHEEN has also acted in such films as Wall Street *and* Being John Malkovich.

MARTIN SHEEN

◆ ◆ ◆

One day in the early 1990s my son Charlie and I visited the Hall of Fame and Museum and Doubleday Field, where baseball is said to have originated. While there he bought a souvenir baseball, tucked it away in his pocket, and went along, looking, gawking, and enjoying himself just like any other pilgrim to Cooperstown. As we strolled along I noticed that a group of youngsters began following us. That's not unusual. Actors are often approached by kids of all ages. What struck me was one kid off to the side, following along but always in the background. No matter where we went, the kids were there—and so was the little boy, always to the rear, never butting in or bothering anybody.

As we started walking in the parking lot, preparing to leave, the kids dispersed—but not the quiet kid. He kept following us, always respectfully distant. Ordinarily, we'd never relate. Fame divides many people. But this was Cooperstown. Baseball unites them.

Ultimately, Charlie reaches into his pocket, pulls out the ball he just bought for himself, gets a pen, turns away from the boy's view, and autographs the ball. Then he turns to the boy, catches his attention, and tosses the ball. The boy caught it, tucked it in his pocket, and just as quietly turned and went on his way. They never actually met, never exchanged a word, never had to. What does baseball mean to me? It means unspoken love.

MARTIN SHEEN broke through at age twenty-four in Broadway's The Subject Was Roses. *Movies include* The Incident, Badlands, *and* Apocalypse Now. *He currently stars in TV's* The West Wing.

Cooperstown, New York, by Otsego Lake. Doubleday Field is in the center. Main Street lies to its rear.

BOB SHEPPARD

◆ ◆ ◆

When I was about ten years old, my brother Jack bought me a beautiful first baseman's glove for my birthday. As a left-handed first baseman, my idols at that time were George Sisler and Bill Terry. I treasured that glove and used it for over ten years. Through sandlot, high school, and college games, it served me well.

Now, after fifty years as public address announcer for the New York Yankees doing over 4,000 games, I still feel a warm glow and a vibrant excitement with every baseball experience. Baseball is in my bloodstream!

BOB SHEPPARD is the Voice of Yankee Stadium, gracing baseball, football, boxing, and other events. He has also been Professor of Public Speaking at St. John's University.

Bill Terry was the National League's last .400 hitter (.401 in 1930). He also managed the Giants to pennants in 1933, 1936, and 1937.

George Sisler got a record 257 hits in 1920 and batted over .400 twice. Said Ty Cobb: "He's the nearest thing to a perfect ballplayer."

HUGH SIDEY

◆ ◆ ◆

I t wasn't the game of baseball itself so much as it was the guy at the far end of the radio waves. He was named Ronald "Dutch" Reagan and resided over in Des Moines, sixty miles away. In the depths of the Great Depression in the mid-1930s it might as well have been Timbuktu for those of us in our tiny town of Greenfield, Iowa. A journey to Des Moines was a major excursion that required meticulous planning and budgeting. Baseball was not a part of such logistics.

There was no big league team in Des Moines. But Dutch was doing the Chicago games on Des Moines station WHO. Had we thought about it we would have realized he was for the most part faking them, getting the play-by-play ticker readouts and supplying the background crowd noise, whacking his pencil on the table for the sound of wood against ball and unleashing his abundant enthusiasm to create a wonderful vocal fiction.

It didn't matter. By the time I began to pay attention, Dutch was a folk hero in stressed-out Iowa, a state beset by depression, drought, occasional dust storms, grasshoppers, and despair. There was something in baseball that seemed to link everybody together in a genial but odd contest of otherwise useless skills like catching a ball and hitting it with a piece of lumber. Perhaps baseball was our answer to gladiators and jousting: minimal cost, low maintenance, and nobody intentionally killed or maimed.

Oddly, baseball in my town took fourth place in high school sports to football, basketball, and track. Yet its disciples kept the flame alive, muscular young men whose biceps bulged from tossing bales of hay and shoveling grain. They would gather in the evenings on idle pastures mostly cleaned of cow pies and sheep droppings. Something about that small ball so smooth on your fingers and nestling in the worn

Ronald Reagan re-created 1930s Cub games over WHO Radio in Des Moines. Reagan later said: "In re-creations and politics, you had to be an actor."

leather glove soothed a tortured soul.

Anyway, if Dutch liked baseball, then most Iowa kids did, too. He was in the broadcast pantheon of Jack Armstrong and Little Orphan Annie. I remember it vividly. The Philco radio sat on the table by the living room windows, always open during the scorching summer days and nights. The sun filtered through the leaves of a huge linden tree in our front yard, turtle-doves gave their soft calls, and down the streets and alleys there was an occasional woof from a friendly but overheated dog. And there was Dutch's voice, rising, laughing, wondering, creating, and full of a hope and life that most of us could barely imagine. It occurred to even a small boy like me that Dutch was one happy fellow and somehow that was connected to baseball.

Years later I encountered him in the White House and he began telling hilarious stories of the perils of ticker tape broadcasting. Once the ticker broke. Dutch knew that if he admitted that fact the audience would switch to another game. Dizzy Dean was pitching. The Cubs' Billy Jurges was at bat. Brilliantly, Dutch turned to the one thing that doesn't get in the box score—a foul ball. For the next ten minutes Dutch set a world record for fouls. Ultimately, the wire was restored and Dutch began to laugh. It read: "Jurges popped out on the first ball pitched."

HUGH SIDEY is formerly TIME *White House correspondent and Washington Bureau Chief. He recently hosted the PBS Television series* The American President.

NAOMI SILVER

◆ ◆ ◆

Growing up, I couldn't imagine that I would become the highest-ranking woman in minor league baseball. I could imagine—in fact, knew—that I loved the game. My dad, Morrie Silver, was President of the Rochester Red Wings. He was involved with baseball before I was even born. So going to the game was the norm, where I went to see my father, and where my mother and I spent our summers. As a teenager, I was at the park.

Young women often ask me for advice about how to enter baseball. I tell them to first learn the game. Follow it when you're young because that's how you grasp it. Baseball is less a job than love if you know what's going on. I was lucky. Born into the game,

Women are a majority of Americans, a fan base we have to nurture.

I knew a lot of baseball people. It wasn't a case of some strange woman trying to crack an old-boys' club. Other women don't have that advantage. That's why I'm glad that clubs are trying to increase diversity. With the Red Wings, eight of our twenty-five front office people are female. Slowly, barriers are falling.

More women in baseball helps the game. Women are a majority of Americans, a fan base we have to nurture. Moreover, women in the front office spur a more professional scene. If there's a woman there, men are a little more dignified. They have to suppress their fun and antics. Male *or* female, I tell youngsters: Get your education, and find a team when you're a college student where you can intern. It's not easy. Front offices in the minors are very young. You have to work hard, there's no downtime, and it takes a lot to prove yourself. But once you have, you've got a job.

What I learned from my father I tell young people: Baseball becomes your life. It takes a special person to get involved. You don't have time for a social life, life outside the park. There are long nights, you don't get rich, but where better to spend your time? To me baseball is everything warm and pleasant. It becomes your center, where you see friends and family. To me baseball is like sitting around a fireplace. If the rest of life was as lovely as baseball, we'd have a better world.

People ask me if we compete against the major leagues. Only in the sense that if, say, a big Yankee

Silver (nee) Red Wing Stadium, 1929–96 home of the Rochester Red Wings. Action from the 1960s.

game is being televised we might lose some fans. Same thing with the Orioles, our parent club. Otherwise the minors sell what they *are*, not who they're *against*. We make the event fun so that regardless of who wins, people leave feeling it was worth it: "I want to come back again." I love the minors. Players are more congenial than the bigs, more hopeful, aggressive, and willing. Too many lose that later on. They also interact with our fans, which is harder to do in huge major league parks. You get to know people who know the game as well as you. "What about this pitcher...why don't we sign a shortstop...did you see that guy try to steal?" Conversation—with friends.

I think this is the reason minor league baseball has boomed in the last twenty years. It's less remote, more intimate and neighborhood—a community. Today you see businessmen try to buy clubs and move them to their hometown: The purchase prices are mind-boggling. That disturbs me: Too many people are getting involved with baseball more for love of profit than love of game. I hope we never lose the family kind of feeling of the O'Malleys and Seligs. Sure, we try to generate revenue to make a profit. It helps us keep ticket and concession prices low. But you can't focus only on the dollars to be made. Baseball is much bigger than the bottom line.

No price tag could buy my memories of growing up around baseball, what it taught me, how it brought me closer to my father. I tell young men and women that it can do the same for them.

NAOMI SILVER is Chairman of the Board and Chief Operating Officer of the Class AAA Rochester Red Wings. In 1994, Rawlings named her Woman Executive of the Year.

BURT SOLOMON

◆ ◆ ◆

I don't know what year it was—sometime in the early 1960s—and I've never wanted to look it up. I remember being with my dad in the ramshackle locker room at Camp Holiday, outside Baltimore, which was a summer camp during the week and a small swim club on the week-ends. The radio was on. Chuck Thompson was speaking in his wondrous, siren-sweet, soothing way. The Orioles were playing the Yankees, in the dying days of summer, and this was the miracle—*they were winning*. It was hard to believe. As long as I could remember, the Orioles had been awful, with a lock on sixth place. Now, suddenly, they weren't. Nothing got by Brooks at third. Luis Aparicio came over from the White Sox, and was like Fort Knox. Hoyt Wilhelm's knuckleball mystified Mantle and Maris. The Yankees were in first place, the Orioles in second—and gaining. Sort of a rite of passage. Since then, nothing has been the same.

Chuck Thompson called the Orioles for nearly four decades. His calling cards included "Ain't the beer cold!" and "Go to war, Miss Agnes!"

BURT SOLOMON, National Journal staff correspondent, is author of Where They Ain't: The Fabled Life and Untimely Death of the Original Baltimore Orioles, the Team That Gave Birth to Modern Baseball.

MICKEY SPILLANE

◆ ◆ ◆

All anyone could afford back then was a softball and a bat. In the fields, baseball lines ran through the weeds and we had more burrs embedded in our knickers than fleas on a dog. If we played in the streets, curb drainage vents were the bases and a manhole cover home plate. This was in Elizabeth, New Jersey, when they started putting in those facilities and paving the streets.

MICKEY SPILLANE is the author of many best-selling mystery books, most featuring his detective Mike Hammer.

Weeds litter Washington's Griffith Stadium, demolished in the mid-1960s.

America's oldest and greatest talking game: Millions listen to the ribbon of narrative of baseball on the air.

CHARLEY STEINER

◆ ◆ ◆

I have three people to thank for putting me in a place where I can tell you *What Baseball Means to Me*. Vin Scully, my mom, and a neighborhood kid named Donnie Sorensen.

I knew what I wanted to be when I grew up, the first time I heard Vin's voice doing a Dodger game on the radio. A Brooklyn Dodger game. Had to be '55 or '56. I was six or seven. I remember hearing the crowd, the crack of the bat, and the voice, that voice, painting the picture. My eyes and ears must have grown to the size of the tubes in back of the big brown Zenith radio. (Think Norman Rockwell.) When I was told that was Scully's job (his job?!), I knew what I wanted to do with my life. There never was a plan B for me.

My mom (to be charitable) is not now, nor has she ever been, much of a baseball fan. Unbeknown to her, she slowed my progress as a ballplayer right out of the

chute. About the time I was falling in love with baseball on the radio she bought me a brand-new glove. Every kid remembers his (or her) first glove, almost as fondly as his (or her) first love. But my first glove and I were destined for a quickie divorce.

You see, I am left-handed (which probably explains more than I care to admit). The moment she gave me that new mitt, I had to go out and break it in. Forget dousing the glove with oil, sticking a ball in the middle of the pocket, wrapping the glove tightly in string and then sticking it under the mattress to sleep on it. That could wait. I had to go out, play catch, and try my new glove. The glove worked fine. But my arm didn't feel right.

The next day and the day after and the day after that, the glove continued to work fine, but I was throwing the ball like a ballerina. I couldn't figure out why, until I missed a toss, and threw the glove in hopes it would stop the rolling ball (it didn't and it never does). I retrieved the ball and threw it back to the kid with whom I was playing catch.

And then an epiphany! I discovered I could throw the ball overhand with an easy follow-through, and with a little more mustard on it. How could this be? I was actually able to throw the ball better without the glove on my hand! Some kinesiological imbalance, perhaps? Nope. I came to discover that the glove (as pretty as it was) was a right-handed glove, which of course goes on the left hand. Mom thought, "Well, my son is left-handed," and so she assumed the glove should go on the left hand. For the first couple of weeks of my ball-playing life I was vainly trying to throw with my right hand. From the very beginning, it was apparent that my future in this game was not on the field.

If there was any doubt, it was erased the first time I played a fungo softball game just around the block from my house. Three kids per team. The elm tree up the street on the right was first base. The elm tree across the street on the left was third base. An old towel was second base. And home plate was a piece of cardboard.

Now, this is where Donnie Sorensen enters the story. He must have been all of eight or nine, an experienced veteran. He hands me the bat and offers up some basic instructions. Toss the ball about shoulder high. When it drops, swing the bat, hit the ball, run to first base (the tree), then second, then third, and then home.

Following the orders of the older boy, I hit the ball. And ran for the tree. Then the towel. Then to the next tree. And then...home. I mean, home. All the way to my *house*. I couldn't figure out why everyone was chasing after me, laughing, screaming, and telling me I was running the wrong way.

I tell you this, because it is with the innocence and pure joy without inhibition of that child, that I can still watch and enjoy this wonderful game.

The first time I heard the game on the radio. The first glove I ever got. The first time I picked up a bat and hit the ball. And ran home.

CHARLEY STEINER is an anchor on ESPN's SportsCenter. In 2002 he began broadcasting the New York Yankees.

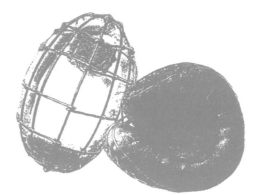

JOHN H. SUNUNU

◆ ◆ ◆

I grew up when baseball was the only sport. For many of us it also involved a very personal relationship. For much of my life it was a lot of my life, and for all my life it has been some of my life. It was a game I learned, a sport I played, a ritual I watched, a bond to community, a tie to friends, and a link to family.

My love affair with baseball started in the glory days of the game in New York City. As home to the Yankees, Giants, and Dodgers, it was the Capital of Baseball. Imagine, of sixteen major league teams, one single city had three of them! Most important, New York was the home of the almost automatic World Series champions, the New York Yankees.

I watched the Yankees–Dodgers 1947 World Series on television standing in a crowd, staring at a round-screened set behind the plate glass front of a radio repair shop on the way home from school. I stood in line with my family, for hours, waiting for tickets to those last two glorious games in 1949, when the Yankees beat Boston twice for the pennant.

I rooted for DiMaggio and Berra, Mantle and Martin, Woodling and Mapes, Raschi, Reynolds, and Lopat, Ford and Turley. I cheered when the Sains and Mizes and Slaughters decided to come to New York to pick a World Series ring before they retired.

In those days, to be an American, a New Yorker, and a Yankee fan was to be triply blessed.

From that moment in January or February 1947 when I made my first public pledge of allegiance by picking my side in a snowball fight (Yankees versus Dodgers, of course) until they fired Yogi Berra as manager after losing the seventh game of the World Series to the Cardinals in 1964, my summer morning newspaper began with the Yankee box score. My baseball card collection (which my mother did *not* throw out) has very few holes from 1947 to 1964!

For me, playing the game was even more important than being a fan. New York City had no Little League

Root, root, root for the home team.

in the 1950s. But I was lucky. There was a vacant lot about a mile from my home. As a fourth grader, I finally managed to talk my mother into letting me ride my bike, glove in hand, to that vacant lot. From that day on, for the next five years, I played baseball almost every spring afternoon after school, on that sandy, rocky, bumpy field.

There were no chalk lines or foul poles. No padded bases, and only occasionally a jury-rigged wooden frame for a backstop. No pitcher's rubber, no umpires, no fences, no grass. It was a field with no trees, and big enough to make every hit playable. It was *our* baseball field.

I learned a lot on that field: the value of friendship, the fun of the competition that came from choosing up sides as balanced as possible, and how important it was to everyone to give everyone a chance to play.

We called our own strikes, safe or out, fair or foul. We didn't always agree, but we called them honestly. We learned sportsmanship, how to settle arguments, the pleasure of winning, the agony of losing and how unimportant those things are in the long run.

In the summer, in the city, we played on the public school softball fields. From sunup to sunset, a half-dozen or even a dozen games. Eventually, we earned the opportunity to play on grass. High school baseball, CYO Leagues, PAL Leagues. Over time, I got comfortable with an honest self-assessment of where I stood in the talent pecking order: great hit, average field, average arm, and no Yankee Stadium in my future.

So, off to MIT to learn a trade. But horror of horrors, in Cambridge, in Boston, home of the hated Red Sox...and, as fate would have it, living on Commonwealth Avenue only four blocks from Fenway Park. Fenway Park, that heaven for a right-handed pull hitter from Queens. That wall alone strained my loyalty, and though I stayed ever faithful to the Yankees, I did fantasize about hitting in Fenway Park.

Life was great in college and even better afterward.

We learned sportsmanship, how to settle arguments, the pleasure of winning, the agony of losing and how unimportant those things are in the long run.

Through it all I tried to keep an even more reluctant body baseball sharp by playing faculty-student softball, or governor's office versus legislature, or in fact, any good excuse to play a game here or there in venues not so competitive as to embarrass myself.

The best part of life came from a great wife and wonderful family of eight children, all of them Red Sox fans, who teased their ever-loyal Yankee fan father and put up with all the strain of the public focus that comes to the family of a public figure. That public focus had the greatest impact on my youngest son, whose entire early life covered those public years.

He was a die-hard Red Sox fan who was never impressed that his father had been Governor or Chief of Staff. Not even when that Chief of Staff arranged lunch for him with Roger Clemens in the White House mess! Or when he put together that gloriously successful conspiracy, with Commissioner Fay Vincent and President George Bush, who also loved the game, to capture Joe DiMaggio and Ted Williams in the White House and *Air Force One* for a Presidential Medal/All-Star Game afternoon. Not even the autographed balls and pictures taken that day gave any aura to the father of a loving, yet tough critic of a, son.

But baseball was too good a friend to let me down. As fate would have it, one day several years after finishing the State House/White House phase of my life, I drove my youngest son to get some batting practice. I watched him do pretty well in the batting cage. I could also feel the urge building in my own creaky bones. I could feel my legs and shoulders timing every pitch. My eyes were laser sharp, watching every ball come off the mechanical arm. Mind and ego were wallowing in memories of a time I could have humbled that machine, and soon the same curiosity that killed a cat had to find out whether the old, tired body, the rusty reflexes, the bifocal eyes could meet the best.

Finally, I could stand still no longer. I got change for a $10 bill, chose a bat, found a helmet to fit, took a dozen practice swings, and entered the cage. For the first ten seconds in the batter's box I felt tense and awkward. And suddenly, as the mechanical arm wound itself up, comfort—so at home, so loose again.

I went through a fistful of change. My hands stung, blistered, and bled. But I continued until the whole $10 was gone. Just like old times. I could see the ball, I could time the pace, and I could control the bat. I was in a zone. Line drive after line drive, almost all neatly pulled to deep left-center.

When I got home I received the real reward of the day, and for a father, one of the rewards of a lifetime. My youngest gushed to his mother, "Mom, you should have seen Dad. He was really pounding the baseballs. He drew a crowd. If it had been at Fenway, he would have been loading the screen over the Green Monster. He was great, really great!"

Thank you, baseball!

JOHN H. SUNUNU co-hosted Crossfire, *CNN's political debate show. The former Governor of New Hampshire was Chief of Staff to President Bush from 1989 to 1992.*

John Mize is the only man to hit 50 homers in a year while fanning less than 50 times.

JAMES W. SYMINGTON

◆ ◆ ◆

My introduction to the game was via my granddad Senator James Wadsworth of New York, who prided himself on the fact he was the only Yale man in history to play first base on the Yale varsity baseball team—and sing first bass on the Yale Quartet. He later played on a semipro team in Geneseo, New York. This was in 1898. In the 1930s, during my early youth as a New Yorker, I followed the Yankees—and could dilate with great precision on the achievements of Manager McCarthy, Lou Gehrig, Gordon, Crosetti, Rolfe, Tommy Henrich, Charlie

Keller, Joe DiMaggio, Red Ruffing, and their associates.

The family move to Missouri in 1938 brought me in touch with the more erratic Gas House Gang, including Pepper Martin. Pepper liked to run in the wrong direction from the trajectory of a fly ball, then race to make a dazzling shoestring catch. Later it was Musial all the way, Stan repaying my individual loyalty by supporting me in my congressional campaigns. I witnessed Joe Medwick and Johnny Mize hit back-to-back homers a few times. Of course, I loved the historic St. Louis World Series in 1944.

In school I played shortstop and sometimes third base. Like many players, I had one unfortunate encounter with a coach. My sophomore year at Deerfield Academy I played third, and though I seldom hit the ball beyond the infield I managed to maintain a fair batting average. For this I depended on generous calls by the plate umpire and some bad hops. In one game, however, the ump kept calling strikes on pitches that barely cleared my ankles. I honestly thought this might have been due to my baggy pants, the elastic of which drooped well below my knees. I thought it might help if I hitched the elastic up to the knee and did so after a second called strike.

This almost innocent gesture incurred the explosive wrath of our coach, who stormed onto the field up to the batter's box and gave me holy hell for "the worst sportsmanship I've ever seen." Chastened into a state of tranquillity, I feebly grounded out on the next pitch and returned to the bench cleansed and pure of heart.

JAMES W. SYMINGTON joined the Marines, was an aide to U.S. Attorney General Robert Kennedy from 1962 to 1964, and from 1969 to 1977 was a U.S. Congressman.

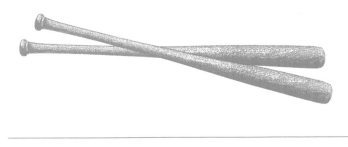

CHUCK THOMPSON

◆ ◆ ◆

One of the great things about baseball is its parks. I spent one afternoon in Fenway that I'll never forget. It was the day (July 20, 1969) Neil Armstrong landed on the moon, and I was working an Orioles–Red Sox game. I'm sure that when that announcement was made anywhere Americans stopped and cheered. At Fenway, Sherm Feller was the

PA announcer—and when he reported it the applause was so overwhelming that it stopped the game. The umpire said, "We've got to wait till this dies down." Brooks Robinson, the due batter, couldn't hear what Feller said and started for the plate. When the umpire explained what was going on, Brooks promptly dropped his bat and joined in the applause. Then down in the left field corner at Fenway Park—what I refer to as No-Man's-Land, where some of baseball's worst line drives have been hit—some leather-lunged fan stood up and started to sing, "God Bless America." No sooner did he start than everybody in that old ballpark was singing. You've never heard it sung so loud by people who were crying. Definitely not just another day at the park.

If you ask him his most embarrassing baseball

In 1954 the St. Louis Browns moved to Baltimore. Memorial Stadium, plain and horseshoed, hoisted three World Series and six pennant flags.

moment, Paul Blair will mention Tiger Stadium. He was a runner at third base. Frank Robinson was the batter. Frank took a swing, missed, and couldn't hold on to the bat. Anyone in baseball knows the terrible experience of seeing a bat fly into the seats. Frank's bat went end-over-end into the seats down the third base side as the park just froze. All of us said a prayer that no harm was done—including Blair, who turned and stared at the stands. Robinson's worried, so he starts that way, too.

When Frank swung and missed, Detroit catcher Bill

My favorite experience was the Orioles' final game at another park, Memorial Stadium (October 6, 1991), the year before moving to Camden Yards.

Freehan caught the ball. All of a sudden, I see Freehan start up the third base line because Paul was standing there looking into the seats. He tapped Blair on the shoulder, and showed him the baseball. "Paulie," he said, "look at what I've got." Paul is called out. He starts arguing with the third base umpire. "You can't call me out." The umpire says, "You're out." Paul says, "You can't do that." He answers, "Why not?"

Blair says, "Because when I get to the dugout, [manager Earl] Weaver's going to kill me."

My favorite experience was the Orioles' final game at another park, Memorial Stadium [October 6, 1991], the

year before moving to Camden Yards. The postgame farewell was the most wrenching feeling I've had at a ballpark. If you haven't seen it, I would invite you to write to the Orioles and ask for their videotape. You'll be crying because of what happened *after* the final out—and without a word being said over the PA system.

First, the background music began from *Field of Dreams*. Then, the first man emerged from the dugout to take his position—Brooks Robinson, at third base—followed by outfielder Frank Robinson, followed by pitcher Jim Palmer. This is how the Orioles said goodbye to Memorial Stadium—asking to come back to Baltimore all former players who could possibly be there. The crowd didn't know this. When it happened, they were stunned.

One after another the players came out—no introduction, just dressed in their era's uniform—and found their position. Luis Aparicio went to shortstop. The first basemen, second basemen, catchers, outfielders—each together. More than seventy-five players positioned around the field—and that music kept rolling. Working with Jon Miller, I looked with binoculars at fellows like Brooks and Boog Powell—and they were, like we were, drained. It was hard to keep from breaking down completely. The thing is that there was no cheering—none. Instead, thunderous applause—and enough tears for a river.

When I left the park that afternoon, I didn't pass a dry eye as I walked to my car. Whoever said "There's no crying in baseball" would have changed his mind that day.

P.S. In this day of the high five in baseball, it did not show up at any time. On this day the players shook hands as gentlemen should. I never saw a high five!

CHUCK THOMPSON first learned baseball in a home, owned by his grandmother, that boarded Connie Mack. He has broadcast the Phillies, A's, Senators, and since 1962 the Orioles.

BILLY BOB THORNTON

◆ ◆ ◆

Baseball is what got me through school. I was pretty unpopular until I became a local baseball hero in Arkansas. I was a pitcher with a good curveball, even slider, and what we then called a screwball. Baseball has been a lifetime passion. Matt Damon and I threw all the time while making *All the Pretty Horses*. I reminded him constantly about 1967 when my Cardinals beat his Red Sox. In the World Series, my heroes were Bob Gibson and Brooks Robinson. I still live the game today.

BILLY BOB THORNTON is an actor, screenwriter, and director. Among his movies are A Simple Plan, All the Pretty Horses, One False Move, *and* Sling Blade.

Bob Gibson won three games in the 1967 World Series. A year later he posted 13 shutouts, 28 complete games, 1.12 ERA, and the Cy Young/MVP.

BOB TRUMPY

◆ ◆ ◆

I love baseball as a broadcaster because I was raised in the middle of Illinois—Tremont, a farming community, population 1,500, which probably hasn't changed fifty people either way in the last 100 years. Why is that, you say? Because each spring, summer, and fall, the last thing I heard before sleep was Jack Brickhouse doing Cub games from Wrigley Field or Harry Caray out of St. Louis. Every night,

every year. It was like one of my parents reading me a book before I went to sleep.

It is odd, in a way, me a football broadcaster, because I have such admiration for baseball Voices. All great broadcasters do baseball, did baseball, or should do it on radio. TV doesn't do the game justice. It's more a sport of listening to than watching. I'm amazed when I go to Riverfront to see the Reds. Thousands

Crosley Field's famed left-wing terrace. "The Reds showed me how to go up the hill,"
said Ernie Lombardi after tumbling. "They just didn't show me how to go down."

are there to *hear* the Reds! They have their transistor radios with the earphone. In no other sport does radio have that pull.

Great baseball announcers don't overplay their hand. Instead, they set the stage: "First and third, nobody out, such and such at the plate, such and such average." There are so many numbers in baseball that you could statistic yourself to death. The greats know this. On radio they create the atmosphere, caress you. As a kid growing up, I had no sense of what kind of people athletes were. All I had were Brickhouse and Caray, painting the picture. They made you think baseball players lived on a cloud and descended to earth just before the game. Hey-hey! Holy Cow!

Baseball broadcasting is very regional: You grow up in an area, and expect a certain style. I remember talking to Caray. He'd talk about the Reds' longtime announcer. "I hated to come to Cincinnati," he said. "Why?" I said. "'Cause Waite Hoyt was here." "What do you mean?" I said. He laughed. "You'd get in a cab, hit a bar, go to a restaurant, all you heard was, 'Hear Waite last night?' 'What about that Hoyt?'" Harry took a sip. "He was the guy I hated the most, but for the right reasons. He had everybody's ear." Any sport would kill for love like that.

I'll never forget the first time I went to Crosley Field, sat in a tiny folding chair on the roof—the press box. They even had ticker tape. I remember thinking, "Hey, this is cool." Or going to Fenway Park, my thought was, "Hey, this is how it was back in the 1930s"—terrific. The thing is, I felt like I'd been there before—Harry brought me there, and Jack and Waite. They made the old ball game come alive—the Polo Grounds, Ebbets Field, old Comiskey Park. *They're* what baseball means to me.

Si Burick, the *Dayton Daily News* columnist, was a good friend who used to drive fifty miles each night to see the Reds. I said, "Why do you come up here?" He said, "When you walk in the press room, just listen."

I said, "Listen for what?" He said, "The noise of the typewriters. It either mesmerizes you, or it doesn't." Typewriters didn't mesmerize me, but baseball on the radio did. Still does, even now.

BOB TRUMPY, a four-time NFL All-Pro, turned to broadcasting in 1977.

PETER V. UEBERROTH

◆ ◆ ◆

Burton Roberts, the famous Bronx judge who sentenced more criminals in a day than many judges do in a year, called me one day and said he would like to go to a baseball game at Yankee Stadium. Since the courthouse is virtually across the street from Yankee Stadium, I knew he had all the tickets he could possibly need. But he wanted to bring

As baseball's commissioner (1984–89), Peter Ueberroth accented marketing, licensing, and corporate sponsorship.

three friends and to sit with me in the Commissioner's box. I said sure and we set the date. My administrative assistant, Bernadette Cannon McDonald, who coordinated my activities, made friends with the judge's assistant and found out he was bringing three young African-American siblings to the ballpark.

The judge had recently sentenced their father to over a dozen years for a murder conviction. He was impressed by how politely the man's wife and three young sons sat through the courthouse proceedings. The judge had admonished the father to be on his best behavior so he could get an early release and help raise his sons. He instructed the sons that they had to help their mother in preparation for the father's return. Six months after the sentencing, Judge Roberts started looking in on the family and became unofficially an uncle.

With this knowledge, I arrived at the ballpark with Bernadette. Soon, the usually highly opinionated judge arrived with three neatly attired young boys. I placed a call to the dressing room and asked for Dave Winfield. Out of earshot of my guests, I told Winfield the brief facts. I asked him to come over and say hello prior to taking the field for the game. Bernadette then alerted the usher not to let other kids run down the aisle.

As the Yankees prepared to go on the field, the big, rangy outfielder ran to my box, looked right past me, and said, "Judge Burton Roberts, I have heard so much about you and respect you so much, I couldn't wait to meet you." The judge was speechless for the first time in his life! Dave then talked to the three boys and told them that they should get good grades, help their mother, and they could be whatever they wanted to be. Then he said, "I am playing the game for the three of you."

Winfield came up in the second inning and immediately had two strikes. The third pitch was a fastball right at his ear that put this gangly ballplayer in the dirt. Winfield got up, dusted himself off, and when the bat met the next pitch, it was obvious that the ball was doing "downtown"—a home run. As he rounded

third base, he looked over at the box, pointed to the boys, put up a finger signaling Number 1, and headed to the plate.

Three innings later, with a new pitcher and one on, he repeated the feat. Except this time, with a wink and two fingers, to his new friends. Winfield tried for a third home run, unsuccessfully, although he did double during this Yankee win. But more importantly, he showed great respect for a very special judge, and positively impacted the lives of three young men.

During my term as Commissioner, I witnessed hundreds of events that never made the media. This was one of those very special events that makes baseball our National Pastime.

PETER V. UEBERROTH headed the 1984 Los Angeles Olympics Organizing Committee, for which TIME *named him "Man of the Year." He later served as the sixth Commissioner of Major League Baseball.*

BOB UECKER
◆ ◆ ◆

To me baseball means eternal hope. People ask why I entered broadcasting. I point to why I'm famous—my [1962–67] career with the Braves, Cardinals, and Phillies. A .200 average helped. I could always talk, which is good. I never was the brightest student. My dad spent more time in the high school principal's office than I did in class. Even now, old friends are amazed that I made something of myself. They think back on me not graduating from eleventh grade.

I knew early where I was headed. I'd sit in the bullpen and talk into a beer cup. Of course, a lot of the stuff you couldn't say on radio. My managers didn't want me in the game. Hell, they didn't want me on the bench. So they exiled me to the bullpen. One week I played four straight days for Philadelphia. Talk about a miracle. Kids ask me who I played for. I say, "Nobody, but I sat for a lot of clubs." I had to fight players to get in games—and fans who wanted to get me out.

One day this fan got to me, saying things that would have killed my parents. Finally, I'd had enough. So I dove into the stands. Figured I had the advantage— had my chest protector and shin guards on. Hey, I'm no fool. I got a couple of good punches in but the bad thing with something like that is a lawsuit. I can remember walking into the courtroom and *she* was sitting with her attorney. She was still pretty well marked up.

Of all the places I played Philadelphia was toughest. Its fans are so tough that when there's no game scheduled they go out to the airport and boo bad landings. But it also had maybe the best manager, Gene Mauch. Gene'd always fight for his players. Sometimes he'd even fight *them*. After the 1965 season I was traded to his Phillies. Later

I was dealt away, and Gene tried to cushion the blow by letting me stay in one game. I got a double—a whole career in one swing. Afterward, he called me into the clubhouse and told me I'd been traded. I said, "For

Bob Uecker, known as Mr. Baseball, is seldom found in the front row.

The Uke that America loved: The Cardinal catcher reaches high for a low and inside pitch.

who?" He said, "Gene Oliver." I said, "You got screwed!"

I was sad to leave because Gene was the manager who best understood me. When I was with the Phillies, he'd say, "Get a bat, and stop this rally." Or, "Forget the bat, and try for a walk." Like me, Gene took it personally when as a hitter I'd look at the third base coach for a sign and he'd turn his back. And the catcher, instead of giving a signal to his pitcher, would yell out what he wanted. I wouldn't say the other clubs regarded me lightly, but it never was reassuring to go to bat with two outs in the ninth inning, look into the visitors dugout, and see everybody in street clothes. Gene stuck up for me when nobody else would. Even my mom was critical of my play. She'd always say, "Why don't you get a job?" Dad, on the other hand, was a real fan. He booed me, too.

In 1968, I retired as a player—a popular decision—joined the Braves' front office, and started on the rubber chicken circuit. I did stand-up stuff about my career—anything for a laugh. When I was getting started as an announcer anyone who saw me play knew I had plenty of material.

After I joined ABC in 1976, Al Michaels asked if I'd ever been thrown out of a game. "No," I said, "but I got thrown into a couple without notice." Al liked my five greatest thrills as a player. Getting out of a rundown. Walking with the bases full to win our first inter-squad game of the spring. Watching a fan fall from the upper deck and then get booed in Philadelphia when he got up and walked away. Showing up for most games. And catching the games on radio that I didn't show up for. But it was worth it. Once, my son struck out three times in a Little League game. The biggest thrill a ballplayer can have is when your son takes after you.

Al is a great guy. He understood me as a person. One game he asked about my father. I told him, "Oh, my dad came from the old country. He was on the soccer team." That made Al wonder if Dad played goalie. I said, "He didn't play anything. He just blew up the balls, and they didn't have pumps in those days. That's where I get a lot of my talent."

BOB UECKER is a cult figure, movie and TV actor, and since 1972 the Voice of the Milwaukee Brewers.

JOHN UPDIKE

◆ ◆ ◆

What baseball means to me is standing as a child on third base of our local softball field and praying that no ball would be hit my way. Even a softball seemed hard to me, and what came up to the plate in a hardball game looked like a bullet. An imperfectly aimed bullet. My admiration for the men who play this game has been intensified by this early revelation of the courage it takes. The courage, too, to stand alone, surrounded by green space, and have your mistakes show in full view of the stadium.

I grew up not far from Philadelphia. What baseball also meant to me was listening by the radio. With its nine defensive men widely spaced on the field, baseball is an easier game to visualize than a fast shuffle like basketball and hockey, and until girls and a driver's license got me by the throat, I spent many an idyllic summer day indoors huddled on the family easy chair next to the hoarse little Philco. The announcers' voices in their glandular shades of excitement, and the wraparound crowd noise, and the sound in the middle distance of the ball being hit—not to mention the uproarious clatter when a foul ball sailed into the broadcast booth—made a vivid picture in ways superior to what I would see when, once or twice a summer, I was bused the fifty miles to Shibe Park's bleachers.

I even kept box scores of my audited games, and listened on the rainout days when the play-by-play of some remote and feeble contest like the Browns against the Senators would be verbalized from a teletype whose chattering could be heard in the lulls. The two Philadelphia teams were pretty feeble themselves, and created the vacuum into which my irrational ardor for the Red Sox flowed. What had led me, as a youth who had never been north of Greenwich, Connecticut, and didn't know Beacon Hill from Bunker Hill or Fenway Park from Park Street Under, to attach my heart to that distant aggregation? Above all, Ted Williams, who was always doing something interesting. I think he was my favorite all-time player. Even on radio, he always seemed the loneliest.

JOHN UPDIKE is a novelist, short story writer, and essayist. His name evokes The Centaur, The Witches of Eastwick, *and Updike's contemporary Everyman, Harry "Rabbit" Angstrom.*

A maelstrom near third base:
The Phillies' Saul Rogovin and Willie Jones
collide, while Andy Seminick watches.

GEORGE VECSEY

◆ ◆ ◆

The question was, what moves me about the game of baseball? The more I thought about it, the more I remembered literally moving experiences, that is to say, the grand link between the automobile and the national pastime.

Either baseball was invented with the car radio in mind, or vice versa—the fustian tones of some local announcer filling your brain with images, in many cases far more inspiring than the actual sight of the game, or what the television camera chooses to show you.

Your car wanders, your mind wanders. Or perhaps you seek high ground in the New York area and put the car into park and listen to a particularly important Red Sox game slipping through the hostile electronic barricades of Yankee City.

The games I've heard in a lifetime of baseball come flooding back at the slightest invitation:

Driving around with my father in 1946 while he moonlighted delivering

registered mail, his muttered response when the St. Louis Cardinals shellac our beloved Brooklyn Dodgers by a score of 10–2. To this day, I think 10–2 is the worst possible score by which to lose.

The warble of young Ernie Harwell. The crisp tones of the nearly forgotten Connie Desmond. The measured drawl of Red Barber. The chatter of Russ Hodges. The perkiness of the new kid from Fordham, Vin Scully. Driving home from the beach with my family and a few of us shouting, "Shut up, Mel," at the Yankee game on the radio.

Standing by my car in the Hofstra College parking lot in 1956 and listening to the last called strike of Don Larsen's perfect game and knowing, just knowing, the pitch had been outside the strike zone.

Then there was the liberating joy of road trips, first ventures outside New York—barreling across Pennsylvania and Ohio one summer evening,

Roberto Clemente had 3,000 hits, won four batting titles, and "treated baseball," wrote Roger Angell, "like a form of punishment on the field."

listening to the Cardinals beat the Phillies, 1–0, circa 1964, and when the Phillie stations faded out, I found that great Midwestern giant, KMOX, and rode it all the way to the final out.

As a news reporter, based in Appalachia in the early 1970s, I would drive through the narrow valleys of Kentucky and West Virginia, following the Reds games on homey WLW, or playing with the dial, trying to fix the signal of the local Reds affiliate in all the small towns, and enjoying the informed comments of a young announcer named Al Michaels.

These games I know I heard on the car radio: Bucky Dent's home run in 1978, while taking our oldest daughter for college interviews in upstate New York; Bob Welch striking out Reggie Jackson, while heading home from another college visit in Boston. Reggie must have been up for fifteen tense minutes while I drove through Rhode Island.

I heard Ernie Harwell calling the improbable Boston rally against poor Donnie Moore in 1986 while I headed to the Mets playoff game at Shea.

Then in 1991 I was driving south on another assignment during the seventh game of the World Series between the Twins and the Braves. During the white-line monotony of the midnight hour on Interstate 95, my mind was totally engaged by Jack Morris and how I wished the game

would last twenty or thirty innings.

For all of my working life, I have been driving home from Shea Stadium after a night game, listening to the Yankee games from the West Coast, or driving home from Yankee Stadium, listening to the Mets games from California:

Phil Rizzuto describing a hit up the alley and blurting, "You describe it, White," much to the surprise of his generally unflappable partner, Bill White. Or Bob Murphy fretting that the Mets need another six or eight runs to be secure. Or the weird undulations of John Sterling.

These human beings are the nervous inner voices of the true fan, the souls of teams, the repository of aural history. The radio games work for children falling asleep in bed in the fourth inning, they work on a front stoop in a muggy evening, but they are at their best on a car radio, both hands on the wheel, and the mind on a runner edging away from first base in a noisy stadium hundreds of miles away.

We keep our eyes on the blinking taillights of the eighteen-wheeler, and the time glides by.

As long as there is a ball game on the car radio, Jackie Robinson is still dancing off third base, Stan the Man is still coiled in his eccentric stance, Roberto Clemente is still throwing out some foolish runner trying to take an extra base on him.

The broadcasters make the miles and the nights pass with a comforting blanket of continuity. We drive, our minds safe at home.

GEORGE VECSEY, the New York Times *columnist, has covered papal conclaves, the Grand Ole Opry, and the World Series. Among his books are* Joy in Mudville; Loretta Lynn, Coal Miner's Daughter; *and* Get to the Heart.

DICK VITALE

◆ ◆ ◆

What does baseball mean to me? I reflect back to my youth. Wow, I will never forget, as a young teenager, an experience when I went to buy tickets to see the Yankees play. Living in New Jersey, I used to go across the river to see the Bronx Bombers—and I couldn't wait to see the pinstripes.

On this day, when going to pick up tickets, my buddy and I couldn't believe it. We were able to get into the stadium and roam around the baseball diamond. Dreams were flying like you could not believe. To think I was on the outfield grass that was patrolled at one time by legends like the Yankee Clipper, Joe DiMaggio. What a thrill it was! Then we ran to the mound and made like Whitey Ford.

Going to sleep at night, I dreamed about those Yankee pinstripes. Baseball. What a sound, to hear the unbelievable roar of the crowd. The sound when the lumber makes contact with that little white ball. It is so sweet. To smell that fresh-cut grass at the ballpark. To hang around and catch batting practice, watching sluggers put souvenirs in the stands. I used to go early and hang out by the right field porch at Yankee Stadium, chasing the BP home runs. What a thrill that was.

Nothing will match that feeling of walking through Yankee Stadium with my buddy. We were even able to get into the locker room, as a maintenance guy let us in to take a look. I couldn't believe it! The jerseys hanging there. It was a thrill of a lifetime. My love and passion for baseball have continued over the years.

During the season, I can't wait to get up every morning to see the newspaper and check out the box scores. I love to see how my favorite players are doing.

Alex Rodriguez turns a double play. In 2001 A-Rod set the big-league record for homers by a shortstop (52).

◆⟨═○═⟩◆

It is awesome, baby, with a capital A!

◆⟨═○═⟩◆

In today's modern era, I love to see how Alex Rodriguez is doing. I can't wait to see what Ken Griffey, Jr. is doing in a Cincinnati uniform. I love to see if Mark McGwire has gone long ball again. Or how Randy Johnson and Pedro Martinez did on the mound.

I'm addicted to baseball. As a kid, I loved to read Dick Young's column in the *Daily News*, looking at his tidbits on the sport. Growing up, what a thrill it was to follow Willie, Mickey, and the Duke! How much has baseball affected me? Everyone knows I have a passion for college basketball, and obviously it is where I make my living. It affords me the kind of money that lets me go out and buy four season tickets for the Tampa Bay Devil Rays. I can't wait to go forty times a year to Tropicana Field and sit in my box in the first row by the visitors dugout.

What a riot it is to get baseballs from the players; even now at age sixty I get to toss them to young fans sitting in the stands. Thanks to my involvement with ESPN and ABC, I have access on the field to watch batting practice by the cage. I see the greats and get to mingle with the people involved. Baseball, baseball. The smell of the hot dogs and peanuts. The excitement of the fans in the stands. It is a place to be. Whenever I go, it is something special. I may be sixty, but when I am at the ballpark, I act like I am twelve!

It is awesome, baby, with a capital A!

DICK VITALE is a former college basketball player and coach who now fuses M & Mers, Quality Time, and PTPers on ESPN-TV.

ELI WALLACH

◆ ◆ ◆

As a kid I used to play stickball on the streets of Little Italy in Brooklyn. The trick was to hit a small ball with the top end of a broomstick. Make it go farther than two sewer covers and you were considered a Babe Ruth. Later, I was a catcher—no mask, no helmet, no uniform—and I have a nose to prove it.

ELI WALLACH is a stage actor, TV performer, and film star. His movies include The Misfits, The Good, the Bad, and the Ugly, *and* The Magnificent Seven.

T-Ball, stickball, and softball mean baseball. A Little League field in Brooklyn.

*Mike Piazza is baseball's best hitting catcher.
His biggest blast won the Mets' first game after
the September 11, 2001, terrorist attack.*

JOHN A. WALSH

◆ ◆ ◆

I grew up with Mel Allen, Red Barber, Vin Scully, Russ Hodges, Bob Prince, and By Saam. When I went to graduate school in Missouri, it was Harry Caray and Jack Buck. And I completed my daily education in baseball by spending full seasons with Al Michaels and Lon Simmons in San Francisco, Jon Miller in Baltimore, and Bob Murphy with the Mets.

I grew up with baseball on the radio every day where the game really matters. Baseball plays ten times as many games as the NFL, and twice as many as the NBA or NHL. From February 15 (pitchers and catchers)

to November 1, baseball is in America's consciousness. Volume is baseball's greatest asset. You follow your team, your favorite players, and now your fantasy teams through *Baseball Tonight*'s ubiquitous highlights. Opening day, trading deadline, home run derby, chasing baseball history—there's always a story line and you can tune in as often as you'd like.

Often the soap operas can make your day: the Rose saga, the tragedy of Howe or Strawberry, Billy Martin, John Rocker, George, Charlie O., A-Rod's wallet, the pine tar on Brett's bat, Sparky's zoo, Ruth *v.* Aaron, Barry's power surge, Sammy and Big Mac, Cal *v.* Gehrig, Clemens *v.* Piazza, Wade's babe, Albert's cork, Fritz and Mike's "trade," arbitration, union appeals, the strike zone, Ichiro, Fernandomania, the Bird, Marilyn and Joe, interleague play, *Eight Men Out, Bingo Long,* Geena Davis, *The Scout,* "Going, going, gone," "It's outta here," "It might be, it could be, it is," Willie, Mickey, and the Duke.

I enjoy baseball in the bigs and at the local town parks, on radio or TV, with friends and colleagues, in arguments on park benches or with instant messaging in cyberspace. We know that baseball can teach, can enhance bonding, can symbolize patriotism, and can even tingle the nerves. In my life, I've found out something very special: Baseball can be a vital part of the fabric of family life and can teach a middle-aged father lessons from a preteen son.

Growing up in the 1950s and 1960s, I was a devout Phillie fan. How devout? The local paper did a profile of my fanaticism and detailed how I could recall the score, winning and losing pitchers, and Phillie home runs for all 154 games each year. Name a date and this was my peculiar Rainman-like talent: I lived and died with Ed Bouchee, Jack Sanford, Joe Koppe, Ted Savage, John Herrnstein, Jack Baldschun, Clay Dalrymple, et al. When the Phillies lost 23 in a row in 1961 to set the consecutive game losses record, I was there.

The first two losses were a twi-night doubleheader;

during the games I was operated on for an emergency appendectomy. When I awoke, the doctor asked, "How are you doing?" My response: "How did the Phillies do tonight?" He answered, "We lost two."

And on that wonderful Sunday afternoon in August when the Phillies finally won a game (John Buzhardt's 7–4 victory over the Braves), I pulled out a straw hat and painted *Phillies* in red on the top so I could wear

it around the neighborhood to celebrate the W.

But I also had a partner in my Phillies fanaticism. My Gramma. She lived with our family, and gave me my first boost of confidence that being a Phillies fan was not only okay, but something worth our time. We ate watermelon on hot summer afternoons, talked about my Wiffle ball exploits almost daily, and listened every day to my blue radio and

By Saam and our beloved Phils.

"How they doing?" "What's the score?" "Who's in first?" "How's Richie Ashburn doing?" "Did Robin Roberts win today?" The Phillies were our bond. Gramma and me. And it wasn't just the Phillies after a while. It was being united against the hated Yankees. It was soaring with incredulity on the front porch listening to Bob Prince call the greatest game ever pitched by Harvey Haddix. It was amazement over 23 innings of the Mets–Giants. And sharing my

A former star in his native Japan, Ichiro Suzuki signs autographs before the 2001 All-Star Game at Seattle. The Classic's leading vote-getter, he became that year's Rookie of the Year and MVP.

Fernandomania! In 1981 Mexican phenom Fernando Valenzuela became baseball's poster child. Here the ex-Dodger pitches for Mexico against the Dominican Republic in a 2001 Caribbean Series game.

enthusiasm for history when my dad brought me to see Don Larsen's perfect game. (Skipping school had to be explained to Sister Mary Arthur. Why did I miss school that day? I was watching history, Gramma observed.)

Gramma was my soul mate, my daily check with the standings, and my assurance that baseball mattered. She made me feel great about what I did, how I spent my time, and what I valued as a preteen and teenager. For almost six months every year, the Phillies were my daily preoccupation and Gramma was my biggest fan. Then one day in early March of 1963, the year before the Phillies almost won the pennant, Gramma was taken on a stretcher out of our house never to return. She passed away soon thereafter and for a few days I didn't pay any attention to the Phils' spring training.

In 1980, the Phillies won their first pennant since 1950—which was four years before I became a baseball fan. In 1981, I got married to the greatest woman in the world whose mother just happens to be the greatest Yankee fan in the world. And in 1988 I moved to New England and ESPN and our family became Red Sox fans. (I now gladly point out to baseball fans how my youthful experience with the Phillies was merely the preparation for being a Red Sox fan.)

My son loves Nomar, Jason, and Pedro as a card-carrying zealot of Red Sox Nation. He has a Nanna, just like I had a Gramma, and his Nanna just can't help herself. She follows every pitch of 162 Yankee games; is a loyal pinstriper; preaches Yankee pride and even has a godson who twice was a pitching coach for Steinbrenner's club. She weaves Yankee fever into casual conversation and she can "Oh, my" with the

best of them over Bronx Bomber feats while she glories in the conquests of her revered dynasty. She's been a true fanatic for a half-century or so (even though her godson has gone on to coach the pitching staffs of the Diamondbacks and Blue Jays), and an inspiration to all around her about baseball.

We make it a point to call each other on the days the Red Sox take over first (rare), the days the Yanks move on top, clinch pennants, or win championships (all too frequent), or whenever there's a fantastic baseball story—Manny joins the Sox, Mussina's a Yankee, Nomar's back in action—and we exchange the appropriate zings and arrows.

When I was growing up, my grandmother showed me the wisdom of the diamond and now that I've grown up, thanks to my mother-in-law and son, baseball keeps us sharp and close.

Ironically, my love for baseball as a boy had its limitations. I couldn't play hardball because I just couldn't see well enough. Did I want ever so much to play baseball, put on a Little League uniform, be one of the guys. But I couldn't.

My best friend played baseball, was a star in the Little League where I cheered every game he played and dreamed that I could catch and hit the ball the way my best friend did. But I couldn't.

So I did the best I could. Wiffle ball in the backyard, slow pitch in the church parking lot where I pitched because I had a hard time catching line drives, and following the games on radio and on the sports pages. The least I could do was know everything that was going on in the big leagues. But I couldn't play catch with a hardball because I was afraid, and every time I tried, it was embarrassing because this was the main playtime activity for my neighborhood and school friends.

One day, somehow I was brave enough to try pitching hardball at batting practice with my buddies at a sandlot stadium. I seemed fearless but, boy, was I scared. There I was going to the mound to pitch a real live baseball. For the first ten to twelve pitches, I threw the ball and turned around to make it seem as though I was looking at where the ball was hit. Actually, I turned around because I didn't know where the hell it was being hit and thought I'd be better off doing that than not doing anything. Then, on the 15th pitch or so, I turned around and the ball was hit right back in my face. The seams of the ball made a visible impression on my cheek for the next week or so. I decided then and there that Wiffle ball and softball were my games, and any career as a batting practice pitcher came to an abrupt end.

So imagine my feelings thirty years later when my son comes home from T-ball and says: "Dad, can we play catch?" He has no idea what that question means to me. Thank God I'm not yet fifty. It's slightly reassuring to me that I've just had cataract surgery and can see a little better and what a blessing it is that he's too young to know how to catch or that his father doesn't really know either. (The hitting part of the game, which always intimidated me because the ball was so small and so fast that I could never see it, was not a problem for me as a father because of batting cages. I had studied the game well enough to make batting practice a real father-son experience.) But playing catch? That was a whole different ball game.

It became obvious early and quickly that our son had his mother's athletic genes. Not only could he play (baseball, football, hockey, golf) but he actually took to the game and made baseball something he cared about.

He had no idea how his father felt every day we played catch. I made sure the background was dark so I could see the white of the ball; the distance had to be long enough to be a catch but short enough so I could learn from my son how to use the glove. I couldn't make excuses, but had to be honest. So there I was in my late forties learning how to play catch. My teacher was my son and he thought I was teaching him something about baseball. Each catch was a new adventure,

a learning experience, and with every experience a confidence-builder. We learned together.

He became a reliable, steady player on excellent town teams and all-star competitions getting better with each year's experience. I learned enough to hold my own, though my son soon realized that his dad wasn't Andruw Jones or Ken Griffey or Barry Bonds. I caught his pitching for a while until he started rifling sixty-mile-an-hour zingers—that's when I retired from the game. And now he's on a whole different level, respected as a regular with the best in his school and his town while his dad fades into the back nine of life, forever grateful that my son taught me how to play catch.

JOHN A. WALSH is Senior Vice President of ESPN, Inc. The founding Editor of the original Inside Sports *magazine, he has also served as Managing Editor of* U.S. News & World Report *and* Rolling Stone.

TOM WATSON

◆ ◆ ◆

Baseball has always been a large part of my life, even though my actual playing experience was limited. After learning to play the game in my neighborhood with my older brother and his friends, I joined a Midget C baseball team and played center field. It was called the Henhouse Chicks. We weren't too successful on the field, but it was sure fun. The following year, I tried out for the Midget B team and was cut, setting the stage for me to try another sport—golf. Even though I missed the opportunity to get better at baseball, I am grateful for being cut so I could pursue golf.

TOM WATSON has won more than fifty tournaments since becoming a professional golfer in 1977. The Kansas City Royals fan has also captained the Ryder Cup team.

PAUL WHITE

◆ ◆ ◆

The '69 Mets.

Amazin'! And if I see Pearl Bailey say that one more time when the highlight reel fills up some rain delay...

I wasn't partial to those Mets, but every time they pop up, the musings and memories begin.

The '69 Mets? I'm not going to lie and become one of the, oh, 33 million who claim to have been there when they clinched the pennant or won the World Series.

I saw them twice, quite by accident.

Hey, you want the exact dates? Well, let's start with July 20.

Doubleheader at Jarry Park in Montreal. Go ahead, look it up.

Miracles? Yeah, right. The Mets lost the first game when Mack Jones, Bob Bailey, and Bobby Wine homered in the same inning. And when Coco Laboy led off game 2's bottom of the ninth with a tying homer, being swept by the expansion Expos was a real possibility. But pinch hitter Bobby Pfeil bailed them out in the 10th.

I know that doesn't mean much. I just like tossing around all those neat names.

Oh, and if the date sounds vaguely familiar it's because Neil Armstrong set foot on the moon that night. I pulled into a rest area on Highway 401 in eastern Ontario during the all-night drive home just in time to see it.

I wouldn't have a clue about the date of that doubleheader were it not for astronauts debuting on the moon the same summer the real Spaceman, Bill Lee, debuted in the majors.

That was a period when baseball had to battle for my attention. Those college years, you know.

If you said Joe McDonald, it wasn't the guy in the Met front office. It was a guy nicknamed Country Joe leading a band called the Fish;

If you said National Anthem, it was Jimi Hendrix at dawn, not Robert Merrill at dusk;

I was more aware of Max Yasgur than Max Alvis;

I, too, had a girlfriend named Mary Jo but I didn't even have a car;

When my favorite player named Hector was Lopez because the Panamian ex–major leaguer was the first nonwhite manager in the eighty-five-year-old International League. Aha! There's one you didn't remember. Just proves I was paying attention;

When I heard the Orioles might not sell out their World Series home games but opted to save money for a march on Washington a month later (never did come up with the cash);

When I got to see the most momentous day (to that point) in Mets history only because my friend got tickets to *The Tonight Show.*

So we planned ahead and got baseball tickets. There was a Red Sox–Yankees game about which I remember little. The big-bucks crap game behind the auxiliary scoreboard was more intriguing, except when Steve Hamilton came in and threw a couple of his Folly Floater pitches.

And we went to a Cubs–Mets game. This one is impossible to forget. September 9, high in the upper deck along the right field line at Shea Stadium. Forget going to the rest room, too many people were sitting in the aisles.

The only good thing about the seats was that they allowed a view of Cub manager Leo Durocher, huddled in the corner of the dugout.

He let the Mets build a 7–1 lead against Ferguson Jenkins rather than walk to the mound and face the "Goodbye, Leo" serenade from the town he once owned as a Giant and Dodger.

By the time Leo sent up pinch hitter Al Spangler in the eighth, this one was long over.

And when Tom Seaver got Willie Smith to fly to right to end the rout, the Mets were a half-game

The 1969 Miracle Mets. New York's Tommie Agee shakes hands with teammate
Wayne Garrett after scoring in the World Series against favored Baltimore.

behind the Cubs, who did not enjoy the last of their 155 consecutive days in first place.

The Mets weren't even in first place but the rest seemed inevitable to any of us 51,448 at Shea that night.

It was, of course.

School started a few days later and, in the first two weeks of October, it didn't really register with me that the Reds hired Sparky Anderson, the Twins fired Billy Martin, and the Cardinals traded Curt Flood.

But the Mets. Wow, they were groovy.

PAUL WHITE helped inaugurate USA Today *in 1982. In 1991, he was named the first and still only Editor of* Baseball Weekly.

SEAN WILENTZ

◆ ◆ ◆

*October 1, 1961: Roger Maris hits number 61.
"If I never hit another home run," he said, "this
is one they can never take away from me."*

Forty years ago, the seats on the New York City subway were woven out of rattanlike laces, and not molded out of plastic. The riders who stood, the straphangers, grasped ceramic handles that actually resembled straps. There was no air-conditioning, but the overhead blade-fans, now retro fashion staples, worked well enough. The color scheme was pea soup green. Many men (and it was a mostly male crowd on the D train up to Yankee Stadium this late Sunday morning) still wore hats. Only boys wore ball caps, like my friend Robby Kritzer. It was 1961, and Robby and I were ten. There was an ad for Camel cigarettes posted above the door between the subway cars: Yogi Berra puffing contentedly.

"Just hope that you-know-who hits you-know-what, you-know-where," Robby and I told each other and our fellow passengers as we pounded our gloves, proclaiming the obvious, as excited kids do.

Some restaurant owner out in California had offered a big cash prize to the person who caught the record-breaking homer. Our ten-year-old's wisdom told us to sit in the right field stands, just to the left of the foul pole, the porch originally built for Babe Ruth—but Robby and I could only afford 75 cents each for the bleachers, and we weren't schooled in sneaking over and into the grandstand.

The crowd was fairly small, considering the stakes and the sunny skies—23,000 odd, the papers said the next day. The Yanks had already clinched the pennant, which might have explained the low turnout.

And lots of people, we knew, wished that Mantle, not Maris, could have beaten Ruth, and they couldn't care less what happened. Still (as I had pleaded with my mother after church, her not wanting me to go to yet another ball game), it would be today or never, the last day of the season. And out where we were, in the right field bleachers, it was packed.

A few of the fans around us talked about the money—the money, and maybe we'll catch the ball. But looking back, I think all of us really wanted to see some history made, back in the pre-mega-hype days before every little thing had become a monstrous media spectacle.

And in the bottom of the fourth, we did see history made. You-know-who *hit* you-know-what, though not you-know-where. The ball landed, as we'd expected, in the right field stands, fought for fiercely and finally claimed by a guy from Coney Island named Sal Durante.

I only saw the speck taking off from Maris's bat, losing all sense of its depth or height: obscured in the skeletal stadium facade, it might have been a homer or it might have been an infield fly. The roar around us was confirmation. So Robby and I yelled and screamed as Maris trotted at a slant around third, headed for home, and then right for the dugout, without the merest tip of the cap. His teammates had practically to lasso him into taking a shy little bow on the dugout's top step.

The Yanks won the game, 1–0. Maris got his record (at the time, outrageously, asterisked). Durante, who caught the ball, got to meet Maris and then got his prize, a whopping five thousand dollars. Robby and I got to go back to Brooklyn on the subway (changing for the A train at 59th Street, smiling agog, just barely reaching the ceramic straps). I held on to my ticket stub as if it were a splinter of the True Cross.

Years later, visiting home from college (or maybe after my folks split up), I rummaged around the basement for that stub but couldn't find it. So now I'm one of the millions of people who claim they were in Yankee Stadium on October 1, 1961, but can't prove it.

It was the first time that I knowingly attended a historic event. That helped change my life—and my life's work forever. Still, I hope that somehow Robby

Kritzer (who moved to California) will read this and vouch for me, assuring the world that we saw an amazing thing happen and assuring me that we weren't just there in my dreams.

SEAN WILENTZ is Dayton-Stockton Professor of History and Director of the Program in American Studies at Princeton University—and faculty advisor to Princeton's baseball team.

GEORGE F. WILL
◆ ◆ ◆

I write about politics, mostly to support my baseball habit. But, then, by its very milieu, baseball is good training for everyone who participates in or studies the great sport of democratic politics in America.

Consider two matters—the basic arithmetic of baseball, and the common law of baseball.

Baseball, like democracy, is a game of the half-loaf. In democracy, no one gets all he wants. Politics is the art of the possible, and in democratic politics, compromise defines what is possible. In baseball, a batter who "fails" only—only!—70 percent of the time is a .300 hitter, and a huge success. A team that wins 10 of every 20 games is, by definition, mediocre. But a team that wins 11 of every 20 games wins 89 games over a 162-game season, and that may well be enough to get it into the postseason.

It has been well said that every year on opening day every team knows it is going to win one third of its games and is going to lose one third, so the whole season is played, in a sense, to find out about the other third. In democracy, too, the contest usually is about, and usually is settled by, small differences.

Furthermore, in baseball, as in any free and decent society, manners matter. That is, much that is important to the civility and sportsmanlike conduct of the game is not a matter of written rules. Rather, it is a matter of a generally understood etiquette—an unwritten code of behavior. You cannot look it up in any book, but you can see it being lived by generation after generation of players. This code is informally taught and, when necessary, enforced by the players and managers.

For example, one tenet of the code is: You don't show up your opponent. Think back to Mickey Mantle circling the bases after hitting a home run. What strikes you about that picture in your mind's eye? That's right—Mantle has his head down, almost as if he worries that he has done something ostentatious.

Respect for one's opponent, and a certain restrained demeanor, are learned early, in the long

acculturation of a player making the climb to the big leagues. If a player has not learned it by the time he gets there—and there are always some slow learners—he is apt to be tutored the hard way when he gets there. The tutorial can involve a stern talking-to by more experienced players on his own team, or a high and inside pitch from the other team.

A while back I wrote a book, *Men at Work: The Craft of Baseball*, during the writing of which I spent many hundreds of hours in conversation—in dugouts, clubhouses, hotel lobbies, team planes—with players,

The Mick (second from left), flanked by (left to right) Mel Allen, Billy Martin, and Joe DiMaggio, at Old-Timers Day at Yankee Stadium.

including some of the best of this era. After the book was published, someone asked me the most surprising aspect of the experience of writing it. I was surprised by my own answer. The most surprising thing, I said, was that I never—not once—heard a big leaguer brag.

Players know how difficult it is to play this game. How often in the course of a season do we hear a baseball broadcaster say, "He winds up and here's the pitch—there's a routine ground ball to second..." Routine? Well, yes, but for the vast majority of Americans—and remember, we are all failed baseball players—there never was any such thing as a ground ball coming at us that seemed "routine."

That much I vividly remember from long ago and far away—in Champaign, Illinois, in the early 1950s—when I was playing, earnestly and badly, for the Mittendorf Funeral Home Panthers. Our color was black. Of course.

GEORGE F. WILL is a columnist for Newsweek *magazine, writes for more than 450 newspapers, and regularly contributes to ABC Television.*

JUAN WILLIAMS

◆ ◆ ◆

On the Orioles' first Sunday of the 1994 baseball season I cried at Baltimore's Camden Yards. The reason was simple emotion tied to my childhood love of baseball. As a poor black kid in Brooklyn, I never thought that I would be able to regularly sit in good seats for major league baseball games.

I grew up watching the Mets on TV. In their first season I was just seven years old. Watching the Mets was part of becoming an American and a New Yorker for me. My mother brought me, with my older sister and brother, to Brooklyn from Panama when I was just

I followed the Mets and their many losses with the deep affection of an immigrant child who identifies with another underdog.

three. I followed the Mets and their many losses with the deep affection of an immigrant child who identifies with another underdog. Actually, my connection to baseball went far beyond the Mets. When my family got our first decent place to live it was in a government-subsidized apartment building erected on the grounds of the old ballpark, Ebbets Field, once home to the Brooklyn Dodgers.

My Aunt Annie was a big Dodger fan from her days in Panama. As a little boy coming to understand the world, Aunt Annie filled my imagination with amazing stories of the daring of Jackie Robinson and Roy Campanella, both as ballplayers and men who stood tall in the face of segregationist rules that once kept blacks and Hispanics out of the big leagues. I was too young to see them play but visions of their strength was a very real family inheritance. Aunt Annie's stories about two black ballplayers gave me role models of dignity during the tense days of riots and marches in the 1960s.

Baseball offered another key to my sense of security and identity as a boy. My favorite contemporary player in the 1960s who did not wear a Met uniform was Juan Marichal. He shared my first name. I can't tell you how special that was for me. Juan was not a very common

name in America in the
1960s. To have a base-
ball star with my name
helped. When I played
stickball on city streets—
nearly every day—I played
pretending to be Marichal or
one of the Amazin' Mets. Even
when I moved up to sandlot and
high school, I played the game fantasizing
about the other Juan, the major leaguer.

But actually going to a big league game
was rare. Once my older brother took me
to the last game of a bad season at Yankee
Stadium. I went to see the Phillies once
during college and caught games in Boston
and Pittsburgh. I always watched on TV.
But I did not go again until several years
after I became a writer for the *Washington
Post*. One of my friends was the Orioles beat
writer and he invited me to join him in the press
box from time to time. Then, I got married and
my wife and I got in the habit of driving up to
Baltimore to catch games. But none of this provoked
any emotion and certainly no tears. The tears came
out of nowhere on a day when I was in my forties
and accompanied by my wife, three young children,
and our in-laws.

We were sitting in box seats on the lip of the upper
deck exactly overlooking first base. These were good
seats. After the celebrated opening of Camden Yards,
a truly beautiful ballpark, I had tried to get good seats.
When the Orioles put their seats on public sale in late
December I was there, standing in cold, even snowy,
weather, and ready to buy. But the good seats were
always gone to season ticket holders and the best tickets
I could get—and did buy—were far down the foul
lines, in the back of the upper deck, or in the bleachers.

But one night, as I walked into CNN's Washington

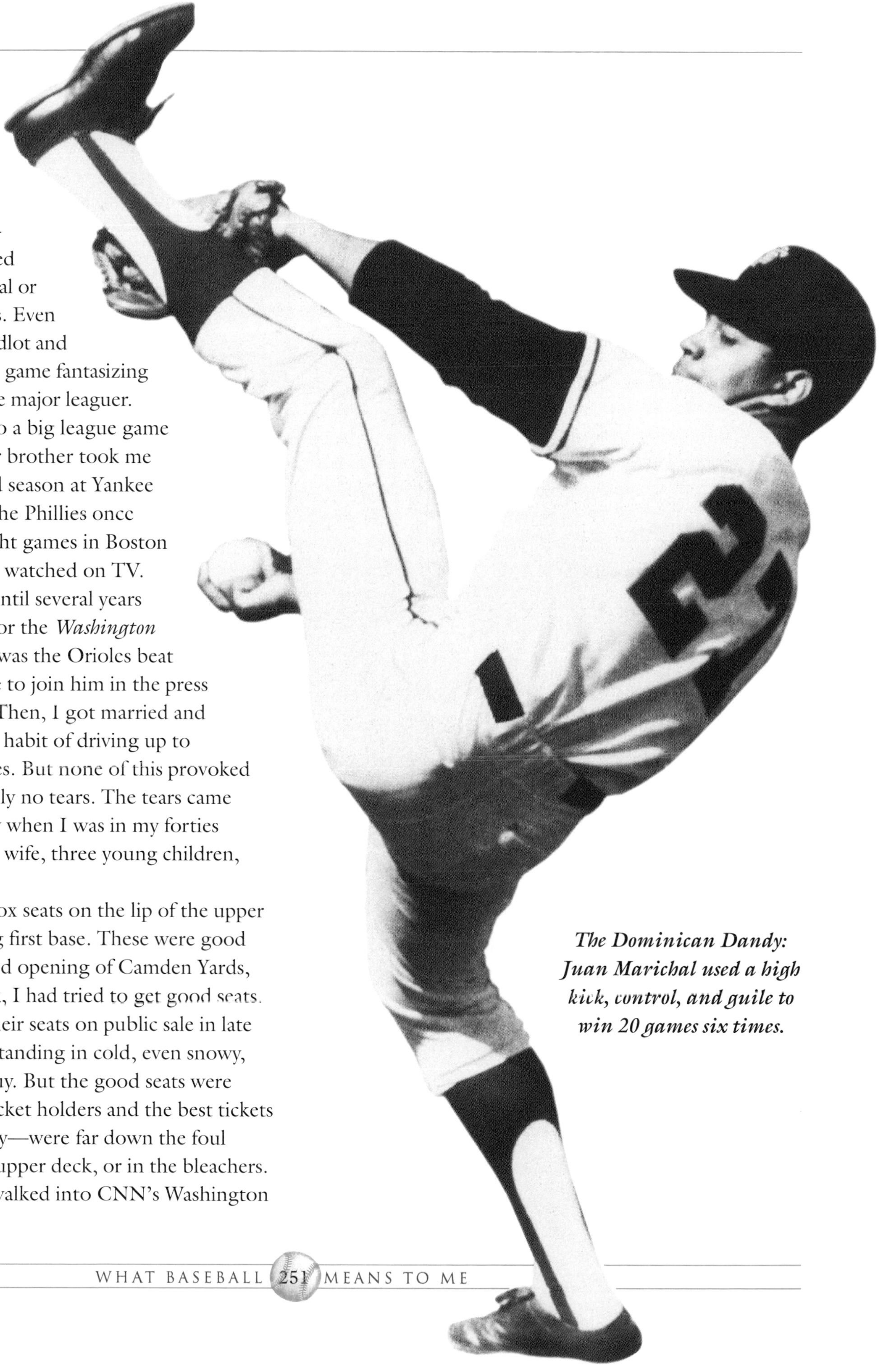

*The Dominican Dandy:
Juan Marichal used a high
kick, control, and guile to
win 20 games six times.*

television studio for the political dogfight *Crossfire,* my co-host, John Sununu, the former White House Chief of Staff, introduced me to a friend he had invited to the studio. He was Eli Jacobs, a financier who was owner of the Orioles. Jacobs came back several months later and then I ran into him at a fancy New York restaurant. He was in the final stages of selling the team when an idea finally struck me. Why not ask Jacobs to help me get good seats? When he returned to the studio a few weeks later I popped the question. He smiled before giving me a name and phone number in the Orioles front office. I had to call back repeatedly, especially after saying I did not want full season tickets but seven seats for Sunday games. I worried the seats would be terrible and after I was told they were in the upper deck I was sure they were terrible.

But on that first sparkling April Sunday, just days before my birthday, I got emotional. As we sat down after the National Anthem I realized that these seven good box seats were mine for every Sunday game. It seemed like a birthday gift from God. Looking over the perfect emerald expanse of a manicured major league baseball field framed by a bright blue sky and Baltimore skyline, the tears quietly came. The immigrant poor kid could not believe it. He could bring his family to the great American game and sit in his own good seats all season long.

My wife was startled when she saw tears on my face and squeezed my hand. She asked why I was crying. I just shook my head. It was too silly. It was too deeply tied to my life, to my experience of being an immigrant kid, and to being black during the civil rights years. It was tied to my childhood fantasies. It was a game but it was much more—it was baseball. It was too much to explain.

JUAN WILLIAMS, an author and former columnist for the Washington *Post, contributes to Fox News Channel and hosts NPR's afternoon call-in program* Talk of the Nation.

TED WILLIAMS

◆ ◆ ◆

What does baseball mean to me? Hell, it means everything. I didn't even consider playing baseball practice. The most fun I ever had in my life was if I was hitting a baseball and if I could hit one— pow!—gee, that felt good to me. And as you get better at something you tend to like it a little more. And the practice, that was the most fun I ever had in my life, and I laugh because I got so much credit for it. When I was a kid I carried a bat from class to class in school. The reason was because it was a school bat. I got there early enough so I could be there to get the bat and ball and wait for the kids to play.

The first thing to do is study the pitchers. Red Ruffing faced me my first game, first time, I struck out. He was sneaky fast. He threw with a little umph and, boy, there it was! If you didn't realize this guy could throw and do so with less motion and effort and excitement, then it was by you. My first key on him was that this guy is faster than he looks. Now I've run into quite a few pitchers that I thought were faster than they looked. One was Billy Pierce, who was a little guy. Dizzy Trout was another. He was a big strong guy, but didn't throw a lot of effort into it. But, boy, he could throw the ball, too.

Rip Sewell didn't throw hard, just lobbed that eephus pitch. Just getting it over the plate for a called strike was hard enough. In 1946, Bill Dickey and I were sitting on the bench at the All-Star Game and here comes Sewell.

He looked in and he saw Dickey and he saw me there. I don't know what he heard or what he suspected, but he said, "You're going to get it!" That's all he said. "You're going to get it!" Of course, he knew what we were talking about. I told Bill, "Nobody can hit a home run off that pitch." Dickey said to me, "You can." I just forgot about it and I did hit a home run off it. He didn't throw it harder than a softball, but he could get it called for a strike. And I swung as hard as I could and the wind was blowing out.

That game was at Fenway Park. Don't forget Fenway was the farthest place from where I lived in San Diego. Boston had snow and it had cold and longer periods of cold. I never did like to play in cold weather. But you get used to things. It's the greatest break I ever got, that I got to play for Mr. Yawkey, who was an absolute gem of a guy. He was one of the truly great owners in baseball because he thought of ways to help the players. One thing he couldn't control was that weather.

Give you another example. My last game was September 28, 1960, at Fenway. Cold, dank. To show you how and why I consider myself the luckiest guy that ever hit, I had hunches and I could guess and one of them was the last time at bat. I'd hit two balls good that day and I thought they were going to go, but they didn't carry. So here I am. I got the count one and nothing and now Jack Fisher's pitching. He laid a ball right there. I don't think I ever missed like I missed that one, but I did. And for the first time in my life I said, "What happened, why didn't I hit THAT one?" I couldn't believe it. It was straight, not the fastest pitch I'd ever seen. I swung, had a hell of a swing, and missed. I'm there trying to figure out what happened.

Here's where the luck comes in. I could see Fisher out there with his glove up to get the ball back quickly, as much as saying, "I threw that one by him. I'll throw another one by him." And I guess it woke me up, you know? Right away I assumed, "He thinks he threw it by me!" The way he was asking for the ball quick, I said, "I know he's going to go right back with

In 1941 Ted Williams became the last man to hit .400 (.406). Fifty years later he received the Medal of Freedom— America's highest civilian award.

The Swing. Williams won his final batting title at age forty. Ted retired in 1960 with a home run, number 521, in his last at-bat.

that pitch." And sure enough here it was. And I hit it into the right-center field bleachers. There's the lucky part right there. He gave the pitch away, practically gave it away. I assumed that just by his actions, and I was right, and I must have given it a little extra something because that one did go.

Study, read as much as you can about pitchers. A dad takes his kid out, the kid's doing pretty good and then he gets in a little better league and now he's not hitting like he used to. Finally, he doesn't even make the baseball team. His father might say, "Let's start playing golf." Maybe even basketball. That's the downfall of most young baseball players. Hitting's a hard thing to do and some guys can talk to you for a month and a half and they wouldn't teach you one thing about hitting. You've got to have good eyes and have athletic ability where you can swing coordinated and quick.

Making good contact with a round ball and a round bat even if you know what's coming is the hardest thing to do in baseball. Maybe it's the hardest thing to do in sports. But if you hit that round ball it's the greatest thing in the world. And I've been around a long time: I know. That's what baseball means to me.

TED WILLIAMS averaged .344, won four home run titles, and was walked more often than anyone except Babe Ruth and Rickey Henderson.

JAMES Q. WILSON

◆ ◆ ◆

For the sixth game of the 1986 World Series, I had to be in California at a meeting. It was the worst possible time to be away from my home near Boston where my wife and I had been glued to the television as the Red Sox battled through five games to a 3–2 lead over the New York Mets. When my meeting was over, I raced to my hotel to hear the sixth game. If the Red Sox won, it would be their first world championship since 1918 and the Curse of the Bambino would have ended. No longer would Red Sox fans have to bear the crushing hex put on them by the sale of Babe Ruth to the Yankees, a sale that seemed to end forever any chance of the Sox owning the baseball world.

In my room, I watched as the Sox battled to tie the score, 3–3, with the favored Mets. Then began the 10th inning, the most famous, agonizing, gut-wrenching inning of baseball that I ever watched. In the top of the inning, Dave Henderson hit a home run. The Sox were ahead! Two more Boston hits added insurance. The Sox were ahead by two runs!

In the bottom of the 10th, the Mets scored. But the Sox still led by one run. Calvin Schiraldi was pitching and managed to get two outs. Bob Stanley took over the pitching duties. One more out and the Sox would own the world. I would be ecstatic, emotionally young forever.

Mookie Wilson came to the plate. It was an extraordinary battle. Stanley got two strikes on him, but not before he threw a wild pitch and a Mets runner raced home to tie the score. But all was not lost. If Mookie were put away, the Sox could score again in the 11th. One more strike on him and Red Sox fans could breathe again. I picked up the telephone and dialed the area code of my home and then the first six digits of our number. When Mookie was put away, I would press the final number and my wife and I could celebrate at least staying alive.

As I held the phone, Mookie hit the next pitch toward Bill Buckner, the Sox first baseman. The ground ball rolled between his legs and a Met runner ran home to win the game, 6–5.

I put down the phone. My youth was over. I was now, at least for baseball, an old man. The Mets won the next game. The Curse lived on.

For the Red Sox, each year is next year: The '86 Mets rejoice after Game 6.

When I got home, a friend called me to commiserate. Things were bad, he said, and then asked if I knew that Buckner, so depressed at missing the ground ball, had leapt in front of an onrushing bus. "Oh, no," I said. "Not to worry," my friend replied. "It went between his legs."

JAMES Q. WILSON, the Ronald Reagan Professor of Public Policy at Pepperdine University, has written fourteen books, including the best-selling textbook American Government.

GEORGE WINSTON

◆ ◆ ◆

When I was growing up in Montana in the 1950s and early 1960s, baseball was my favorite passion. My favorite team was the Detroit Tigers and my favorite players were Al Kaline and Rocky Colavito. I used to even bat with a split grip and point the bat at the pitcher like Rocky did. I played every day with my friends in the summers in various vacant lots. It was easy to start a game anytime—there were so many kids of all ages on every block and so many vacant lots then. I also played two years in Little League in Billings in 1960 and 1961, when I was eleven and twelve years old. I pitched and played third base as a twelve-year-old. Billings had a minor league team in the Pioneer League that my friends and I used to go and see as much as possible. I remember one time when I was ten and somehow a "magic bat" fell into my lap. It was an old bat and was about thirty-six inches—big for a kid that age. I hit better and farther than I ever did before or since in the sandlot games, even hitting a home run farther than the fourteen- and fifteen-year-olds. One day it cracked and I tried everything to fix it—taping it up, nailing it, putting screws in it—but it wasn't the same. It finally completely broke in two, and I was back to hitting normally after that.

   After my family moved from Montana

Rocky Colavito looked like Valentino, threw like Carl Furillo, and hit 374 homers from 1955 to 1968.

to Jackson, Mississippi, I played in the Pony League from 1962 to 1965, and then in the Babe Ruth League as a pitcher and an outfielder. My late father came up with a novel idea to help keep base runners close to second base. I pitched right-handed, but could throw pretty well with my left hand, so he had me practice slipping my glove off my left hand, quickly transferring the ball to my left hand from my right hand while in the stretch, stepping with my back right foot off the pitching rubber toward second base, and throwing to the base with my left hand while dropping the glove.

My most profound baseball memory was the great 1960 World Series between the Pittsburgh Pirates and New York Yankees. Game 7 was unbelievable, a seesaw game with many dramatic moments, like when Mickey Mantle was on first base and Yogi Berra hit a hard ground ball to first. The first baseman, Rocky Nelson, fielded it, stepped on first for the out, and looked to second base to get Mantle tagged out. Mantle fooled him. In an amazing spontaneous move, he dove back to first base.

Our teacher, Alma Kenyon—bless her heart—let us watch it in my fifth grade class on TV, as it was an afternoon day game. We had to go home for lunch— I was in Montana, Mountain Standard Time—so I bicycled home quickly to watch the seventh and eighth innings. I biked back to school as fast as I could after lunch to get back in time for the afternoon class, and to miss as little of the game as I could in the ninth inning. Just before I got to school, I heard over the loudspeaker at the Buttreys shopping center the wrap-up of the game. Just minutes before, Bill Mazeroski had hit the home run to win this amazing game, 10–9. I will never forget that game and the moment I heard the wrap-up.

I followed Mickey Mantle's and Roger Maris's great home run race in 1961 to top Babe Ruth's home run record. I rooted for both of them to break it— I love it when records fall. (It's also great to see the ultimate home run king, the late Josh Gibson from the Negro Leagues, getting more recognition now.) I especially remember the Chicago White Sox' dramatic winning of the American League pennant in 1959, ahead of Cleveland and the Yankees after not winning it in forty years. That was also the one year I endeavored to collect all the Topps Company baseball cards, and almost had all of them. There were six groups of cards,

called series, and after getting them all they came out with the seventh series late in the season that summer, and it was hard to find them all. You had to buy package after package of wrapped bubble gum to see what cards were in them. That seventh series was rare.

I lived far away from the major league baseball cities and all I could do was watch the *Game of the Week* every weekend, but I did get to see one game live—the Los Angeles Dodgers against the Pirates at Pittsburgh in 1962, while visiting my uncle. It was the Dodgers' Don Drysdale's best year (he went 25–9 and won the Cy Young Award), and he was pitching that day, with that great sidearm fastball. It was also the year the Dodger shortstop Maury Wills broke Ty Cobb's long-standing record of 96 stolen bases in a season by stealing 104. He stole a base that day, which my dad got a photo of. We also went to a Yankee game, but it was rained out. I remember the great Dodger pitcher Sandy Koufax emerging at this time as an unstoppable force, and his tragic early retirement.

Baseball was great to me as a kid. I am grateful for it—it inspired me and taught me a lot about discipline, the competitive nature of human beings, and sportsmanship. I am most pleased to be able to contribute solo piano versions of baseball songs to Jeff Campbell's baseball theme albums for his recording label Hungry for Music, the proceeds from which benefit inner-city kids. (His Web site is www.hungryformusic.com.) I have recorded four songs for the four baseball albums issued thus far—and have had the pleasure of playing solo piano concerts at Grandstand Theatre, the auditorium of the Baseball Hall of Fame, as a tribute to the late great jazz pianist Vince Guaraldi and the late great Charles Schulz. Baseball is great to me now.

GEORGE WINSTON's songs recorded for Jeff Campbell's albums are Vince Guaraldi's "Baseball Theme," "Charlie Brown and His All-Stars," "Take Me Out to the Ball Game," and "The Mind Is a Strange Thing."

BOB WOLFF

◆ ◆ ◆

What baseball means to me should be answered in triplicate. Truth is, I've led three lives—player, broadcaster, and person—all baseball-related, all bound together. For me, the national pastime is not a pastime: It's a full-time vocation and avocation.

Life one brought me to Duke University, viewed as a springboard to the majors. A broken ankle interrupted my playing baseball, but not my talking about it. The local CBS-WDNC broadcast crew invited me to join them for on-air comments, and life number two as a broadcaster was underway—until World War II put everything on hold.

After graduation, I became a Navy supply officer for the 11th Special Sea Bees Battalion, training at Camp Peary, Virginia, before overseas duty in the Pacific. At war's end, the *Washington Post* restarted my career by hiring me as a sportscaster for radio station WINX. In 1946, I became Washington's first TV announcer on DuMont's WTTG. Next year I made the majors as the TV broadcaster for the Washington Senators.

Baseball is like life: Breaks matter. In 1956 the Gillette Safety Razor

Bob Wolff broadcast the 1947–60 Washington Senators, who never made the first division and finished 482½ games out of first place.

Company chose me for play-by-play on the All-Star Game in Washington. That year I was asked to broadcast my first World Series. What a thrill to be on the microphone to call Don Larsen's perfect game! If baseball wanted to reward my passion for the game, it couldn't have bestowed a finer gift. Later, I did the 1958 and 1961 Series and NBC's *Game of the Week* from 1962 to 1964 with Joe Garagiola, an informative and entertaining partner. Now in my seventh decade of sportscasting, I still cover baseball daily. There's no other occupation I'd rather have.

Think about it: I talk for a living—about baseball—and get paid for going to games, mingling with the players, expressing my views, and airing the excitement of a winning homer, a tremendous throw, a fantastic catch, or a superb pitching performance—all of which I'd be exulting about even if I weren't on the mike. Still, I never gave up my zest for playing—as a story shows.

The Senators gave me a uniform, and whenever possible I'd pitch their batting practice. They even let me bat in spring training. One day I surprised everyone by drilling one off the fence in left. Little did I dream of the prank the players had in store for me. That night at the team hotel, the players put on a mock show of not speaking to me. Finally, one told me, trying to suppress a laugh, "That was a horrible thing you did to that pitcher, Bob. After you slammed that pitch, they released him. They said that if Wolff can hit him, he must have nothing left."

Undaunted, after moving to New York, I kept playing press-radio-TV games. These were unpublicized games on off days at Yankee Stadium when the Yankee or Met coaches and front office athletes would go all-out to show journalists how the game should be played. My last pitch at Yankee Stadium was two feet over then player-coach Yogi Berra's head. Berra's bat came right up like a periscope rising out of the sea as he clubbed a double to right. It's not in the record books, but I savored his agility.

I mentioned three lives. Life three has brought great rewards. First came marriage to beautiful Navy nurse Jane Louise Hoy, whom I had met and fallen in love with at the Sea Bee camp before going oversees. The wedding took place at the Bethesda Naval Hospital Chapel after my return. Our three children have kept the baseball tradition going. Jane and I have watched and rooted for them at every level of their competition.

Bob was a pitching star at Princeton before becoming a doctor. Rick, a top-notch second baseman at Harvard, played in the Detroit organization before entering the writing-broadcasting field. Margy, an award-winning high school athlete, got her nursing degree from Alfred University. Each is married with three children. As grandparents, we cheer for our all-star nine.

What a terrific day in 1995 when we were all together in Cooperstown to share my induction into the Hall of Fame. For me, baseball is a wonderful game—and life.

BOB WOLFF has the distinction of having broadcast the play-by-play of the four major pro championships— the World Series, the NFL, the NBA, and the NHL.

Babe Ruth gives actress Teresa Wright pointers on how to throw a curve.

TERESA WRIGHT

♦ ♦ ♦

I will always be grateful for the role of Lou Gehrig's wife in the movie *The Pride of the Yankees*. The amazing thing is that I didn't realize until recently how wondrous this game is.

For years I literally knew nothing about it. Then, in the winter of 1980, the Yankees called me. They were going to honor Lou Gehrig's birthday, and wanted to know if I would throw out the first ball. That began my love affair with baseball. Quickly I discovered what I'd missed. I now fully understand why America loves it. Each year baseball is our rite of spring.

Baseball is like theater: The more you know, the better you appreciate it on so many levels, with plots

Eleanor and Lou Gehrig. The Iron Horse remains an American hero. Writer Jim Murray called him "Gibraltar in cleats."

better than any play. It's wonderful to read about. On television, you also catch the panorama of the field. For years I could never understand why people kept talking about baseball after the game, or season. Now I understand.

Like the theater, there's so much to review in baseball. I'm so grateful that I finally found this game.

TERESA WRIGHT was nominated for an Academy Award in 1942 for her performance as Eleanor Gehrig in The Pride of the Yankees. *She left film for TV in the 1950s, receiving three Emmy nominations.*

BROCK YATES
◆ ◆ ◆

Bob Masterson. First base, number 11, bats and throws left. Cleanup hitter for the 1948 Lockport, New York Cubs of the Class D Pennsylvania–Ontario–New York (PONY) League.

The first true hero in my young life.

Those hushed summer nights sitting in awed witness of Masterson and the Cubs remain a luminous memory, although the man, his team, the stadium, and the entire league have long since been swallowed by time.

A struggling left-hander cursed with leaden feet, I was vicariously attracted to the great southpaws of the game; the immortal Babe and Stan Musial, while lefty power hitters Gehrig and Williams were always favored over righties like Hank Greenberg. There being no

Lockport or Chattanooga (shown, Engel Field), minor-league parks are more intimate than the majors'.

television, exposure to these distant stars came only through murky black and white photographs in magazines and newspapers. But Masterson was real, moving with purpose and fleetness on the manicured grass of Lockport's Outwater Park; raw evidence that athletic prowess was almost—but not quite—a little boy's reality.

He never made it. No plaque in Cooperstown. No mention in the encyclopedias and histories of the game. Perhaps a failure to hit the slider. A weak arm. A wrecked knee. Disease. Personal demons. Death. I have no idea of his fate. All I know is that this young man, long forgotten, served somehow to activate in me a desire to excel and achieve, if not on the diamond, at least in some of life's higher purposes. Wherever he is, number 11 is enshrined in my own Hall of Fame.

BROCK YATES, Car and Driver Editor at Large, has written books and several Burt Reynolds movies and done TV commentary for CBS and TNN.

MASATO YOSHII

◆ ◆ ◆

Millions of people around the world will never forget the 1998 season. I know I won't. My first year in the majors was also the year Mark McGwire broke Roger Maris's single-season home run record. I couldn't believe I was in the same league as Big Mac. In mid-August, the Cardinals came to New York to play the Mets. McGwire was at 49 homers and it was my turn in the rotation. Somehow, I managed to keep him in the ballpark, just

Mark McGwire at Wrigley Field. On September 8, 1998, he broke Roger Maris's single-season mark. Big Mac ended with a then-record 70.

like I had done in my other start against the Cardinals that year. The next day, Big Mac hit number 50, a towering shot down the left field line at Shea Stadium. I remember exactly where I was when he hit number 62. I was in the dugout at Shea Stadium and we were playing the Giants. I looked up at the scoreboard and the game came to a stop. Players in both dugouts came out and gave a standing ovation. It was awesome to see that many people clapping and cheering for something that happened a thousand miles away. People know Big Mac in America, in Japan, and everywhere in between. Now that I look back on it, I wouldn't have minded giving up a home run to McGwire during that memorable year.

MASATO YOSHII embodies major league baseball's growing diversity. The pitcher was born in Osaka, hurled 13 years in Japan, and made "The Show" in 1998.

Masato Yoshii, here pitching for the Mets. Baseball is truly a global sport.

Tom Williams of Stone Ridge, New York, hurled four no-hitters in Little League.

FUZZY ZOELLER

◆ ◆ ◆

In Little League, I once pitched a no-hitter. Our team lost, 9–0. You figure it out.

FUZZY ZOELLER has won the 1979 Masters and 1984 U.S. Open and thrice made the Ryder Cup team. In 1985, he won the Bobby Jones Award for sportsmanship.

JOHN ZOGBY

◆ ◆ ◆

Ultimately, you know, for boomer-age men, everything reduces down to Little League. It's the benchmark for all experiences in our lives—all the successes, failures, hurts, and realizations that just because someone has a receding hairline and gray hair, it doesn't make him smart. We, of course, can all pretty much confirm that today.

My lawyer is an old friend from grade school. Every year we go out together for dinner with our wives and some other couples. We eat too much and drink a little too much wine.

About ten years ago, Bob (obviously not his real name), who stands six-foot-five and was a standout basketball player in high school and college, told us how he was the last player picked for Little League and never got a uniform.

Not only were we all in tears about his humiliation, but his booming voice happened to be sharing this sad experience with several other tables of dining guests. By ten o'clock we were holding the most pathetic seminar about Little League slights, hurts, and pain with pretty much the entire dining room.

But there were the good moments, too. I hit three home runs when I was twelve. But, as with some other joys in life, you always remember the first time. Hitting a home run over the fence was the ultimate answer to every Little Leaguer's dreams. It was also the subject of so much conjecture. Short pop-ups to the shortstop became near–home runs (you know, "*If* the wind had been blowing the way it was yesterday" or, "That was a line drive that was on its way up when the shortstop caught it"). For me, my first home run came in the 10th inning, my family had gone home, and the rain had already begun to fall. Our Little League had a rule: If the ball hits the center field scoreboard above the fence line, then it would be ruled a home run.

So, to empty stands and an umpire who was already very late for dinner, my home run hit about six inches above the fence line and, of course, had to be disputed. By the other team's coach, by my rivals on both the other team and my own team, by everyone it seemed. Except the umpire. I was patiently standing on second base when it was ruled a home run. I then got to do

that obnoxious trot that I (and all my friends) had been practicing since I was five.

I have thought so many times about Little League. In fact, as so much of my life intersects with the world of politics in Washington I think about how so much of the behavior I see and experience is so similar to the jealousies, intrigue, and moments of triumph of those early years.

As the author once wrote, we may have learned everything we needed to know in kindergarten. But for so many of us guys, it all boils down to Little League.

JOHN ZOGBY, a leading U.S. pollster, appears on many network nightly newscasts and is a political commentator for CBC and BBC.

Timeless tableau: Hope swings eternal.

EXTRA INNINGS

Each of the banal and towering, self-assured and unself–confident, devious and trustworthy people that are the people of the United States have something basic to their life. For Franklin Roosevelt, it was paralysis; Sam Goldwyn, the immigrant experience; Enos Slaughter, the bruised tailbone of poverty. "Back home, even among the adults," Willie Morris reminisced in his autobiography, *North Toward Home,* "baseball was the link with the outside." For many, it is spectral, if not central.

Draw an American football field: each, 100 yards from one goal line to another and 53 1/2 yards wide. Fix your favorite pro hoops court: each, 94 feet by 50 feet, its basket 10 feet high. A tennis court is 78 feet long by 36 feet wide: Even height net and serving box size are identical. Custom decrees 90 feet between bases and 60 feet, 6 inches from home plate to the pitcher's mound. Elsewhere, look backward, angel. "Thanks to Alexander Cartwright," says former baseball commissioner Bowie Kuhn, "the distance to the outfield, height of fence around the field, or territory between seats and foul lines" swaps sameness for array.

Let me thank contributors to and friends of *What Baseball Means to Me* for shedding sameness. A Chinese proverb says: "One generation plants the seed. Another gets the shade." Rick Wolff, Executive Editor at Warner Books; Dale Petroskey, President, National Baseball Hall of Fame and Museum; and former Hall Vice President Frank Simio planted this book's seed.

I have written of numerous presidential libraries and halls of fame. Cooperstown's is *primus inter pares*—first among equals. One reason is its staff: W. C. Burdick, Manager, Photo Services; Bill Francis, Senior Researcher; Jim Gates, Librarian; Bill Haase, Vice President, Business and Administration; Greg Harris, Director of Development; Jeff Idelson, Vice President, Communications and Education; Bruce Markusen, Manager of Program Presentations; Patricia Kelly, Director of the Photograph Collection; Scott Mondore, Manager, Museum Programs; Helen Stiles, Accessions Associate; Ted Spencer, Vice President and Chief Curator; and Tim Wiles, Director, Research.

Officials throughout major and minor league baseball were most helpful. Michael Levine enriched the contributors list. Dan Ambrosio of Warner Books was invaluable in keeping the project on course. Nicholas Wyatt and Theresa LaPietra, students at the University of Rochester, supplied research. My literary agent, Bobbe Siegel, helped create the book. My wife, Sarah, nursed it to completion. Our two children, Olivia and Travis, show promise as left-handed pitchers.

"Give me a child until he is seven," said St. Francis of Assisi, "and you may have him afterward." I wish to finally thank the reader. Be glad that baseball has you—and is unlikely to let you go.

—Curt Smith

THE MANAGER

Curt Smith is an author, radio-television commentator, and former presidential speechwriter. NBC broadcaster Bob Costas says: "Curt Smith stands up for the beauty of words."

What Baseball Means to Me is his tenth book. Others include *Voices of the Game* ("monumental," said *Publishers Weekly*), *Storied Stadiums* ("a vastly entertaining voyage through time," hailed *Booklist*), *Windows on the White House* ("elegantly written": the *New York Daily News*), *Long Time Gone* ("entrancing": *TIME* magazine), *America's Dizzy Dean*, *A Fine Sense of the Ridiculous*, *The Storytellers*, *Of Mikes and Men*, and *Our House*.

Mr. Smith hosts two public affairs series on Rochester, New York, CBS Television affiliate WROC: *Perfectly Clear* and *Talking Point*. He also hosts a series for Fox TV's Empire Sports Network, does daily commentary for Rochester AP affiliate WYSL, and is Senior Lecturer in English at the University of Rochester.

Mr. Smith's commentary for Rochester NPR affiliate WXXI has been voted best in New York State by the Associated Press and the New York State Broadcasters Association. He has written and co-produced prime-time ESPN documentaries based on his book *Voices of the Game*—and helped write and research ABC/ESPN's *SportsCentury* documentary series.

Formerly a Gannett reporter and *The Saturday Evening Post* Senior Editor, Mr. Smith wrote more speeches than anyone for President George Bush. Among them were the "Just War" Persian Gulf address; Nixon and Reagan Library dedication speeches; and the December 7, 1991, speech aboard the USS *Missouri* on the fiftieth anniversary of Pearl Harbor.

Leaving the White House in 1993, Mr. Smith then hosted a smash series at the Smithsonian Institution, based on *Voices*, before turning to radio and TV. Raised in Caledonia, New York, he graduated in 1973 from SUNY at Geneseo and has been named among the 100 Outstanding Alumni of New York's State University System. He is a member of the Judson Welliver Society of former White House speechwriters and lives with his wife, Sarah, and children, Olivia and Travis, in Rochester.